Change Up

HOW TO MAKE THE GREAT
GAME OF BASEBALL EVEN BETTER

BUCK MARTINEZ

WITH DAN ROBSON

HarperCollins*Publishers*Ltd

For my granddaughters, Zoe and Lara,
who have re-energized me with their wonderful spirit

CONTENTS

FOREWORD
by Chris Berman

IT WAS SEPTEMBER 6, 1995. We had just shared the ESPN broadcast booth with President Bill Clinton for an inning. Of course, it was a labor of love and a privilege for us, but we could readily see that it was the same for the president. He was at a ballgame, talking baseball—just like we were.

This wasn't just any game. Joe DiMaggio was there, representing his teammate Lou Gehrig. Baltimore legends Earl Weaver and Brooks Robinson visited us for an inning as well. America was dialed in on this Wednesday evening at Camden Yards. We know, because it was, and always will be, the highest-rated baseball game ever shown on ESPN.

There was magic in the air. The Baltimore Orioles were hosting the California Angels. It became an official game when the Angels were retired in the top half of the fifth inning. Then, and only then, were the huge numbers 2131 unfurled on the warehouse beyond right field.

Cal Ripken Jr. had passed Lou Gehrig's record for consecutive games played. He had reached the unreachable star.

There was an explosive roar from the fans. Everyone went from cheering wildly to crying, to cheering and clapping, to crying, back to cheering. Cal made his way around the ballpark, shaking hands and high-fiving as many people as he could. In the broadcast booth, we were silent for 23 minutes. Maybe we were smart enough not to say anything, or maybe we were too overcome with emotion—it doesn't matter. It was a glorious night for baseball. It was a glorious night for *America*. Many times, I looked over at my broadcast partner and thought to myself, "There is nobody better to be sharing this experience with than Buck Martinez."

John Martinez is a baseball lifer. Signed in the '60s as a teenager from baseball-rich Sacramento, Buck caught in the big leagues as a 20-year-old. He played for almost two decades with Kansas City, Milwaukee and Toronto. From behind the plate, he could see it all ... sometimes through his catcher's mask, sometimes from the dugout and clubhouse, sometimes from the bullpen, and sometimes with a broken leg.

His playing days ended in 1986, but his baseball days never stopped. His broadcast career has lasted longer than his playing career, although it was interrupted once, for good reason: He managed the Toronto Blue Jays.

Buck played and managed, and now broadcasts, from the heart. A baseball heart. He's never tried to succeed in all three of these baseball careers with any flourish. The soul of the sport is too important to him for an embellishment. To Buck, baseball properly played is a game that will properly embellish itself. He told me long ago that he wasn't a great player, but he knew what one looked like.

As you read the pages that follow, know that you are joining a baseball lifer who only wishes that baseball, in its next life, is better than baseball in its current life—if that's possible, because we all feel that baseball has been pretty darn good.

Buck used to tell me before our broadcasts, "Boomer, you handle the entertainment. I'll handle the baseball." So thanks to him, here's the baseball. Enjoy it.

1

THE VIEW FROM HERE

As a broadcaster for the Toronto Blue Jays, I sit above the field and talk about a game I love with baseball fans who love it as well. I get to travel to diamonds around the league and chat with the great minds—players, managers, coaches and scouts—who live and breathe baseball. It's a wonderful job, with a wonderful view.

Today, I see the game from a different vantage point than I did as a manager in the dugout. And that perspective, in turn, was much different from the one I had when I crouched behind home plate as a catcher, playing major-league ball in three decades. My job in all three places has always been to watch and learn. To understand the game and share what I see. To learn and evolve. To adapt.

This book is the culmination of those experiences.

In my view, it's clear that the game has lost sight of past lessons and that franchises are suffering because of it. More and more, teams are collections of individual brands, concerned more about building up their stats. They are more worried about the bottom line—or upcoming free agency—than winning as a team. Contracts are signed based on showcase skills, resulting in one-dimensional players. Instead of developing talent, organizations pay mercenaries to try to boost their odds of winning championships or even playoff berths. The idea of *the team*, of players wishing for the team's success more than their own, is becoming extinct.

With all this change, people forget that the essence of winning has always been the same. It's pride in the jersey you wear. It's despising your opponent, just because they are on the other side of the field. It's fire. It's heart. It's pitching and defense. Old-school baseball.

If you look at some of the most successful managers in the game today—guys like Buck Showalter, Mike Scioscia, Joe Maddon and Bruce Bochy—they're old-school baseball guys. They're carrying on traditionally in an era that is dominated by analytics. We see teams position their defenses according to spray charts alone, without watching for the little hints, making small adjustments, reading the way a batter is fouling off the ball over the course of a game. Teams are reading numbers, but they aren't reading the game. They don't know how.

Many people would like to dismiss the notion of old-school baseball. It seems outdated. Everything has to be quantifiable in baseball—right? To some, there is little value in the history of the game. The feel of it, the instinct, the *way it once was*—that's just a collection of worn-out stories told by ballplayers long past their best-before dates.

But that attitude is wrong.

Yes, baseball *is* a numbers game, but it is also a game of puzzles that the equations alone can't solve. We know more about how players and teams perform than we ever have before. We have a good idea of how they will perform in the future, based on the past. But the very best baseball people today know how to marry statistical analysis with a grasp of the unquantifiable elements of the game. It's with both of these ingredients that great franchises are grown. It's not one or the other. It never has been. It never will be.

THERE ARE MANY MISCONCEPTIONS about the approach to building a franchise that has come to be known as "Moneyball." The principles of Moneyball are smart. On a restricted budget the Oakland Athletics' general manager, Billy Beane, looked at the game from an analytical perspective, focusing on statistics that were traditionally ignored (or unknown) and using them to piece together a winning team on a budget. Oakland's analysis showed that on-base percentage was a better indicator of a hitter's value than his batting average, just as slugging percentage was more telling than the number of runs a player batted in. The A's used these and other undervalued statistics to build a team more economically than most other winning organizations were capable of. In 2002 the Oakland A's had a payroll of around $44 million while the Yankees paid their players more than $125 million that season, the highest in Major League Baseball. Beane also found a way to pick up these undervalued players and trade them at (or just before they reached) their peak value, receiving future talent in return.

Oakland's model yielded some success. The team won the American League Western Division title in 2002 and 2003, losing the American League Division Series both times. (The A's had also lost the ALDS in 2000 and 2001.) In 2006 Oakland made it all the way to the American League Championship Series, but lost in four straight to Detroit.

Billy Beane is an exceptional general manager who was a pioneer in using sabermetrics to build his team. Today, there is little debate over the value of advanced statistics. But the teams that combine this new era of statistical analysis with learning from the game's old lessons are the ones that have continued to have the most success—most notably, the San Francisco Giants and St. Louis Cardinals.

This is often a polarizing conversation, with fiery opinions on both sides of the fence. Some traditionalists want to dismiss sabermetrics out of hand as overhyped nonsense. On the other side, some people look at the game's older minds as geriatric fools hollering at them to get off their field.

But the truth is there is value in both perspectives.

The greatest minds in the game have always thought about baseball beyond conventional wisdom. With all due respect to the ideas of Moneyball, no one in baseball was more revolutionary than Branch Rickey. We can trace his influence to the modern era. The formula for success hasn't changed.

With the help of some of baseball's greatest minds, this book will attempt to marry the past and present, searching for the secrets to building a winning franchise. This is the game I've grown with through six wonderful decades. These are the lessons it has taught me, and the lessons it's still revealing to me. But before we can find the solution to what's lost, we need to remember why this game matters at all. We need to go back to the beginning.

WHEN YOU WATCH YOUNG PEOPLE play baseball today, from tee-ball to high school, it reminds you how, when things change, the stakes get higher. The familiar joy is there at the start: playing catch on a sum-mer afternoon, hearing the pop of your first hit, the cheers when you thump across home plate. But somewhere along the way the game starts to lose itself. Far too soon, it becomes a business. An investment. Or, really, a lottery ticket. The dream was once about making it to the major leagues and starring for your favorite team, in the position of your favorite player. It was about the thrill of competition and the pride of winning. And for many young players, it still is. But far too often these days, the dream is now a signing bonus. It's a lucrative, record-breaking contract. Of course, it was *always* about the fame. But more than ever, now, it's about the fortune.

We all started in the same place, as players or as fans. We were drawn to the diamond for a reason: for the pure and simple joy of it. Baseball was fun. And from that first game of catch, that first hit, the joy of it grew. Most of us can remember watching our first major-league game in a stadium. We remember feeling dwarfed by the magnitude of it, but at the same time feeling included—feeling connected—to something so huge. It was exhilarating.

Every ballplayer has felt a version of that kind of joy and allowed it to evolve into relentless passion. Not every ballplayer has that kind of joy now, though. It's often something that's shed along the way. This is a business, not a game. And loving baseball? It might be something you talk about—something you tell reporters in scrums, or seem to say in your bright smiles as you pose for pictures with fans—but it's not something you actually feel. Some, for sure. But not all.

A real baseball player needs to truly love the game and to remember why they played it to begin with. The first key to creating a winning team is to fill it with people like that.

I want you to know why I love the game. I want you to know why it bothers me that so much has changed. It's important; there's a very good chance you have a story just like this. I want you to remember why you first loved the game too.

Baseball has always been a part of my life. I have a picture of myself in my living room when I was about two, in a full woolen baseball uniform, holding a little bat. That was the beginning.

I grew up in Redding, California. It was a small town of some 10,000, in the foothills at the end of the Sacramento Valley. The Redding Browns, a Class-D minor-league team in the Far West League between 1948 and 1951, played in a stadium right across the street from our house when I was young. We were right down the left-field line, with the foul line pointing directly to our home. I was playing outside one day when a ball rolled into the gutter—it had been hit straight over the fence, onto our street. I picked it up and thought, "Wow! A real pro baseball!"

After a few years there we moved to an old ranch house next to an orchard, across the street from one of the newer subdivisions in Redding. We lived on Layton Road. We grew apricots, peaches and cherries in our orchard, and beyond our house there was nothing but oak trees and then fields.

My three little brothers, Jim, Jerry and Jeff, all slept in the same room, but I was the oldest, so I had my own room. My father, John, was a handy guy, and he made bunk beds with drawers underneath for us to put our clothes in. We didn't have much, but it was good enough for us. We didn't care much about the inside of the house anyway. The best part was on the outside.

When I was eight, in 1956, my father built a baseball diamond in our backyard, next to the orchard. He was a repairman for Bell Telephone. He brought home some old telephone poles that were being replaced, and he used them to build a backstop with chicken wire. Big oak trees lined the property and served as our home-run markers. We went down to the Sacramento River and loaded up the pickup with loam, silt and sand, and used it to make the infield. It was fine, gray dirt. It wasn't soft. But to us it felt like it was a major-league diamond. I learned how to drive our '48 Ford pickup by using it to drag the infield.

All of my friends called it Buck's Field. (The nickname "Buck" had been in my family for generations. We also called my uncle Buck. My father started calling me it when I was very young, and it stuck with me.) There were at least a dozen kids playing baseball in my back-yard every day—all of the neighborhood kids. Some of the bigger kids were even able to hit the ball over the oaks. We collected Coke bottles to return for deposit to replace the asbestos shingles we broke on the house near left field. We had gunnysacks full of balls, but we always had to go hunting for more.

We had real bases—padded white bags. They were perfect. And there was a bag of bats too. Many of the bats had been cracked, so we ham-mered in nails to repair them. Then we taped over the cracks and nails for more stability. We'd also collect broken bats at the Browns games. We'd find them after the games and cut the ends off so they would be shorter. Our batting helmets consisted of plastic earflaps secured to your cap with an elastic band. I had a little black first baseman's glove that I thought was the coolest glove in the world. My parents ordered it from the Sears or Penney's catalog. That's how we got everything back then. (I didn't get a new glove until I was a senior in high school. It was a Ted Williams model from the line of sporting goods he endorsed for Sears. My parents gave it to me for graduating.)

The games on our backyard diamond were the best way to learn the game. When we didn't have enough guys, you weren't allowed to hit the ball to right field. If you did, you were out. That's how we learned to place our hits. We played every variation of the game that way. If we only had three people, we'd play two on one. We'd only use home plate and second base, and the batters would run back and forth. It was called "one-eyed cat." If we had four guys, we'd play the same game, two on two. We'd also play "pickle," which was a rundown game between the bases. A runner would run back and forth between two fielders, trying to avoid getting tagged. Talk about getting exercise! We'd just go back and forth, back and forth. You'd slide to avoid the tag (or, sometimes, just run the guy over). The point was that we learned how to slide properly. We learned "hook slides." Sometimes we would put down a plastic sheet and drench it with water to practice sliding in all different directions.

Redding is hot, one of the hottest places in the country. We'd be outside, sliding in the gray dirt, getting filthy, and my mother, Shirley, would bring out a gallon of Kool-Aid for everybody and make lunch. It was just something she always did. All the kids were there, and we'd take about five minutes to consume whatever she brought out—venison jerky, sandwiches, fruit—and then we'd be back on the diamond in the hot sun.

I learned basic skills of the game on that backyard field, but I really learned *how to play* the game in Redding Little League baseball. Back then, we only had one Little League for all the kids, regardless of age, so I was eight years old, playing with 12-year-olds. I was on the Coca-Cola Red Legs. I'll never forget getting my first uniform. They were wool, major league–style uniforms. We played at Coca-Cola Field, a beautiful ballpark with lights for evening games and a concession stand. It also had a press box. They'd announce your name when you went up to the plate. The press box was probably 20 feet high, but it looked like a pro stadium. Beyond right field was the McColl's Dairy factory. It was right over the fence, just across the street, and every once in a while somebody would hit one over there and it would bounce off the building. We always thought that was pretty cool.

Back then, I was actually a decent hitter. I hit my first home run when I was eight. That year, our coach, Johnny Crotto, told me I was playing a new position and handed me a piece of curved plastic.

"What's this?" I asked. "It looks like a face mask."

"No, this is your protective cup," he told me. "You're going to be a catcher."

I didn't even know what a catcher was.

During one of our first games, batting against a 12-year-old, I turned into a pitch and it caught me right in the stomach. It hurt. A lot. I decided that I'd had enough and wanted to quit playing. I went home and told my parents, and Dad said, "If you want to quit, that's okay. But you'll have to turn your own uniform in to your manager." My mother washed it, folded it all up and put the socks and the cap on top. I took the uniform down to the diamond, walked up to our manager and said, "Mr. Crotto, I don't want to play anymore."

But Johnny Crotto wouldn't let me quit. He was about my father's age, around 40. He was a really nice, very soft-spoken guy. He was just one of those soothing kind of coaches. Not a screamer or a hollerer. Winning wasn't everything back then. Crotto wanted everybody to play and have a good time. He told me to stick with it. "You're just learning," he said. "It's a fun game. And you're going to be good at it. We really want you to be on the team."

He kept me on the team. He kept me in baseball. And I can't thank him enough.

In 1958, when I was ten, we moved to Sacramento, about 140 miles from Redding. My father's family lived in the area, and he'd gotten a promotion from the phone company to move there. It was his chance to give his boys a better opportunity in life. After we moved I joined the Parkway Little League. It was a big upgrade from what I had known in Redding. We lived in a poorer part of town, but the ballpark was in a new, upscale subdivision in South Sacramento. The community put on a parade for Opening Day. I played for the Dodgers (all the teams were named after major-league teams). We had even nicer uniforms than I had back in Redding.

At that time I had never thought about playing professional baseball. It was just a game to me, a fun game that consumed much of my life. But still, it was just a game. The year we moved to Sacramento, I went to my first major-league baseball game. The Giants had just left New York for San Francisco. Instead of the hallowed Polo Grounds in Washington Heights, they now played in Seals Stadium at Bryant and 16th in the Mission District. (Candlestick Park was still under construction.) The San Francisco Seals of the Pacific Coast League had started playing in the stadium in the early 1930s—Joe DiMaggio hit in 61 straight games when he played for the club in 1933. When the Giants arrived in '58, the Seals moved to Phoenix and became a Giants affiliate.

I saw my first game with my cousin Leo, who was a fireman in San Francisco and a big baseball fan. He took us to a game against the Cardinals on July 5, 1958. We sat on the right-field line, exactly in front of the Cardinals bullpen, in the first row. Lindy McDaniel started for the Cardinals and Mike McCormick was pitching for the Giants. McDaniel was only 22 years old at the time. (I couldn't have dreamed then that I would one day catch for him in the majors—but we would become teammates in 1974, when he was 38.)

At the time, I hadn't seen much pro baseball on television yet.

We learned about the game on the radio and in the paper, reading the box scores. That was the big thing. But I did know that Willie Mays was my hero, and he was out there playing in center field. During the game, Stan Musial struck out several times. I remember Larry Jackson getting up in the bullpen and warming up, right in front of us, in the ninth inning when the Giants were losing. I remember thinking, "Wow, that's a major-league player." It was special just to be that close to a real pro. The Giants came back in the bottom of the ninth, scoring two runs off Jackson to win, 5–4. It was incredible. When the game was over, we got to walk across the field, because the exit was in center. Here I was walking, walking on a *real* major-league field.

I remember it all, because I was just a baseball fan then. I loved the game.

A few years ago, I went back to find our old house in Redding. It's still there. Those majestic oak trees still mark the outfield wall. The left-field fence is still there, but there's an apartment built where the orchard was. The gray dirt and backstop made of old telephone poles are gone. The basepaths are overgrown. Our diamond is gone. The space is empty now, but I can still imagine a game playing there.

I still feel the hot Redding sun and see myself at the plate, tightening my grip on an oversized bat and swinging for the oak trees.

2

HOW SHOWCASE SKILLS ARE
HURTING THE GAME

Felipe López—do you remember him? He was a serviceable major-league infielder who played for eight teams (two of them twice) through his 11-season career, which started with the Toronto Blue Jays in 2001. He was once rated as the top defensive high school shortstop in the United States by *Baseball America*, and the Jays took him with the eighth-overall pick in the 1998 Major League Baseball draft. Over the span of his career, López was never able to scratch the surface of his capabilities. He made $17 million in his career as a ballplayer.

I don't think anyone should begrudge players the money they make today. They are given what the market dictates. But the reality is that when a marginal player can make a lifetime's wages in a relatively short career, it creates two problems.

The first is motivation. The $17 million that Lopez made isn't a lot by major-league standards. Most people accustomed to current salaries would read that figure without thinking twice about it. If anything, it seems low. But the comfort that comes with such a financial cushion can easily create a crisis of motivation. In today's game a guy can have a terrible year, and it doesn't really matter, because he still walked away with $5 million.

This is a new wrinkle in the long history of the game. These conditions didn't exist until the great Marvin Miller blazed a trail for player rights and secured the kind of compensation players had been robbed of for generations. Miller created one of the strongest unions in America in the Major League Baseball Players Association.

But when winning isn't tied to survival, when a marginal player can walk away with a king's ransom, how can a team get the most out of that player?

The second problem is the erosion of talent. Players get paid more than ever these days, but their instincts for the game have diminished. I've spoken with many scouts about this over the years. In North America we have become obsessed with radar guns, home-run bat speed and leg speed. Focusing on these details has skewed the way we evaluate talent. It rewards showcase skills; players get noticed by excelling against simplistic measures of their ability.

In Latin America you find well-rounded ballplayers because these young players have developed their skills on sandlots and in fields. They have played baseball, pure and simple. They have grown up in the game. In North America we don't play sandlot games anymore. We play showcase tournaments and area-code games. Our young players leap from team to team at the behest of their parents, who are searching for the best opportunity for their kid to get discovered. Because of that, these young players often miss out on building lasting relation-ships with their teammates, which is an essential experience. Some-thing important is developed in the connection between teammates. It's not the same anymore, in Little League *or* the big leagues. These days, it's rare for a player to wear the same team's uniform throughout his career. In an era of free agency, the concept of being part of a team is lost. Winning a World Series is great, but signing a contract worth $20 million per season is considered to be *much* better.

This is the new reality. Prospects look for signing bonuses. Estab-lished players try to boost their numbers to improve their arbitration cases. If you put up good numbers in the right categories, you're going to get rewarded. Your actual baseball sense means little. The art of actually *playing the game* has been de-emphasized.

Some people will try to dismiss my viewpoint. They'll try to say that baseball never really was a team sport. Or that players hunting for lucrative contracts makes them better players, and collectively, that makes for a better team. But they are wrong. (The importance of team unity is something we'll return to.) Despite what many cynical pundits say, the state of the clubhouse matters. Having a roster full of drones who think only about hitting the longest home runs or throwing the fastest fastball doesn't actually translate to team success.

We don't create instinctive baseball skills. We're not teaching these young players enough *baseball*. Yeah, prospects can hit the ball nine miles, but they can't hit a breaking ball, and they can't bunt, because these aren't skills that are valued at showcase events, where young athletes are put in front of a group of college and professional scouts for a short tournament. (In some of these showcases, young people pay hundreds of dollars just to participate.) We clock a player's speed between the bases, but we don't assess how well he reads a pitcher or how intelligent he is with the leads he takes off the bag. They have these showcase skills, but they haven't learned how to play the game of baseball in a competitive atmosphere. And that's what's missing with a lot of players today: They don't have that competitive edge. They don't have the game instinct.

Mel Didier knows more about this than pretty much everyone in the game. Didier has spent 65 years in and around Major League Baseball. You can spot his wide-brimmed straw hat towering above all the other heads at minor-league games across North America. The man has an encyclopedic knowledge about baseball, which he'll happily share in his warm southern drawl. If you're lucky enough to meet Mel, take the time to chat. He just loves the game. "I married baseball," his wife jokes.

The son of a college baseball coach, Didier pitched in the minor leagues back in the late '40s, first with the Stroudsburg Poconos in Pennsylvania (affiliated with the Cleveland Indians) and then Georgia's Thomasville Tigers (affiliated with the Detroit Tigers). A shoulder injury shortened his career. Unable to play, he moved to scouting, working with the Detroit Tigers, Milwaukee Braves and Atlanta Braves, and became one of the top scouts in the history of the game.

Didier became the first scouting director of the Montreal Expos, from 1970 until 1975. He was the guy who made sure Gary Carter remained a catcher when he was in the minors. Didier had placed Carter with an affiliated team in West Palm Beach in 1972 after the Expos drafted him as a shortstop. The manager of the team was Lance Nichols, who had been a catcher in his playing days. Didier believed Carter would be a great catcher and wanted him to learn the position from Nichols. But after about ten days Nichols called Didier and said he didn't think Carter could cut it behind the plate because he couldn't catch anything. Mel wasn't happy. He told Nichols that if he saw Gary's name listed on a score sheet at left field or at first base, he'd be fired. "You make him a catcher," Didier said. "Every morning at ten, you bring him out and teach him how to catch. You make him work!" Of course, Gary Carter became a Hall of Fame catcher—and Lance Nichols became a successful farm director, never forgetting the lesson he learned from Mel Didier.

Didier became a scout with the Dodgers under Al Campanis in 1976. Campanis, who played parts of seven seasons in the Dodgers minor-league system in the 1940s and seven games under Leo Durocher with the Dodgers in 1943, would construct a Dodgers team that went to three World Series in the 1970s before finally winning it in 1981. (Campanis's time as the Dodgers' GM ended after his terrible comments to Ted Koppel on ABC-TV's *Nightline* in 1987 about black players not having the proper attributes to be successful baseball managers.) Later in the decade, Didier was responsible for the Dodgers signing outfielder Kirk Gibson when he became a free agent in January 1988.

That same season, playing with two injured legs, Gibson went on to hit a home run off Dennis Eckersley of the Oakland A's to win the first game of the World Series. Before the series, Didier had written a report on Eckersley, claiming that with a 3–2 count and a left-handed hitter at the plate, the pitcher was certain to throw a backdoor slider. Gibson would later recall that he could hear Didier's advice in the back of his head as he stepped back into the batter's box with a full count and readied for the pitch. He knew exactly what was coming. That was the only at-bat Gibson had in the series, because of his bad knees, but he made the most of it, helping the Dodgers beat the A's four games to one to win the World Series.

After the Dodgers, Didier worked with the Seattle Mariners and coached at the University of Southwestern Louisiana. In the late 1990s he joined the front office of the Arizona Diamondbacks, helping to piece together a team that won the World Series in 2001, just three years after the expansion team began play. He later worked as a scout for the Baltimore Orioles and Texas Rangers before becoming a special advisor to the Toronto Blue Jays. At almost 90 years old now, he remains an integral part of the team's brain trust.

In short, Didier knows the game of baseball inside out.

He's also seen it change.

One of the most recent changes, he says, has been at the plate. Almost all young players want to be home-run hitters. The fascination with the long ball started back when Babe Ruth captivated the sports world with bombs, including his record-setting 60 in 1927. Of course, there were great hitters before Ruth, like the incomparable Ty Cobb and George Sisler. But with his moon shots, the Great Bambino created a mythology all his own.

Others followed: Hank Greenberg, Joe DiMaggio, Ted Williams, Stan Musial, Mickey Mantle, Roger Maris, Willie Mays. The game's best hitters captivate our imagination. They become our heroes.

But it wasn't until the last 20 years—in the midst of the steroid era and skyrocketing salaries—that hitting home runs became an obsession in the game. The slick-fielding shortstops and second basemen, who pick up decent batting averages and on-base percentages by making contact, slapping out singles and driving in runs, don't draw the same kind of salaries that players who crush the ball do. There are exceptions, of course, like Derek Jeter and Dustin Pedroia. But for the most part these days, the money goes to the sluggers. So naturally, that's what everyone wants to be.

As a result, the most attention in a player's developmental years is spent on offense. Defense is still taught, Didier says, but kids spend more time in batting cages than ever before. To really excel on defense, young players have to work at it on their own time, because most of their formal training focuses on driving the ball. "We've carried this into professional baseball," says Didier. "We spend a great, great deal of time on the offensive side of the game."

Well, sort of.

It would be great if every aspect of offense were taught with the same attention that slugging the ball received. But it doesn't happen that way. For example, Didier points out that bunting isn't *really* part of the offensive toolbox that young players develop. It exists, of course, but the real fundamentals of the skill aren't stressed the way they were when Didier first started scouting players. Even players who excel on the field and between the bases can't seem to get the need to hit homers out of their minds.

"We have to remind our minor-league players—guys that are, say, 5-10, 5-11, 165, 185 pounds—that they're not going to be home-run hitters," says Didier. "They're all trying to hit home runs because they want to get the big pay."

In high school and college you'll find a lot of big, strong kids who can hit the ball a mile. They also strike out constantly. Hitters aren't learning to look for the right pitches. "They are swinging from their tails," says Didier. They are looking to hammer the ball out of the park. I believe there is a connection between this approach at the plate and the remarkable increase in strikeouts we have seen over the decades.

Consider these numbers compiled by Stats Inc.: Since 1958, when I saw my first big-league game, strikeouts have gone from an average of 5.02 per game to 7.88. In the American League the average has gone from 4.87 strikeouts per game in 1958 to 7.53 in 2015. In the 1920s the average batter struck out once every 12.22 at-bats. That rate dropped

HOW SHOWCASE SKILLS ARE HURTING THE GAME

in each of the next four decades, reaching 5.92 at-bats per strike-out in the '60s, when pitchers dominated the game. In 1968 scoring reached an historical low of 3.42 runs per game. The pitcher's mound was lowered the following season, and scoring shot up 19 percent to 4.07 runs per game. Through the '70s and '80s, the strikeout rate hovered around 6.5. But since 2010 the average major leaguer has struck out once every 4.58 at-bats.

These are alarming statistics. Yes, we have entered an era dominated by excellent pitching. And yes, players today have the added challenge of facing specialist pitchers with fresh arms, coming into the game more frequently. That might explain the rising strikeout rate in part. But not completely. In fact, the number of at-bats per strikeout has continued to decline steadily each season for the past five years, from 4.82 in 2010 to 4.42 in 2015.

In 2014 when Mike Trout hit 36 home runs and was named the American League's Most Valuable Player, he struck out 184 times—the most by any batter in the American League. (By comparison, when a 22-year-old Joe DiMaggio hit 46 home runs in 1937, he struck out 37 times all season.)

I have little doubt that the rise in strikeouts is correlated with the modern hitters' focus on swinging for the fences. Of course, no one can argue that home runs are a bad thing. But when power hitting is overemphasized to the detriment of a more intelligent approach at the plate, it diminishes the game. It clearly takes a lot more than home runs to build a winning franchise. You can't field a team of huge, slow guys who do nothing but hit the long ball.

Still, the attitude Didier finds among a lot of young players after they strike out is "Well, what's the difference? If I hit a pop fly or hit a groundball, I still get out." It doesn't register on them how important it is to just put the ball in play. Making contact puts the onus on the defense. Grounding out or flying out is always better than striking out. If you put the ball in play enough, the other team will make errors or open up holes in their coverage that give your team a chance to win the game.

This is basic, fundamental baseball. And we're getting away from it.

TWO-TIME SILVER SLUGGER and nine-time Gold Glove winner Torii Hunter credits the irascible Tom Kelly, his former manager with the Minnesota Twins, with hammering the fundamentals into him on the field and at the plate. He watched Kelly take players off the field when they missed the cutoff man or botched an easy play because they weren't focused. At the plate, if he told a batter to hit to right center, but the guy pulled the ball every time he was at bat, that player could expect to sit the next day. With Kelly it was never about showcase skills; it was about fundamentals—and having players who could do what he needed them to get done. Hunter credits Kelly's insistence on the basics with guiding him through such a successful career. "I look back, I say, 'You know what? Because of him I know how to play this game,'" says Hunter, a five-time All-Star. "I know how to go the opposite way, and you can't just do a shift on me, because I'm going to shoot it the other way. He taught me that." ("The shift" is a defensive alignment that repositions the fielders to overload the side of the field that a batter has a demonstrated tendency to hit to.)

Hunter also had the fundamentals drilled into him while he played in the Minnesota Twins' minor-league system. Showcase skills didn't cut it then. They ran through basic drills, "over and over and over again"—hammering Hunter and his counterparts with the baseball instincts that would make them actual ballplayers instead of fading away as one-dimensional and undeveloped draft picks.

"They were serious about that, and that's why you see the finished product today," says Hunter, who made his major-league debut in 1997 and returned to the Twins in 2015 at the age of 40. "I might not be as athletic as I was, but still I try to do everything the right way, as far as hitting the cutoff man, going first to third, knowing what's going on and being a student of the game."

Tom Kelly's influence was apparent in game two of the 2015 American League Division Series between the Blue Jays and the Texas Rangers. In the top of the first, the Rangers took a quick 2–0 lead, and with one out, they had Prince Fielder on third base. Josh Hamilton hit a bouncing groundball toward Jays first baseman Chris Colabello. Colabello had faced the same situation in spring training with the Twins a year earlier but had messed it up, quickly making the out at first but allowing the runner on third to score. Kelly, who has been working as a special advisor to the Twins since he retired as manager, took Colabello aside later to walk him through what had gone wrong and to show him a better way to keep the runner from scoring. In that playoff game with the Jays, Colabello thought back to what Kelly had taught him. He kept his eyes locked on Fielder while running toward the first-base line to intercept Hamilton with a tag. Fielder stopped in his tracks, not knowing what to do. After making the out on Hamilton, Colabello charged across the diamond toward Fielder, who was stunned like a deer in the headlights and was easily tagged out. The heads-up play ended an inning that threatened to put the Jays in an enormous hole right from the start. So Toronto can thank Tom Kelly for that one.

That's the fundamental baseball intelligence that is being forgotten at the developmental level of the game in North America today.

Aside from hitting bombs, pitching for the radar gun has become a major showcase-skill obsession among young players. And just as swinging for the fences is an unfortunate distraction from the true art of hitting, throwing for speed works to the disadvantage of pitchers as they develop. But it's not their fault. It's such a challenge for a youngster trying to make it on the mound these days. If he doesn't light up the radar gun now, he's basically got no chance to play pro ball.

EVERY YEAR, DIDIER SPEAKS at high school coaching clinics around the United States and Canada. About 15 years ago he started to hear more and more from people who would marvel at how hard teenagers were throwing. To be a top prospect, you'd need to have a fastball hitting 95 miles per hour.

"Man, we didn't have kids throwing like that 20, 30 years ago!" he'd hear them say.

"Well, we didn't have radar guns then," he'd always reply. "So we don't know."

As a pitcher, Didier never had a clue how hard he threw the ball. And throwing smoke really wasn't the goal anyway. It was about control. To get noticed today, pitchers focus on one trick: speed. But that speed doesn't guarantee anything. "As soon as scouts hear those numbers—93, 95—they don't worry about how well he can pitch," says Didier.

And because there is a premium on pitchers, as with home-run hitters, everybody wants to be one. A high school coach from California recently told Didier about a widespread trend he was noticing. Excellent defensive players, like shortstops and center fielders, who demonstrate in high school that they have great arms but aren't power hitters, are being told by their coaches that if they want to get noticed, they need to get on the mound. So instead of developing into great defensive infielders or outfielders, they become pitchers. Great pitchers are a coveted commodity in the major leagues, and so they go higher in the draft. According to Baseball-Reference.com, just over 47 percent of players taken in the first round between 2011 and 2015 were pitchers. And teams looking to acquire veterans at the trade deadline must give up a bounty of pitching prospects. At the 2015 trade deadline, 62 major-league players were traded, 38 of whom were pitchers. That's more than 61 percent. Of those pitchers, 12 had ranked among the top ten on a franchise's list of top prospects at some point in their young careers. The Blue Jays acquired five players at the deadline—Troy Tulowitzki, LaTroy Hawkins, David Price, Mark Lowe and Ben Revere—by moving 11 pitchers, eight of whom were 22 years old or younger. Other trades across the majors that involved such key veterans as Cole Hamels, Ben Zobrist, Gerardo Parra, Johnny Cueto, Scott Kazmir, Aramis Ramírez, Sammy Dyson, Juan Uribe, Kelly Johnson and Yoenis Céspedes involved 14 top pitching prospects.

"So all of a sudden, instead of being a shortstop who has a great arm, good hands, can't hit, gets drafted in the 15th round for $25,000, he moves to the pitcher's mound," says Didier. "And all of a sudden, he gets drafted in the third round and gets $800,000. Or if he's a first rounder, he gets $2 million."

That's a difficult incentive to argue with. There is a lot of pressure to be a high draft pick because it guarantees a significant payout. In the first two or three rounds of the draft—around 100 picks—about half will be pitchers with good arms. But the return on those investments isn't always great. The cost, for the teams and the players, can be high. "The good arms disappear quick," says Didier, with a foreboding tone. "I mean, those college arms and those good high school arms—they disappear *quick*."

And when they don't have the speed, many are left with nothing.

The alternative is a guy like Mark Buehrle, one of the most consistent pitchers in the game. Never a flamethrower, Buehrle was an afterthought who was cut from his high school team as a sophomore in St. Charles, Missouri. He went on to pitch at Jefferson Community College, where his velocity topped out at around 80 miles per hour. He put on a bit of weight and managed to get his speed up through his freshman year, but his game plan was never to blow batters away with his speed. After one of his games, scouts came down to chat with him. They loved his command and control. Buehrle assumed they were there to see the team's ace, a hard-throwing lefty. He told them they had the wrong guy. But each time he pitched for Jefferson, more and more scouts came out to see him. The Chicago White Sox eventually drafted him, in the 38th round in 1998.

From his first season as a starter, in 2001, until 2014, Buehrle pitched more than 200 innings every year. He fell just short of that mark in 2015. He has won a World Series. He has pitched a no-hitter. He has pitched a perfect game. He has been one of the game's best pitchers for a decade and a half. And in his mid-30s, Buehrle is still going strong. He has done it by being a workhorse with an arsenal of pitches who doesn't overthink the game. He never shakes off his catcher. He wastes no time between pitches.

"[If] you throw 95-plus, you've got a better chance," says Buehrle.

"But for me it was location and movement and, you know, throwing your off-speed pitches behind in the count when the hitter thinks a fastball's coming—and the confidence to throw pretty much any pitch, in any situation. I think that's what's gotten me where I'm at today."

When the Jays traded for him in 2013, Buehrle took on a mentorship role with many of the team's young arms. One of his most common nuggets of wisdom is to remind them not to overdo it. If they throw 95 miles per hour, they don't need to try to crank it up to 97. He has found himself in jams where he has tried to power his way out. Instead of hitting his spots at 83 miles per hour, he has tried to crank it up to 86, and the ball just sat over the middle of the plate. "That's when you get hurt," says Buehrle. "You've just got to stay within yourself."

He has been baffled when hitters have told him they'd rather face a guy throwing 100 miles per hour instead of a pitcher like him. "I'm like, 'How is that possible?'" he says. But if the ball is coming in straight, major-league hitters can always catch up to it. With movement, though, it doesn't matter if the pitch is coming in at 80 or 90 miles per hour—hitters hate dealing with it. So Buehrle's advice to the new guys is simple: "Just worry about location and movement," he tells them. "Don't worry about velocity."

Wise words from one of the best. But even Mark Buehrle feels lucky to have had the chance to show what he can do without firing bullets in college. Today, so much potential is overlooked because of our obsession with the radar gun. I think it's time to holster it for good.

But that will take an enormous shift in how we view the game. It will require us to look beyond showcase skills to evaluate talent.

There's no easy solution. It's hard to argue with the mindset of youngsters who dream of making a million dollars just by getting drafted, not to mention becoming one of the game's biggest stars—and receiving a potential bounty worth the GDP of a small country. Kids will dream of being sluggers and aces because that's exactly what the game rewards.

No, the kids can't be expected to change. They only do what they're being told is most important.

The showcase culture won't change, unless there is a fundamental shift in the way franchises develop and evaluate talent.

3

WHY BRANCH RICKEY IS STILL
THE SMARTEST MAN IN BASEBALL

This book is not about trashing the game today. Baseball is a flourishing sport, enjoying terrific popularity and financial success. It has survived as a beloved pastime, captivating our imaginations for more than a century. Recent scandals like the influx of steroid use tarnished the game's reputation and converted a generation of fans into skeptics who wrinkle their brows at every 400-foot home run and every 40-home-run season put up these days. But the game will go on, just like it did after the Chicago White Sox gambling scandal in 1919. In fact, I believe we are seeing a resurgence in our passion for the purity of the game because of the steroid scandal. People want to get back to the basics. Don't get me wrong: Baseball is big business, and as long as money is its driving force, the sport will face many more scandals. There will always be people who find a way to cheat. But the game will *always* survive them.

That's because, at the heart of it, this game is really about the joy of playing. It is about the memories I shared in the first chapter. It is about dirt and grass and a fresh summer breeze. It is about imagination. From the mid–19th century to today, that part—the heart of the game—remains *exactly* the same.

So this book isn't intended to make it seem like there is something inherently wrong with baseball. It's more of a counterargument to those who think baseball has somehow changed for the better. In the last 20 years we've heard constantly about how the game is being redefined, as though a deluge of statistics has somehow altered the way it's played.

I have wondered if the people who came up with batting averages and earned run averages felt that they had changed the game, the way we sometimes talk about stats like on-base percentage and WHIP (walks plus hits per inning pitched) as being revolutionary. The numbers have always been important. They are a way to interpret. They attempt to tell us *what*. But they can never tell us *why*.

This book is an attempt to explain the *why*. But it is also an attempt to reflect on what has made teams great in the past, and how those same principles can be applied today. The game is still great, but it needs a changeup. So many new factors have come into play over the past few decades that it's difficult to realize that this is not a sport that hinges on reinvention. At least I don't believe it is. Rather, it is a game that builds on past lessons.

In baseball it's all been done before. We've forgotten that. Today, we are trying to reinvent the wheel. We can't. Baseball is a game that doesn't allow you to do that. We are introducing more and more stats, coming up with new algorithms that say exactly what we've known about the game for decades. Some of the stats are helpful, others are not—they are just a distraction. The bottom line is that in baseball, you've got to catch it, you've got to be able to pitch it, and you've got to be able to keep the other team from scoring. If you do those things, you're going to be in the contest; you're going to be in contention.

THERE ARE LINKS THAT CONNECT the great franchises in the game. If you look at the most successful organizations, reaching way back, the principles of building a winner are all the same.

In my mind, the model franchise started with Branch Rickey. No one in the game has had the impact that he had.

Rickey played ball in the early 1900s, but he never had much of a career as a player. He was a staunchly religious man who famously refused to play on Sundays and abstained from the vice of alcohol. In history, he'd be best known for signing Jackie Robinson for the Brooklyn Dodgers. And while that was certainly his most important contribution to the game, Rickey's legacy goes well beyond his challenge to the racist mold that infested the sport.

Branch Rickey was also baseball's greatest innovator. After his playing career, while he was coaching at the University of Michigan, Rickey was obsessed with teaching the art and science of baseball. He ran his players through bunting and base-running drills, and showed his catchers the proper way to flip off a mask when chasing down a fly ball. He created sand pits where he ran his players through proper sliding techniques. He tried to keep hitters from taking long strides by placing a shot-putter's toe board at the front of the batter's box, so they couldn't step beyond it. Several of his players sprained their ankles, so he was forced to reconsider. He also tried to tie a rope around the players' ankles, but found that didn't work either. That was just the beginning of his innovative approach to training players.

After coaching at the college level Rickey started out as a front-office executive with the St. Louis Browns, where he most notably signed a young George Sisler, whom the Pittsburgh Pirates claimed as their property, but whom Rickey successfully kept for his team. Leaving the Browns, Rickey purchased a small stake in the St. Louis Cardinals and served as team president and business manager, a precursor to the more modern concept of general manager.

The Cardinals were a notoriously cash-strapped team, operating in an era of massive checkbooks. Baseball was already a rich man's hobby. Rickey always believed that the presence of limitless cash was a bad thing for baseball. It made owners try to buy championship teams instead of developing them.

Operating as a poor man, Rickey had to be creative. In 1919 he held an open tryout at Cardinal Field, allowing hundreds of hopefuls from across the Midwest and South to make the trip at their own expense and see if they had what it took to make the majors. Out of the experiment, he found a coal miner's son named Jim Bottomley. The kid was rough around the edges, but he showed the athleticism that Rickey believed a professional ballplayer needed. He also had a decent left-handed swing. After a few years of development, Bottomley spent a decade as the Cardinals' regular first baseman. He hit .310 through his career and was elected into the Hall of Fame in 1974.

Branch Rickey also persuaded the team's majority owner to buy into two minor-league franchises so that the Cardinals could have first crack at their players. He was the first to realize that if his team couldn't afford to buy its players, they'd have to develop their own. In doing so, Rickey essentially created the farm system, where players learned how to play the game the way an organization expected, in terms of skill and demeanor, and as such introduced the concept of building a team of homegrown players. Despite facing widespread criticism, as well as direct opposition from commissioner Kenesaw Mountain Landis, Rickey's system created a crop of players who were brought up in the Cardinals organization. From Dizzy Dean and Pepper Martin to Stan Musial and Enos Slaughter, Rickey's farm system harnessed and developed talent that would direct the course of one of the most successful franchises in the history of the game.

Rickey did much more than develop talent. He had a keen sense of his assets and how to manage them. His grandfather had been a horse trader during the Civil War, a fact he was always proud of. He remembered his grandfather telling him that it was more important to know *your* horses than it was to know the other guy's. If you don't know what you're trading, Rickey believed, you're always going to come out on the short end.

What Rickey had was Rogers Hornsby, one of the best players in the game. And the New York Giants wanted him—badly.

In 1919, after a game between the Cardinals and Giants, Rickey found himself at the same local tavern as Giants owner Charles Stoneham. Stoneham offered him a drink, which Rickey politely declined. Then he declined Stoneham's $175,000 cash offer for Hornsby. Mistaking Rickey's rejection as a play for more money, Stoneham upped his offer to $300,000, plus a $50,000 bonus if the Giants won the pennant with Hornsby in the lineup. Rickey wasn't interested.

Stoneham scoffed and questioned how the Cardinals' business manager could face his stockholders, having rejected such an enormous sum for a single player. (The offer was worth more than the equivalent of nearly $5 million today.)

Instead of being bullied into selling Hornsby, Rickey made a counter-offer.

"Maybe I will consider dealing Mr. Hornsby if you offer me a new player of yours, Mr. Frank Frisch," Rickey replied. "In fact, I'll offer $50,000 for him."

At the time, Frisch was a rookie with no minor-league experience who had just graduated from Fordham University. At just 155 pounds he was an incredible athlete, having played on both the baseball and football teams at Fordham. Rickey saw great potential in Frisch, even though he would only bat .224 in his first season with the Giants.

He was trading horses—knowing the value of what he had.

"You haven't got $50,000," Stoneham huffed as he left the tavern. "You haven't got a quarter."

But the Giants' interest in Hornsby only increased when the New York Yankees bought Babe Ruth from the Boston Red Sox at the end of the 1919 season. (The next year, Ruth would hit 54 home runs for the Bronx Bombers, more than any other *team* in baseball. The St. Louis Browns were the closest to the Sultan of Swat, with 50.)

Desperate to keep up with their crosstown rivals, the Giants again tried to get Hornsby from the Cardinals in 1920, this time offering five players. Again, Rickey declined. He held on to Hornsby, his only true star, who demanded to be paid like one and was a constant source of grief when it came to practice, exhibition games and contracts. Still, he was one of the best in the game.

Rickey's patience paid off. In 1926, led by Hornsby, the Cardinals beat Babe Ruth and the mighty New York Yankees to win the World Series.

The Cardinals' ownership eventually soured on the ever-difficult Hornsby, and Rickey was forced to move him. Once again, the Giants were after him. And this time, they were willing to move Frisch, who had become a .300 hitter and was among one of the league's best base-stealers. Exactly as Rickey had predicted.

In the end, although he didn't want to lose Hornsby, Rickey got his man Frisch. And because he hadn't taken the bait all those years earlier, he also had a World Series title.

Frisch would become player/manager of the famed Gashouse Gang, the nickname the powerhouse Cardinals earned in the 1930s as a Depression-rocked nation looked to baseball for its heroes. The team was made up of players who had developed through Rickey's farm system: Dizzy Dean, his brother Daffy Dean, Pepper Martin, Ducky Medwick, Ripper Collins, Bill DeLancey, Spud Davis and Burgess Whitehead were all among the colorful names that the Cardinals turned into top talents.

They won the World Series in 1934.

Rickey's farm system would also develop Hall of Famers Slaughter and Musial, who debuted in 1938 and 1941 respectively. Rickey's innovative approach to player development harnessed talent that would set the course for one of the most successful franchises in the history of the game. St. Louis won nine National League titles with players signed and developed during Rickey's tenure. He made the Cardinals the benchmark for success.

In 1942 the Cardinals had their most successful season in franchise history, winning 106 games and another World Series title.

The pipe-smoking, Sabbath-respecting general manager moved on to the Brooklyn Dodgers in 1943, taking over as the team's president and general manager. As I mentioned earlier, it was with the Dodgers in 1945 that Rickey signed Jackie Robinson, the first black player in the major leagues in the modern era. Robinson led the Dodgers to the pennant in 1947, his first year with the club. Rickey's efforts to break the color barrier paved the way for Robinson's courage. His innovative methodology for building a successful baseball franchise has had more impact on the game of baseball than anything since.

RICKEY UNDERSTOOD THAT PERSONALITIES are what make the difference between a winning and losing franchise. At the team's core there must be the right mix of personalities, all of whom are willing to buy into the team's system and mindset. Without that, you have nothing.

Along with finding the right personalities, Rickey understood that the most important areas to address on the diamond are speed, pitching and defense. He believed that a team will win games if its players learn how to catch and pitch the ball effectively. He was talking about this just after the First World War. The bottom line is that you've got to catch it and you've got to pitch it—you have got to be able to keep the other team from scoring.

Rickey's influence can be seen in almost any successful franchise since the 1940s. You could see it in the Yankees Way that emerged with Casey Stengel and the Yankees of the 1950s. You can see it in the speed and defense of the remarkable Royals team Dayton Moore has pieced together in Kansas City today. And you can see shades of Rickey in the moves Alex Anthopoulos and the Blue Jays made in 2015, when, after two decades of mediocrity, they picked up an MVP-caliber player in Josh Donaldson, over whom they will have control for the next four years. It took a young third baseman and three pitching prospects to make the deal, though no one can argue that the cost was too high. The Jays also signed a veteran catcher in Russell Martin, a proven clubhouse leader with playoff experience. And during the season, Anthopoulos orchestrated a series of trades that saw the departure of 11—11!— pitching prospects in exchange for ace David Price and the game's best shortstop in Troy Tulowitzki, solidifying a team with enough talent to finally win a World Series. Without harvesting top pitching prospects like Jeff Hoffman, who went to Colorado for Tulo, and Daniel Norris, who helped bring over former Cy Young Award winner Price, the Jays would have had nothing to begin with. Anthopoulos was trading horses too. And those moves wouldn't have happened without a well-developed farm system.

One key point about Rickey was that his system didn't just develop assets, as essential as that component was. You can put the best individual players, the best numbers, together on a team and they might not be a top team. Rickey always emphasized what he called "pepper-pot players"—those who would never give in to being against the odds and never thought about anything other than winning. In Martin and Donaldson, Anthopoulos brought in players with the values that a winning organization needs. It's about more than raw numbers.

4

WHAT WE CAN LEARN FROM
THE ORIOLES WAY

There are some men in baseball whose ability to push against the game's stubborn conventions has had a lasting influence on the game, one so strong that it can still be witnessed on the field today.

Harry Dalton is one of those guys.

When Dalton first joined the Baltimore Orioles front office in 1954, he was just a fresh-faced 25-year-old looking to pursue a dream. He had served in the United States Air Force during the Korean War, and returned to a brief run as a sportswriter in Springfield, Massachusetts, in the region where he grew up. But when the St. Louis Browns relocated to Baltimore in 1954, the place where Dalton's parents had recently moved, he saw it as a perfect opportunity to hook himself into the game he loved. He worked in the front office in a position that paid so little he had to drive a taxi at night to make ends meet.

When Paul Richards was hired as the Orioles' manager and general manager in September of that year, he brought with him a firm philosophy on how an organization should be operated. Richards had been an excellent major-league catcher starting in the 1930s with the Brooklyn Dodgers, New York Giants, Philadelphia Athletics and Detroit Tigers, with whom he won the World Series in 1945. Holding both positions was very rare at the time, but it allowed Richards to implement his ideas without any resistance. He wanted a uniform system of baseball instruction throughout the franchise's farm system. He wanted everything to operate in tune with a singular vision for success. He also wanted to develop talent that would grow within that system.

Richards signed and traded for young pitchers with strong arms and solid defensive players. In 1955 he was part of a 17-player trade with the New York Yankees, which is still the biggest swap in baseball history. And he signed such talented youngsters as the great Brooks Robinson, one of the best third basemen in the history of the game. (They nicknamed him Mr. Hoover, after the brand of vacuum cleaner, because nothing got by him. Robinson would win 16 consecutive Gold Glove Awards while manning the Orioles infield.) Richards also picked up young pitchers such as Steve Barber, Milt Pappas and Chuck Estrada. Under his leadership, the Orioles developed a solid base of talent after several years of mediocrity and showed the early signs of what would come to be known as the Orioles Way. In 1958 Yankees executive Lee MacPhail became the Orioles' general manager, allowing Richards to focus on managing the team.

Meanwhile, Dalton worked his way up from the lowest rung of the Orioles front office, learning how to scout and how to foster the organization's minor-league system, until he became the team's farm director in 1961. MacPhail and Richards had stocked the Orioles' farm teams with young talent including Dave Nicholson, Pete Ward, Ron Hansen, Boog Powell and Dave McNally. By the early 1960s, the Orioles had become American League pennant contenders. MacPhail implemented strict quality-control methods in the Orioles scouting department, including the dogged crosschecking of scouting reports on the same player before offering a contract.

In the fall of 1965 Dalton was promoted to general manager when MacPhail left the Orioles to join the league commissioner's office. One of Dalton's first moves, in December of 1965, was to acquire the already-legendary Frank Robinson from the Cincinnati Reds in exchange for pitchers Milt Pappas and Jack Baldschun and outfielder Dick Simpson. (MacPhail had been part of the early discussions around the trade before he left for his new post.) It was a bold move that diverged from the steadfast path of fielding homegrown talent, but there was obvious value in giving something up for the All-Star outfielder.

Shortly after Dalton took over as general manager, another eager but inexperienced young man came looking for his dream job. Twenty-five-year-old John Schuerholz wrote a letter to Jerold Hoffberger, the president of the National Brewing Company and the owner of the Baltimore Orioles. As a kid he had gone to school across from Memorial Stadium on 33rd Street in Baltimore, and he used to look out the window during class and dream of working there one day. Now he was just finishing up his graduate studies in administration and supervision at Loyola College and had already entered the workforce as an educator. But Schuerholz decided to take a wild stab at his dream job. In his letter to Hoffberger, Schuerholz explained that throughout his youth he had harbored aspirations of spending his life in the game of baseball. He had played baseball at Towson University in Baltimore and had a burning desire to stay in the game. (The baseball facility at Towson now bears his name.) He explained his passion, his love for the sport, his deep knowledge of baseball history, and the abiding joy the game brought him. "That's all I could tell him," Schuerholz recalls. "I didn't know what the hell I could do."

The letter was just enough to get him in the door. Schuerholz was called in for an interview with general manager Harry Dalton; Frank Cashen, the head of baseball operations; and Lou Gorman, the team's new director of player development. He walked in without a clue of what they would ask him or whether there was even a job opening at all. Despite the blind circumstances, young Schuerholz impressed them all. The team was looking for someone to work as an assistant to Gorman. They offered Schuerholz the job.

UNDER HARRY DALTON, the Orioles had become the preeminent scouting and player-development organization on the planet, Schuerholz says. It was a carryover from the days of Paul Richards. Working for the Orioles was an invaluable education for Schuerholz. He eagerly read all of the in-depth reports on the players in the Orioles organization, at each level of the minors. He pored through the team's filing cabinets, reading every bulletin he could, bringing himself up to speed on the ins and outs of building a franchise.

At first, Schuerholz didn't realize how good the Orioles team he was working for actually was. Baltimore had one of the best defensive infields in the majors, with Brooks Robinson at third and the great

Luis Aparicio at short. Davey Johnson was at second and Boog Powell played first. The pitching rotation was developed entirely within the Orioles' robust farm system, and it featured such young guns as Dave McNally, Wally Bunker, Steve Barber and 20-year-old Jim Palmer, who went on to win three Cy Young Awards and earn a spot in the Hall of Fame.

Dalton's big off-season acquisition paid off too. Frank Robinson hit .316, with 49 home runs and 122 RBIs in 1966, winning the Triple Crown and earning the American League MVP Award.

It didn't take long for Schuerholz to realize his lifelong dream of being part of a World Series–winning team. The Orioles won 97 games that year and went on to win the franchise's first world championship with a four-game sweep of the Los Angeles Dodgers, a team that had one of history's great starting rotations with Don Drysdale, Claude Osteen, Don Sutton and Sandy Koufax on the mound. However, it was the Orioles' pitching staff that secured the victory. Baltimore threw three shutouts in the final three games. The Dodgers didn't score after the third inning of game one of the Series. (In that game, Moe Drabowsky took the mound in relief of McNally, with two out in the third, and pitched the rest of the game, allowing one hit and striking out 11, including six in a row.)

The firepower came from within the Orioles' development system. On the 1966 world championship team, the entire starting rotation was homegrown. And with the exception of Frank Robinson and Luis Aparicio, every man in the Orioles lineup was a product of the Baltimore system.

That was the key factor in the Orioles Way. The organization scouted talent better than any other team. And developed that talent better than any team. Under Harry Dalton and the Orioles Way, Baltimore made it to the World Series four times in six seasons. In 1969 the Orioles won 109 games but were upset by the New York Mets—the "Miracle Mets"—in the World Series. Baltimore returned to the World Series in 1970, after winning 108 games in the regular season. This time the Orioles faced the Cincinnati Reds' "Big Red Machine," managed by Sparky Anderson and starring Tony Pérez, Joe Morgan, Bobby Tolan, Lee May, Johnny Bench and Pete Rose. Led by two home runs from Frank Robinson in the fifth and deciding game, the Orioles won their second world championship. Baltimore went for back-to-back titles the following season but lost a heartbreaker to Roberto Clemente and the Pittsburgh Pirates in seven games.

With Dalton's Orioles, Schuerholz saw how the team's culture, from top to bottom, ingrained a sense of pride in the organization. The expectation was to be the best. Of course, every organization claims that it wants to be the best, but this was different. This was about a unified culture. It was about how everyone in the organization carried themselves. "It was second nature," says Schuerholz. "That's the way they talked, the way they acted. The way they expected everybody in the organization to perform and produce."

He watched how Harry Dalton, Lou Gorman and Frank Cashen conducted themselves at the helm of the organization. He watched how they worked together, how they spoke to others, what the expectations at all levels were, and whom they surrounded themselves with. He learned from them the way a resident doctor watches surgery. There was a precise way of doing things.

The "secret sauce" behind the Orioles' success was made up of the homegrown players and having the right people placed across the organization, Schuerholz says. You want a team that is created and constructed to get to championship games, but that doesn't happen in a season. It takes time. With the Orioles, Schuerholz says he learned that a successful team puts quality people in all of the areas required to build a successful baseball enterprise: scouting and player development at the grassroots level; scouting and player development at the amateur level; scouting at the professional level; player development all the way from Rookie league to Triple A. The idea is to actually get guys ready to play in the big leagues, and then to play well when they get there.

That's the central focus of a good organization. Today, you may see many organizations trying to trade or sign their way to a championship. They'll try to buy talent instead of developing it. Buying talent is important, at the right time and at the right price. But without a system built on good people at all levels, you won't have the foundation needed to be a real winner. Harry Dalton knew that. He knew that the most essential ingredient to a winning franchise is what your system is developing. "It's all about the players," says Schuerholz. "It's about their skills and abilities, it's about their physicality, it's about their character, it's about their work ethic, it's about the whole circle that the Orioles had."

And Dalton's Orioles found plenty of creative ways to define and evaluate exactly what it was they were looking for. All of their scouts carried around sheets of paper that were used exclusively in the team's assessment of talent. On each page was a circle with a line across the middle, sort of like an equator splitting it in half. Above the line were all of the physical things you can see. For a pitcher, it was how hard he threw, how sharp his breaking ball was, what kind of movement the guy had. For fielders, there were indicators for how agile the player was and what kind of speed he had. For a catcher, how he blocked the ball and the kind of a game he called.

All of this was basically standard, of course. Every organization evaluated those areas. What set the Orioles apart, however, was what appeared beneath the line. The scouts were asked to gauge each player's psychological characteristics—the player's work ethic, team mentality and other personality traits that were fundamental to the Orioles Way.

"We were asked to be always mindful, when we were sending our scouts out, to find players that would fit the Oriole mold," says Schuerholz. The Orioles scouts and coaches brought the evaluation charts everywhere they went. They were proprietary to the team, developed by a few of the organization's most established scouts. Nobody on the outside was allowed to see exactly what they were looking for or how they were assessing those traits.

Because the Orioles had such a well-balanced approach to uncovering prospects, they were able to create one of the most robust farm systems in the game. But they didn't just have players who put up great stats at the plate and in the field. They recognized the value of personality and understood the effect it had on an individual's ability to grow as a player.

Even today, I believe that Dalton and his Orioles staff understood development better than most. With their carefully selected stable of youngsters, they implemented a culture that permeated all levels of the organization. They defined what it meant to be an Oriole.

DON BAYLOR, WHOM I WOUND UP playing winter ball with, was one of the young prospects in the organization in the late 1960s. He was drafted as an outfielder by the team in 1967. He was in the team's minor-league system for three years before reaching the major leagues in 1970

(around the time we played together in winter ball). As a youngster in the Orioles system, he had firsthand experience with the culture that the organization had established from top to bottom. The Orioles had just won the World Series, and even the brand new prospects shared a sense of pride in the victory.

"It permeated all the way down to the minor leagues," says Baylor. "You were proud of the organization. You wanted to make it to the big leagues, but you had to understand how to play."

Cal Ripken Sr. was one of the excellent coaches in the Orioles' minor-league system. Joe Altobelli was another. After spending 11 years developing as a manager in the Orioles' farm system, Altobelli went on to manage the San Francisco Giants, later managing the Orioles and the Chicago Cubs. Under Ripken and Altobelli, Baylor remembers spending days in the field, practicing relay plays over and over again. They worked on gripping the ball properly at the seams and knowing exactly where the cutoff man needed to be. "It wasn't high school anymore," says Baylor.

The farm system was about developing fundamentals and fostering character. Even in the minors, players looked up to Frank Robinson as a leader within the organization. Robinson was the example, the standard for excellence that the Orioles expected of everyone. "The leadership just really fell on him," says Baylor. "He took the responsibility with his bat, he backed it up on the field . . . it kind of gave the Orioles' young guys a push."

That culture created an environment where the players pushed each other and coached each other. There was accountability among teammates. Baylor came up through the minors with several players who would become key parts of the Orioles' future. He was teammates with second baseman Bobby Grich, catcher Johnny Oates and outfielder Roger Freed. "We watched out for each other," says Baylor. "We got on each other when you didn't play the game right." If a player missed a cutoff man, or didn't run out a hit, chase down a fly ball or slide hard into second to break up a double play, his teammates were on him. They played hard even in the minors. Each of them was pushing to make the big leagues, and pushing each other to get there too.

So, what can teams today learn from Harry Dalton and the Orioles Way? Well, it's a model that you can see replicated in so many successful teams on so many levels. But the takeaways from Dalton's Orioles are:

- The need to create a winning culture within the organization, raising expectations at every level, from the lowest rungs of Single-A ball to the big leagues, demanding accountability and cultivating pride in the organization. To do that, a team needs a scouting system that not only evaluates talent but also assesses character. And not just in a passing sense. Prospects need to have the right mindset to be part of your organization. If they don't fit with the team mentality, they aren't as valuable to you.

- From a quality scouting system, you need a system that fosters youth. Homegrown players are the "secret sauce," as John Schuerholz says. A good team grows into a winner; it doesn't rely on mercenaries.

- Developing talent, of course, requires the creation of a coaching system that follows a philosophy of the game that is uniform from top to bottom. One that focuses primarily on defense and pitching and stresses the fundamentals.

These elements make up the foundation of a team that is simply great at winning.

5

HOW THE KANSAS CITY ROYALS
BUILT A FOUNDATION FOR WINNING

B aseball is simple at its core, but creative minds have always found ways to get ahead of their opponents by thinking differently. Branch Rickey was never afraid to go against convention. His innovations changed the game. Creativity can be the difference between developing a mediocre franchise and building a winning one.

I didn't really understand the difference until I arrived in Kansas City, where I grew up in one of the most innovative organizations the sport has ever seen.

When Charlie Finley's Athletics left for Oakland after the 1967 season, Major League Baseball granted the city another franchise that would join as part of a four-team expansion in 1969. The other new teams were the Montreal Expos, the San Diego Padres and the Seattle

Pilots, who became the Milwaukee Brewers in 1970. The new Kansas City team was owned by Ewing Kauffman, a local entrepreneur who had built his fortune in pharmaceuticals. An innovator from the start, Kauffman started his company, Marion Laboratories, in the basement of his home in Kansas City (Marion was Kauffman's middle name), where he made calcium tablets by grinding up oyster shells.

Kauffman was an incredibly proud and loyal citizen of the city. He believed that it deserved to have a major-league baseball team. With the Royals, Kauffman quickly erased the pain the city felt in losing the A's to Oakland. He also set out to build a brand new stadium to replace the old Municipal Stadium that the A's and the Chiefs of the American Football League had been playing out of.

When Kauffman purchased the rights to the city's new franchise, he approached the venture with the same creative mindset and relentlessly competitive spirit that had helped him flourish in the pharmaceutical field. He had paid $11 million to get 40 players nobody else wanted.

So to improve, he *had* to be an innovator.

Kauffman took much the same approach to building his franchise as Harry Dalton had as general manager of the Orioles. In fact, Kauffman took the same people. Shortly after the end of the Orioles' season in 1968, Lou Gorman walked into John Schuerholz's office. "John, I've got really exciting news," Gorman told him. "We're going to Kansas City."

"What the hell are you talking about, Kansas City?" Schuerholz said. "And what is this 'we' stuff?"

Kauffman had set out to hire the most forward-thinking minds in baseball. First, he recruited Cedric Tallis as the Royals' general manager and told him to build the best management team possible. Tallis had been a minor-league general manager for several organizations before becoming the California Angels' business manager in 1961. He knew the ins and outs of the business. Inspired by Baltimore's well-known success with minor-league talent, Tallis approached Lou Gorman to run the Royals' farm system. He and Schuerholz had worked closely, overseeing the Orioles' successful scouting and minor-league system. Gorman wanted Schuerholz to come with him, but the young executive was apprehensive. He was a city guy, born and raised in Baltimore, and the Orioles were just attaining the peak of their success. When Schuerholz thought of Kansas City, he pictured cows walking up and down the street and people tying up their horses to go and pick up groceries at the general store. He wasn't interested in making the move, but Gorman was persistent. They had a chance to be part of something brand new—something they could grow from the ground up, using the Orioles' philosophy. Plus, they had a local owner who was eager to try new things. Eventually, Gorman persuaded Schuerholz to take the job, and they set out to build the Royals.

Tallis also hired Charlie Metro to be the Royals' director of personnel. Metro was an old-school baseball man who had played briefly in the majors with the Detroit Tigers and Philadelphia Athletics, but who had spent most of his playing career in the minors. He briefly managed the Chicago Cubs but then returned to the minors as a scout and manager. He was a scout with the Cincinnati Reds when Tallis offered him the job with the Royals.

One of the first things Gorman and Schuerholz did in Kansas City was to implement a similar scouting system to the one they had been using in Baltimore. These methods had been exclusive to the Orioles, but since Gorman and Schuerholz had created them, there wasn't much that could be done to prevent them from using them. They altered the evaluation categories a bit—in line with the collective ideas of Tallis and Metro—but they essentially followed the same philosophy in grading the characteristics they wanted in a baseball player.

This was how the Royals went about building their first roster and filling their system with future talent. "That was the bedrock for the organization we were creating, the bones of that organization around which we intended to build something very good—which we did," says Schuerholz. "And in a short time, we became the most [successful] expansion team in the history of Major League Baseball." The Royals made the playoffs more quickly than any new major-league team ever had before.

Ewing Kauffman epitomizes the way an owner should operate. You need someone at the top who invests in the team because of a true passion. Often, when a corporation takes over a team, you can see how it gets tangled up in the bureaucracy of the company. People who know little about baseball try to make baseball decisions. It rarely works. In his business, Kauffman had distilled his management philosophy down to three main points: Treat others as you want to be treated; share life's rewards with those who make them possible; and give back to society. He took this philosophy with him into his new baseball venture. After he bought the franchise Kauffman announced that he was creating a profit-sharing benefits package for non-playing team personnel. He wanted to bring in employees who were motivated to build a winner because they had a direct stake in the team's success.

Kauffman also knew that if he was going to bring in the right baseball people to build his team, he couldn't be afraid to pay them for it. Kauffman had no problem paying for top coaches and scouting staff throughout his farm system. Nor was he afraid to sit back and let them do what they did best. He respected their expertise but also confidently provided his own ideas about building success—something he knew a great deal about, given what he had done with Marion Laboratories. He had the intellect to envision and construct his own company; he wanted to accomplish the same thing with the Royals. By the time he was done hiring, the Royals' minor-league system had more coaches and managers than any other team.

"He didn't know anything about baseball, but he knew about leadership and he knew about working together and creating good collaboration and partnerships in business, and he brought those attitudes to us," says Schuerholz. "He hired a bunch of young guys, and some of us were not really experienced, and he said, 'You know, I trust you—you're the guys that have been selected. Here's what we want to accomplish. We want to become world champions.' The goal was crystal clear."

Kauffman was also unique in his approach to the kinds of people he brought in to be part of his team. He was baffled by baseball's traditionally slow process of scouting and drafting players. The baseball establishment was stubbornly resistant to change, which he found counterintuitive and completely at odds with his experience in the business world. Reacting to that, Kauffman wanted to take a scientific approach to baseball. He wanted to show that technology and innovative ideas could improve the game.

As one of his first innovative moves, Kauffman hired Dr. Raymond Riley, a research psychologist who had worked for NASA and the Office of Naval Research. Riley had no sports experience. So in Kauffman's eyes, he was perfect.

Kauffman then called Bob Howsam, the general manager of the Cincinnati Reds, and asked if he could have someone evaluate his players. Kauffman was wise enough to know that if they were going to build a winner in Kansas City, they had to look at what other teams were doing right. He knew the Reds were going to be a success. Remember, this was right before the Big Red Machine took off in the early '70s. Kauffman wanted to understand what Howsam had discovered in those players.

Howsam agreed, and Dr. Riley went to study the Reds. He also studied many of the players in the Royals' minor-league system. Riley evaluated the vision, psychomotor response and psychological makeup of the players. In his evaluation of star players like Johnny Bench, Riley came up with four characteristics that he believed to be necessary for a potential player to have success: exceptional running speed, fast reflexes, excellent body balance, and strong eyesight and depth perception.

After evaluating the Reds and other players, the management team, coaches and scouting staff that Kauffman had assembled to run his franchise met at the old Continental Hotel in downtown Kansas City. Kauffman sat down in the conference room with the group, rolled up his sleeves, said, "I want to learn about baseball," and then sat through the entire meeting just listening as they talked through the plans for the team's inaugural season. Near the end of the meeting, Kauffman finally spoke up. "You know, gentlemen, we give all these bonuses out to these young players, but how do we know how well they can see? Did we test their eyes?" The room went silent. Everyone just stared at each other, not knowing how to reply. The answer, of course, was no. Kauffman was simply baffled that eyesight was an attribute that scouts and coaches somehow overlooked.

IN 1969 THE ROYALS traded outfielder Steve Whitaker and pitcher John Gelnar to the Seattle Pilots for a 26-year-old rookie named Lou Piniella. He had been signed by the Cleveland Indians as a free agent in

1962, when he was 18. He was picked up by the Washington Senators in the first-year draft later that year. (This draft, which existed between 1959 and 1964, allowed teams to claim a minor leaguer who had just completed his first year in pro ball.) The Senators traded him to the Baltimore Orioles, who then traded him back to Cleveland, and the Seattle Pilots picked him up in the fall of 1968 in the expansion draft. Through that time, Piniella played only in ten major-league games. The Royals traded for him right after spring training in April 1969, and that's when everything finally took off for him. Piniella was a terrific athlete. Aside from baseball, he was also a great basketball player. And he could run like the wind. He was the kind of athletic player Kaufmann loved.

Piniella was also a maniac in the field, in a good way. He loved to play and was competitive as hell. He thought he should always get a hit and never get called out. Seriously, he was intense. He wanted to win *every* game. If he didn't, he just went crazy. But he was funny too. He'd be intense one minute and hilarious the next. He was always doing goofy things. Once, in the on-deck circle, a weighted ring got stuck on the barrel of his bat and he just kept pulling away at it in an attempt to free it—while 30,000 people were watching. Finally, someone threw a bat out from the dugout and Lou used it to hammer the weight off of his bat. He regrouped and calmly strode to the plate. Everybody loved Lou, and he carried that right through his career. He played his ass off every day, and boy, he could hit.

In 1969 he hit .282 with a .741 OPS (on-base percentage plus slugging percentage). He won the American League Rookie of the Year Award. The Royals really knew how to spot talent. After all, I was a rookie with the team that year too . . .

I had a front-row seat for all of this. I saw how the Royals built their organization, how they pieced together a team that could actually win. They found undervalued players from other organizations and brought them into a new atmosphere. By 1971, the Royals had their first winning season, finishing with 85 wins and 76 losses, good for second in the American League Western Division. They were the first of the four teams from the 1969 expansion to post a winning record.

AFTER MY FIRST FULL SEASON in Kansas City, I stayed in town during the off-season to work for the ballclub. As part of Mr. Kauffman's desire to build a franchise that had a real connection to the community, he established a group called the Royal Lancers, a bunch of successful businessmen in the Kansas City area whom he persuaded to go around to local businesses and sell season tickets. The Lancers wore royal blue blazers with the Kansas City Royals emblem on the pocket. The one who managed to sell the most season tickets was given a free trip to spring training.

My job was to go along with the Lancers and knock on doors. For example, we'd go to a bank and meet with the manager and sell a package of tickets—they'd be introduced to a player and we'd talk about how great the upcoming season was going to be. It was a very successful initiative, and the ticket holder got a chance to see that the players were actually a part of the community—that we lived there, and we planned to be there for a long time. We weren't just in town to be part of the Royals; we were there to be part of Kansas City. That was real community building, and Kauffman had an excellent grasp of how valuable it could be.

You don't really see that today, beyond the few mandatory philanthropic events a team takes part in through the season. What fans see are clips of their favorite athletes cleaning out their lockers the minute the season is over and heading straight for the airport. With the exception of a few players, there is often no demonstrable connection between the guy on the field and the families in the stands.

There is nothing better for a team and its fan base than when a real sense of connection has been developed between them. In those situations the experience is about more than entertainment—it's about pride. The team and the players represent the people and the community. The passionate support of the fans absolutely has a positive impact on a team's performance. It's more than ticket sales and television ratings. It's simple psychology. Kauffman understood the economic and psychological importance of his team being ingrained in the community. It's something that gets lost today.

Obviously, the economics are much different now. Part of the reason we stayed in Kansas City was that we couldn't afford another house. My first salary in the majors was $10,000, which is about $65,000 a year today. It stayed like that for about five seasons. Every year, I was on a one-year contract. Raises were negotiated in increments of about $500! The players were also paid in the off-season, on "personal services contracts." They paid me around $1,000 a month during the off-season to call on season-ticket holders and get them to renew.

I can remember when Wayne Garland signed a ten-year contract with the Cleveland Indians for $2.3 million. More than $200,000 a year—it was unheard of. And everybody's response was "Oh my God! Are you kidding me?" That was in 1977, which was the first season of large-scale free agency. However, Garland failed to reattain the heights he reached in 1976, when he went 20–7. His record over the rest of his career was 28–48. The Indians waived him after the 1981 season, just five years into the deal.

KAUFFMAN CONTINUED TO INFUSE the Royals with innovative ideas through those early years of the franchise. He had already stocked his team with some of the best scouts in the game and hired the best coaches to develop the minor-league system. In 1971, remembering the research he had gleaned from the Reds, and that eyesight was one of the key traits Dr. Riley had identified among the talent in Cincinnati's organization, Kauffman decided to take his investment one step further by adding a vision expert to join his staff. That's how Dr. Bill Harrison got his start in professional baseball.

Harrison was an optometrist who focused on athletic performance. He had played baseball for the University of California, Berkeley, during his studies, so he had a rich background in the game. Later, Harrison developed an instrument to measure the strength of the right and left eyes. He also tested for color blindness—the inability to distinguish between colors. But the real key to his work was measuring a player's depth perception. Harrison found that depth perception was vital to hitting, particularly in night games, and he believed that it could be trained and improved on.

(One prospect who failed the Royals' eye tests ended up being drafted 13th overall by the New York Mets. He never made it past Double A.)

In December 1971 the Royals brought Harrison to Kansas City to work with 18-year-old George Brett, whom the Royals had selected in the second round of the '71 draft, 29th overall. He was in his first season in the minors, playing in Billings, Montana. At the time, Brett didn't really stand out as a prospect. He was very good, but no one knew just how good he could be. But Harrison identified Brett's remarkable ability to *see* the ball. "I think the thing with George that was hidden when he was 18 is no one saw the desire he had," says Harrison. From the start of spring training, Brett was open to working with Harrison on a series of drills that improved that vision. And because of that willingness to try something new, he was able to improve on the vision he already had.

Brett, of course, went on to become one of the best hitters in the history of the game, one of only four players to have more than 3,000 hits, 300 home runs and a .300 career batting average. In 1999 he was inducted into the Hall of Fame.

Not a bad first student to have.

"He was incredibly consistent in his way of going about the things he believed in and the things he did," says Harrison. "I was spoiled in those years because it's not as easy today to get players like George."

Since then, Harrison has spent more than 40 years in Major League Baseball, conducting sports vision analysis on generations of the game's best teams and biggest stars.

Kauffman was pleased with the results the doctor obtained with the Royals' positional players and wanted him to do the same with the team's pitchers. So in January 1973, Harrison started to work with guys like Bruce Dal Canton, Dick Drago, Steve Busby and Paul Splittorff. He worked with them on visualization—centering themselves on the mound and increasing their focus, which is such an important part of pitching. I remember being on the Royals' bus, watching Splittorff going through Harrison's material and going over his instruction. Paul created a tape that he would play the night before a start. He would talk his way through the entire lineup he was going to face the next day. He would visualize each at-bat for each hitter, so that when it happened, he'd already have gone over it in his mind. Paul went on to be one of the most consistent pitchers in Royals history.

If you want to be the best, you have to develop the best. This was the philosophy that Kauffman instituted. You can't draft talent and expect it to grow without providing the proper opportunities and instruction to get the most out of it. This *has* to be the mentality of a franchise that wants to win consistently. Bringing in an eye doctor was certainly not an idea shared by other ballclubs. But it was the right one. Every aspect of a player can be improved. It takes a true innovator to look for unexpected ways to make good players great.

THE ROYALS WERE A BRAVE organization from the beginning. Mr. Kauffman was wise enough to know that if they were going to develop a franchise the right way, they needed to emulate the teams that had already done so, and then they needed to improve on the model. Kauffman hired the Orioles' brain trust in Lou Gorman and John Schuerholz. He found the scouts he wanted and the coaches he wanted, and he developed a franchise with an infrastructure that would support future success. That's exactly why the Royals became *the Royals* and their success spanned so many years. We saw it before them, with Branch Rickey and the Cardinals, and then with the Dodgers. You can see it in the Yankees' success with Casey Stengel through the '50s. And then with Harry Dalton and the Baltimore Orioles. In the four decades since, so many great teams have emulated the same core principles. There are no shortcuts. Once you realize that, it's easy: You follow a tried-and-true model. The foundation is simple: Focus on scouting, develop homegrown talent, double down on pitching and defense, and you're always going to be in the ballgame.

A little creativity helps too. Sometimes the winning edge comes from thinking outside the box. I believe that one of Kauffman's greatest contributions to the game was a grassroots experiment that was widely criticized at first. He called it the Kansas City Royals Baseball Academy. It's long forgotten now, but I believe that if dusted off and tweaked with some modern twists, it could actually change the way successful teams are built today.

6

HOW THE ROYALS ACADEMY
REIMAGINED THE FARM SYSTEM

The dilemma confronting Ewing Kauffman in 1968, when the Kansas City Royals franchise was granted, was that it had cost him a lot of money—$11 million—to receive a bunch of players through the expansion draft that, really, no one wanted.

Eleven million was a preposterous amount of money for a new franchise in 1968. When the Toronto Blue Jays joined the American League nine years later, in 1977, the franchise only cost $7 million. But Kauffman was willing and able to foot the bill.

Aside from the expansion draft, the only real source of talent available to Kauffman was the amateur draft. (He could buy players from other teams, or trade for them—though as a brand new team, the Royals didn't have many players with trade value.) Kauffman believed that to build a contender the conventional way would easily take 10 to 15 years. Knowing that he didn't want to take that long, he needed to come up with another approach.

Kauffman's premise was that there might be an untapped pool of talent—athletes who had been overlooked in the draft and who could be developed, by coaches who had the right tools, in the Royals' mold. He decided to have his top-notch team of scouts and coaches evaluate overlooked players from across the nation by holding a series of open tryouts. From those who attended these tryouts, the Royals would select a small group to attend the Kansas City Royals Baseball Academy in Florida, where they would be immersed in baseball education on and off the field and play together in Florida's Gulf Coast League, an established rookie-level minor league.

The concept wasn't entirely new. Other teams had flirted with similar ideas in the past. Branch Rickey was one of the first, utilizing his sliding pits, batting tees and pitching machines to teach the fundamentals of the game. Around the same time, in the 1920s, National League president John Heydler discussed having the league sponsor a baseball school to improve player development, but nothing came of it. In the late 1930s, Chicago Cubs owner Philip K. Wrigley hired Coleman R. Griffith, a pioneer in sports psychology, as a team consultant. Griffith studied new methods of analyzing the game and tried to build a scientific training regime for the players. He filmed players batting and fielding, and he documented their progress using diagrams and charts. He made changes to batting and pitching practices to make the experiences better resemble in-game situations. But Griffith only lasted two seasons with the Cubs. He clashed with the two Cubs managers he worked with during that tenure, Charlie Grimm and Gabby Hartnett, both of whom disregarded the work he was doing. By the end of his time with the Cubs, Griffith had produced 400 pages of reports and documentation on player development. His work would later become well respected in the baseball community.

Later, in the 1950s, a psychologist named David F. Tracy was employed by the St. Louis Browns to work with players during spring training, using relaxation techniques and hypnosis in hopes of improving their performance. In the same decade, Casey Stengel created a preseason baseball camp for his New York Yankees, hoping to better develop young players who had already made it to the professional level. Mickey Mantle was one of those who took part in the Yankees' preseason camp. So was minor-league pitcher Syd Thrift, the man Kauffman would appoint as the first director of the Royals Baseball Academy.

In the 1960s, Philadelphia Phillies owner Bob Carpenter funded a study by researchers at the University of Delaware that ran from 1963 until 1972. The scientists studied the intricate aspects of hitting, measuring bat acceleration and bat speed. They also researched fielding and pitching, as well as studying player vision. But tradition-minded scouts mostly dismissed the findings.

KAUFFMAN OFFICIALLY UNVEILED his Baseball Academy in September 1969. The Royals would build a brand new 121-acre campus just outside of Sarasota, Florida, next to a pair of big lakes that Kauffman had stocked with fish and which were crawling with alligators. The campus featured five baseball diamonds, each built to the exact specifications of the field that was being built at the new Royals Stadium, which was scheduled to open in 1972. The facility had eight pitching machines and enough space in the bullpens for eight pitchers to warm up at once. The locker rooms were enormous and could hold up to 254 players. There were 50 dormitory rooms for the players to stay in, offices, lecture halls, laboratories, tennis courts and a swimming pool. In all, the facility cost about $1.5 million to build.

Thrift was named as the school's director. After his minor-league career with the Yankees, he had become a scout in the Royals system. His experience in the minors had helped make him a remarkable judge of talent. Many give him credit for coming up with much of the Academy's methodology.

Thrift wanted raw athletes with an ability to learn. "People say that we can execute better than teams that have been together for only six weeks," he told *Sports Illustrated* that year. "Heck, you can execute all day and never win if you have players who have weak arms or are slow runners. Our players have good arms and speed."

The Royals embarked on an enormous public relations campaign to get the Academy off the ground. They hired a marketer named Sam Ketchum, who put together a questionnaire and brochure and sent it to nearly 8,000 high schools around the country. The club wanted to hear from everyone and anyone—especially coaches and athletic directors—who thought they had an athlete with untapped talent, regardless of what sport they played. Before tryouts in each city, Ketchum had flyers posted in stores and on lampposts around town.

These brochures and flyers outlined the fundamental requirements for applicants to the program: "An applicant must (a) have completed his high school eligibility, (b) be less than 20, (c) be able to run 60 yards in 6.9 seconds in baseball shoes [the average of major leaguers is somewhat about 7.0], and (d) be neither enrolled in a four-year college nor have been drafted by a major-league team."

The advertisements also promised that the Royals would use the most scientific and modern methods to identify talent and that prospects would be given first-class treatment.

The Academy found plenty of candidates who boasted a wide range of experiences. There was a high school sprinting champion from Missouri and a high school state wrestling champion from New Mexico. They had a bowler, and a weightlifter, and a high school quarterback who had set a school record in the javelin throw.

By that June, Royals scouts had evaluated thousands of young players at tryout camps in 41 states across the country. At the tryout in New Orleans, a skinny 18-year-old catcher named Ron Washington showed up, not really certain what it was all about.

At the time, Washington was playing American Legion ball, which is a nationwide amateur league for teenagers. He was one of 166 hopefuls who showed up at the diamond to run through a series of drills, vying for a shot at being part of this new Royals Baseball Academy, which was still just a crazy idea at the time. Washington ran a 60-yard dash, fielded one ball at second base and took one swing of the bat before he was pulled aside by one of the Royals' scouts, who told him he could go home. The camp continued without him. Later, Washington was told that he had made the cut. He was the only candidate selected from the New Orleans camp.

Washington was in elite company. The Royals' scouts looked at a total of 7,682 baseball players across the United States. They narrowed that group down to 43 players, who were invited to be part of the first Royals Academy. None of the players who made the first team had been scouted by a major-league ballclub. Eight hadn't played baseball at the high school level.

FOR COMMITTING TO STAY with the Academy for at least ten months, students were paid between $100 and $200 a month. (This would increase to $500 a month in the second year.) They were all given free room and board, three meals a day, health and life insurance, and a round-trip ticket home for Christmas. It cost the Royals about $1,000 to keep each student in the Academy for a month.

Instruction at the Academy included two years of college courses at nearby Manatee Junior College, paid for by the team. The courses were geared toward skills the students would use as ballplayers, including courses on nutrition, finance and public speaking. The players took classes in the morning and played baseball in the afternoon. The intent was that living together and attending classes together would build a unique camaraderie among the players.

Each course counted as a college credit. This wasn't just an education tacked on the side of baseball instruction. The education *was* baseball instruction. The Royals wanted to develop well-rounded players who were more than just physically capable of being professional athletes. Understanding how overlooked education had been in the course of a prospect's development, the Royals wanted their players to have the educational tools to succeed. On days that the students didn't have class in the mornings, they were given in-class baseball instruction at the Academy. After all, being a professional athlete is about so much more than your performance on the field. (That's another thing that is often forgotten in the game today.)

Kauffman hired Buzzy Keller to manage the Royals Academy team, which played in the Gulf Coast League. Keller had played baseball at Texas Lutheran College and played minor-league baseball for a few years before returning to his alma mater as head coach of the baseball team. He then served as the athletic director at Texas Lutheran from 1966 to 1970, before Kauffman asked him to manage the Academy team.

The Academy also had several full-time staff members, all of whom had played major-league baseball. Steve Korcheck was the Academy's coordinator of instruction. He had been a catcher with the Washington Senators, shuttling between the minors and majors through the 1950s. Johnny Neun, another former player with the Washington Senators, was also hired as an instructor. The Senators' manager, Jim Lemon, joined the staff too. Joe Gordon, who managed the Royals through their inaugural season, left his post in Kansas City for a position at the Academy. Former Red Sox and Senators pitcher Chuck Stobbs was there too. So were former big-league pitcher Bill Fischer and former Yankees right fielder Tommy Henrich.

THE ACADEMY WAS SET to make its debut in August 1970. From the start, the experiment was met with much derision in baseball circles. Some old-school executives simply ignored it; others sneered at it as an affront to tradition. Others quietly worried that it just might work.

Every game the Royals' farm team played represented a divide between the old way of doing things and a new vision for how a team could be developed. Consider the cost of the signing bonuses paid out to the drafted players on the opposing teams. The Royals Academy players were a bargain compared to the elites they played against, and other teams resented that.

Once, after the Royals Academy lost a game, their opponents ran a victory lap around the field to rub it in.

"Buzzy, that's not baseball," one of the players shouted to Keller, the manager. "That's Mickey Mouse!"

But Thrift and Keller didn't let the chirping get to them. Seeing the talent that had emerged from the open tryouts, they knew the Royals Academy was on to something big. The negativity just increased their resolve. Letters from the baseball establishment criticizing the outlandish experiment as a waste of time were posted on the walls of the complex.

Kauffman also heard the criticism. He didn't like that his idea was being laughed at, but what he disliked more was the idea of backing away for that reason alone. He sent Art Stewart, one of his top scouts, down to assess how things were going. Stewart had heard a lot of things from his colleagues in the scouting community, most of it negative. Admittedly, he didn't know whether Kauffman's experiment would work. But it didn't take long for him to realize the potential talent the Royals were fostering down at the Academy. For starters, they had 18-year-old Orestes Minoso Jr. in center field. His father, Minnie—nicknamed the "Cuban Comet"—had been a star in the Negro Leagues before being signed by the Cleveland Indians as the color barrier began to fall in the late 1940s. He then became one of the most popular players on the Chicago White Sox. The younger Minoso appeared to have some of his father's ability.

The Academy's biggest find, however, was a player who basically grew up in the Royals' backyard. As a youngster, Frank White had grown up ten blocks away from Municipal Stadium in Kansas City and had gone to school right across the street from the stadium. He had played in local baseball leagues throughout his youth, but didn't play in high school, where he stood out as a football and basketball player.

When he found out about the Academy, he wasn't going to try out, but his wife pushed him to go. He took a day off from his job at a sheet metal company. Like Ron Washington, White was quickly picked for the camp.

At the age of 20 White became a swift shortstop for the Academy Royals. He was the prime example of what the Royals believed was possible through the Academy. During his first season, White stood out as the best shortstop in the Gulf Coast League. Thrift believed there wasn't a player at that level who could go deeper in the hole and throw out a runner at first better than White could. He was a pure athlete.

NEEDLESS TO SAY, Art Stewart was very pleased with the progress they were making at the Academy. After hearing the positive report, Kauffman went down to Florida to see for himself. He arrived in a big blue Cadillac one day, just before the Academy Royals played the Pittsburgh Pirates' Gulf Coast League team. Kauffman and his wife sat in chairs right behind the backstop, next to Art Stewart. He watched the game, smoking his pipe, with a big smile on his face as he asked Stewart questions about players on the field, wanting to know where they came from.

Stewart knew all the players on both teams. He pointed out to Kauffman the bonuses that had been paid out to the Pirates' players—"the shortstop signed for $35,000, the left fielder for $20,000," and so on. All of the Royals had been signed for next to nothing.

The Academy beat the Pirates soundly, and afterward Stewart and Kauffman heard the Pirates' coach giving it to his players for losing to a bunch of nobodies. Both men smiled. They were doing it the right way.

The Academy was loaded with quality coaches who hammered the fundamentals into the players, like elementary school teachers making their students memorize their multiplication tables. The fundamentals were essential. Instructors were available to work one on one with any player who wanted to focus on a specific weakness in his game. On the field the Academy students addressed the flaws in their game with careful attention to detail.

Every day, the students were also given at least 20 minutes of hitting practice against a pitcher, which is something most players in the majors wouldn't get in a week. On top of the time spent swinging at real pitches, the Royals had Charley Lau on staff, one of the best hitting coaches in the game. He went down to Florida to do video work with the Academy players, wheeling a dolly loaded with a 50-pound yellow videotape recorder onto the field to tape batting practice. Lau taught hitting like a professor. He retooled many of his philosophies about hitting using information he gleaned from the video work he did with the players in the Academy. The Royals even brought in Ted Williams to give a lecture on hitting.

Joe Tanner specialized in bunting, helping batters perfect their technique so that, instead of popping the ball up, they could direct it exactly where they wanted to place it. The players practiced bunting constantly. (If only teams would do that today. Bunting is a lost art. It's a skill so many players lack.)

Along with solid hitting and bunting fundamentals, students at the Royals Academy emphasized intelligent baserunning. Basestealing was considered essential to the Royals' offense. Instructors set out to improve the team's basestealing by taking a studied approach to leading off the base. An average runner, they said, should take a 12-foot lead off of first base. Faster runners could take slightly larger leads. For second base, they established that a 20-foot lead was ideal. Prospects also practiced scenarios such as delayed steals or double-steal attempts.

The Royals' instructors also thought outside the box when it came to using traditional tools. They turned the pitching machine around and fired groundballs and line drives at their fielders. With the balls going to the exact same place, on the exact same arc every time, they were able to re-create the same play over and over, allowing the fielder to perfect his technique. They could move the machine closer or farther away and specify exactly how the ball would bounce off the dirt. To mix up the bounces, the coaches would sometimes use the curveball machine. Every player's reaction to each scenario was measured and compared.

The Royals also hired experts from outside the baseball world to work on specific areas with their players. They had Bill Harrison, the optometrist, come down to work with some of the players on improving their depth perception, just as he would later do with George Brett. Dr. Raymond Reilly came in to conduct regular physiological and psychological testing with the players.

With Dr. Harrison and Dr. Reilly, the players learned visualization and meditation exercises. They were taught to take a few moments before each at-bat to visualize positive results at the plate. This was another era; sports psychology hadn't really taken off yet. The Royals were way ahead of their time in this regard.

Olympic track star Wes Santee, who specialized in the 1,500-meter race, came in to show the players how to run more effectively. The Royals also hired Bill Easton, who was a track coach at the University of Kansas.

Off the field, the Royals Academy emphasized resistance and weight training, when it wasn't really something that professional ballplayers were focusing on. Mickey Cobb was the team's athletic trainer. He would remain in the organization for two decades and would later spend time as the Royals' trainer. George "Pee Wee" Bourette, who had been a high school football coach in Missouri for 26 years, joined Cobb as a strength trainer. They used inner tubes from tires as resistance bands to give upper-body muscles a workout.

The Academy tried pretty much anything and everything to get an edge. No idea was ruled out. And some seemed perfectly outlandish, like the time they brought in a trampoline expert to hammer home a point about the importance of working directly with an instructor. The players were divided into two groups, split between those who figured they already knew how to do a flip on a trampoline and those who had never been on one before. After a few days of practice, they came back together and demonstrated how the guys with no experience, but who had then had professional instruction, were already better at doing flips on the trampoline than the group that thought it knew what it was doing.

In the end, the Royals Academy players found themselves immersed in an unparalleled baseball experience. Everything they did was geared toward turning them into major-league players. "Working on fundamentals, classroom work, it was really different," says Washington. "It was more than just baseball. They wanted to try to help us complete the education also."

Naturally, the discipline learned and the classroom skills gained were applicable to life even if the players didn't turn into professional players. Remember, this was a free education for many players who could never have afforded one. It was a remarkable opportunity.

And it was a success.

The first class at the Royals Academy won the Gulf Coast League championship in its first season, playing against the rookie teams of the St. Louis Cardinals, Pittsburgh Pirates, Cleveland Indians, Chicago White Sox, Cincinnati Reds and Minnesota Twins. Eight of Minnesota's top ten picks from the summer free-agent draft played on the Twins' Gulf Coast League affiliate. They finished 17½ games behind the Royals.

Part of the Royals' success was due to the team's speed and prowess on the basepaths. There wasn't a team in the league that could touch them when it came to stealing bases. Manager Buzzy Keller wasn't afraid to make daring calls. He had his players stealing constantly and frequently called for double-steal attempts, which they had worked on in practice. During their inaugural season in the Gulf Coast League, the Royals had 103 stolen bases in 53 games. The team with the second-highest number of steals was the Cleveland Indians' affiliate, with 55. Incredibly, the Academy Royals were caught stealing only 16 times that season.

The Academy team also finished first in team batting average, at .257, and first in team ERA, at 2.07.

Before they graduated in December 1971, the first Academy Royals team had won 162 of 241 games, good for a .672 winning percentage, playing against other major-league affiliates, against college teams (which they played before the season) and in a tour through Latin America. The high volume of games played was an intentional development strategy. The best way to get better is to play as many games as possible.

Fifteen members of that first Academy class were promoted to higher levels within the Royals' farm system.

"They used to say you can't make a man run faster or throw harder, but we showed that you could with the right expert instruction and the right kind of practice," Thrift once told the *New York Times* about the Academy's success developing players.

The Academy's second class was limited to just 20 players, between the ages of 17 and 19. Players already in the Royals' farm system were assigned to the Academy for two months after the end of their regular season to provide further training (in a similar fashion to Casey Stengel's preseason camps with the Yankees).

In their second season the Academy Royals had 41 wins and 22 losses in the Gulf Coast League and finished tied for first with the Cubs' rookie team. The Royals again led the league in batting average, at .257, and on-base percentage, at .365. On top of that, they stole an incredible 161 bases. The best player to come out of the second season of the Academy was Rodney Scott, who went on to have a decent major-league career in which he built a reputation as one of baseball's premier basestealers. Scott was actually drafted by the Royals in 1972 in the 11th round and sent to the Academy to begin his career.

Unfortunately, the Royals Academy team struggled in its third season, finishing second last in the Gulf Coast League with 27 wins and 28 losses. The team still led the league in stolen bases, with 96.

In just a few years of operation, the Academy had 14 players who eventually made it to the major leagues, certainly comparable to the success rate of any other farm system out there. Given that these were athletes who had slipped under the radar of the traditional scouting system, Kauffman's crazy idea proved to be a great one. He publicly stated that the Academy would remain in operation for at least another five years. But it didn't have full support among the Royals' management team. Some viewed it as a drain on resources that could go toward developing the players the Royals had drafted and traded for through traditional means. In 1972, frustrated that the Academy didn't receive much support from management (beyond Kauffman), Thrift resigned as the director.

IN MAY 1974 the Academy was shuttered for good. Buzzy Keller received a letter from Ewing Kauffman explaining the decision to end the grand experiment. By then, Keller was working as the coordinator of instruction at the Academy and was no longer managing the team. The letter thanked Keller for his work with the team in Sarasota, and then went on to explain confidentially that a drop in stock values at Marion Laboratories had pushed Kauffman and the company's board to find ways to cut costs. Kauffman's personal stake in the company had lost significant value. He would either have to get rid of the Academy or get rid of the Royals.

It was a more difficult decision for Kauffman than some might think. The Academy had cost about $700,000 a year to operate, but it also developed assets. The players that had been mined from high schools across the country turned into talent that could be sold to other teams—it was the old model of owning talent and selling it that had funded the independent minor-league teams for decades.

But when Kauffman first bought the franchise, he promised Kansas City that the team would not move in his lifetime. The Royals were his gift to a city he loved, and he wasn't about to go back on his word.

It's too bad that Kauffman wasn't able to find a way to keep the Academy going. His inventive approach to developing players had the potential to change the way much of the game's old guard thought about baseball. He was a pioneer in much the same sense that Branch Rickey was. And his outlandish ideas undoubtedly worked. Today, you can see the Academy's basic principles in play in affiliated programs that major-league teams have in markets throughout Latin America, in the Dominican Republic and in Venezuela.

And those principles still have untapped value.

Kauffman later said that closing the Academy was one of the biggest mistakes he ever made.

The benefit of the Royals Academy was most evident from 1978 to 1983, when graduates U.L. Washington and Frank White played beside each other at shortstop and second base for Kansas City. White became a five-time All-Star and an eight-time Gold Glove winner. He was a key member of the Royals team that won the World Series in 1985.

For his part, Ron Washington played in the minors for about a decade, mostly in the Los Angeles Dodgers system, where he was traded in 1976. He went on to play for the Minnesota Twins, Baltimore Orioles, Cleveland Indians and Houston Astros before embarking on a successful career as a coach with the Oakland Athletics and as manager of the Texas Rangers. Even today, Washington looks back on his time with the Royals Baseball Academy as the reason he's spent his life in the game. For him, it was as simple as being given the opportunity. It was about being chosen. And it was about being part of something.

"We learned what camaraderie was," says Washington. "They wanted to get a group of guys together, [get them to] believe in one another, trust one another, and they believed that even though we weren't drafted players we could be successful, and we were."

As long as he had the uniform on, he never doubted his ability. He was a part of a unique family. That's how it felt, Washington says. "In the Academy, that's what it was."

7

WHAT I LEARNED AS A
MAJOR-LEAGUE ROOKIE

got my first shot at pro ball when I signed a contract with the Phila-delphia Phillies in June 1967. I was 19 years old and had just finished my freshman year at Sacramento City College. I signed, and then I flew to Oregon to join the Eugene Emeralds, the Phillies' Short Season Class-A team. It was the first time I had been on a plane. I walked to the back of the DC-6 and sat down in an empty seat next to a guy who was clearly a baseball player and was several years older than me.

"Where are you going?" I asked him.

"I'm going to Eugene," he said.

"Really? I'm going to Eugene too," I said. "What are you going to do?"

"I'm going to play with the Phillies," he said, proudly. "I just got sent down from Bakersfield, and I'm going up to Eugene to play in the Northwest League." (Bakersfield was in the Class-A California League.)

"Well, I'm going up there too," I said.

"I understand we're going to have a real good team up there," he went on. "We just signed this great catcher. He's supposed to be a really good player and he's coming up there."

It was like a punch to the stomach. "Well, that's no good for me," I thought. "I'm not even going to play. Why the hell am I going up there?"

I spent the rest of the flight worrying and wondering who this hotshot catcher was that the team was bringing in.

The next day, I showed up at the field, looking around for the other catcher. It took me longer than I wish to admit that the guy on the plane had actually been talking about *me*.

There are moments like that in a professional career, moments when it suddenly feels like the grand dream you've been visualizing since you were a kid is finally about to come true. When I reached the minors, I felt like it was just a matter of time before I stepped on a major-league field. The dream felt so real.

But once I got to the minors, it was a culture shock. I had never been out of California. The Emeralds' manager was Bobby Malkmus, who had played for the Milwaukee Braves, Washington Senators and Philadelphia Phillies before becoming a minor-league coach and scout.

I remember being given a brand new glove. Eddie Bockman, the Phillies' scout from the Bay Area, gave it to me before I got on the plane to fly north. (Bockman also signed Dennis and Dave Bennett, Larry Bowa and John Vukovich.) That was the biggest thing. He also gave me some big-league bats. In Eugene they handed me some undershirts and a wool baseball sweatshirt, which weighed about five pounds. It was made of very thick wool—it was like a blanket with long sleeves.

That year, I signed my first contract with Hillerich and Bradsby for Louisville Slugger bats. They gave you a set of golf clubs for signing with the company. We thought that was the coolest thing. Just about everybody got a contract. H&B would sign you and give you golf clubs, just hoping you got to the big leagues. I'm not really sure what the contract meant, other than that you got your name on a bat. They took your signature from the contract and burned it into the barrel of the bat.

I hit .357 that year in Eugene. I had 96 hits in 77 games but couldn't run a lick. The next year, I received notice that I had been drafted into the army. I missed spring training as I stayed in school to keep my student deferment, and I didn't join the Phillies' affiliate in Spartanburg, South Carolina, until June. As a result, I played in just 44 games in 1968.

IN DECEMBER 1968 the brand new Kansas City Royals picked me up in a trade with Houston, who had just claimed me in the Rule 5 draft a couple of weeks before. The Rule 5 draft allows teams to pick up young players from other clubs' farm systems, the object being to prevent teams from unfairly stockpiling youth. The Phillies had left me unprotected, trying to sneak me through the draft so they wouldn't have to put me on the major-league roster.

As a Rule 5 player, I wasn't expected to stick with a major-league team. The Royals planned to sit me on the bench and keep me there for the season, and then send me down to the minors the following season, where I'd get my time in and everything would be great. As before, I didn't go to spring training that year because I had to keep my student deferment.

My first taste of the big leagues was during a Royals road trip to Oakland in April of 1969. It was surreal. There were a lot of young guys on their team. I remember being given my uniform. They had these heavy old-fashioned wool uniforms at the time.

When I went out for batting practice, the coach said, "Hey, let the rookie take some swings." But the guys didn't give me a chance to hit. "Screw him," one said. "He ain't going to play anyway."

"Oh God," I thought. "This is going to be miserable."

Later, I took the infield during fielding drills. I remember being nervous throwing to first base. I could feel it in my body. The highest level I'd played at before was A-ball—I had played in the Carolina league, and I hadn't played many games. Now I was in the big leagues and I was taking the infield. I wasn't on the active roster at the time, but I knew I was going to join the team in June. The coach running the drills was Harry Dunlop, who was from my hometown. He was very nice. He and Joe Gordon, our manager, kind of took care of me. They were from Sacramento, like me. After the infield workout I remember walking up the long stairs that led to the clubhouse. They're still the same today. When I got to the clubhouse our third baseman, Joe Foy, asked me how my first practice went.

"How did it go, rookie?" he asked.

I told him it had gone well.

"And how do you like your uniform?" he asked, with a smirk. Foy was 26 and had already played three seasons with Boston before being picked up by the Royals in the expansion draft. He was a nice guy, a leader on the team.

"It's a cool uniform, it feels great," I said, looking down at the gray jersey with *Kansas City* written in script lettering across the chest. "It's really nice."

"What do you think about the socks?" he asked.

It was a setup. I stepped right into it.

"Well, you know," I said, "they're a little low and they're a little tight."

Foy turned around and announced to the whole clubhouse, "Hey! Rookie doesn't like his socks!" And the whole team started to give me the gears. "Well, you don't have to worry about it," Foy laughed. "You're not playing anyway."

I wanted to crawl into a hole. But Dave Wickersham, a 33-year-old relief pitcher—a religious man, a real nice guy—came over to me and said, "Son, don't worry about that. None of us like our socks."

In the end, it was good fun. It was the way of the clubhouse in those days. Rookies had to know their place. Of course, I still had a lot to learn.

I made my first appearance in a game with the Royals on June 18, 1969, during a doubleheader against the Oakland Athletics at the old Kansas City Municipal Stadium. I was in the bullpen, warming up our relievers late in the first game, when the phone rang. It was the ninth inning. Moe Drabowsky, our closer, answered the call. It was our manager, Joe Gordon, a future Hall of Famer. Drabowsky hung up and looked at me.

"Rookie, go down there," he said, nodding to home plate. "You're pinch-hitting. Go hit a home run."

I was 20 years old. I had spent a couple of seasons in the minors after being drafted in the second round. And now, here I was, John Martinez from the sandlots of Redding, California, about to take his first major-league at-bat.

I was floating on a cloud as I walked down to the dugout. I wasn't nervous. "This is something else," I thought. "Wow." There was this sense of calm. I was going to get a hit. *I knew it.* It was a rush.

The ballpark was pretty much empty. There were two out in the bottom of the ninth. We were losing, 16–4. There weren't a lot of fans left in the stands. The Athletics had actually just moved from Kansas City to Oakland. Charlie Finley had bought the team in 1960, made himself the de facto general manager and moved to Oakland the year before. Finley's A's were a pretty good team at the time. They had the makings of the Oakland team that would go on to win three straight championships in the early '70s with Vida Blue, Catfish Hunter, Rollie Fingers and Blue Moon Odom on the mound. They had Sal Bando at third and Bert Campaneris at short. Reggie Jackson and Joe Rudi were in the outfield. All of them were homegrown talent.

I took a deep breath as I walked up to the plate. Chuck Dobson was on the mound for Oakland. I made contact. I hit it really well. It felt perfect. The ball soared high over second base and into the outfield. It was deep. The center-field fence was 421 feet away, and it looked like the ball was going to carry over it. "Oh my God," I thought, as I watched while jogging to first base, "I hit a home run."

But it fell into Rick Monday's glove, just short of the warning track. Game over.

It didn't take long for me to get another crack at it. In the second game of the doubleheader, the same thing happened. It was like déjà vu. I wasn't expecting to get back in, but a call came through to the bullpen. We were losing, but it was only the fifth inning. Blue Moon Odom was on the mound. Again, I was calm and confident. And again, the stadium was almost empty. But I felt like I was going to get a hit. I just knew it.

I made contact again. This time the ball lined over the mound, past the second-base bag, into center for a single. It was no home run, but I was on base with my first major-league hit. I went to second base on a wild pitch during the next at-bat. Dick Green was the second baseman. He was a veteran, and he knew I was a rookie. He also knew that I'd just had my first hit and that it was a significant moment for me. Green came over to me as I stood on the bag. "Way to go, kid," he said. "There's a lot of hits right there up the middle, so stay hitting it right there."

When I got back to the dugout that inning, none of my teammates said anything. It wasn't the same faux silent treatment you see today, when the team pretends to ignore the guy and then everyone celebrates with a laugh. We just didn't make a big deal out of things like a first hit back then. And besides, veterans barely spoke to rookies except to give them the gears.

I got my first start behind the plate later that month, on June 28, 1969, at home against the Minnesota Twins. Galen Cisco, who would later become the pitching coach for the Montreal Expos and the Toronto Blue Jays, among other teams, was on the mound for us. We were up 1–0 in the fourth inning. The Twins' left fielder, Bob Allison, started the inning off with a single. George Mitterwald, the catcher, popped out. But then Leo Cardenas, the shortstop, smashed a double into the gap in left-center field. Allison charged around from first and rounded third. I should mention that Allison was once a fullback for the University of Kansas football team. Our center fielder, Bob Oliver (father of retired pitcher Darren Oliver), collected the ball and rifled it to Jackie Hernández at short. Allison barreled toward home plate. Hernández threw a bullet to me, just as all 225 pounds of Bob Allison smashed into me. We crashed hard into the dirt and my head smacked against the ground, but the ball stayed in my mitt. While I was down, I saw Cardenas break from second for third. I pushed Allison off of me and managed to throw the ball to Joe Foy at third. Cardenas ran back to second—and then I passed out. The trainer had to use smelling salts to bring me around. Today, I'd have been back in the medical room, taking concussion tests and everything else. But it was a much different era. When I was conscious again, I put my mask back on and got ready for the next batter. He flew out.

I was first up to bat the next inning, facing Dave Boswell. I was hitting fifth in the lineup. Despite the lingering headache, I felt pretty good about myself. The shake-up at the plate seemed to jolt something in me. I led off the bottom of the fourth and connected to left center for my first major-league home run.

The next day, we played the Twins again in a doubleheader. I sat out the first game but started the second. All-Star pitcher Jim Kaat was pitching for the Twins. I picked up three hits in the game. I felt like I was on top of the world. Unfortunately, we got our asses beat, 12–2, but I had a hard time containing my excitement. In two days I had hit my first home run and picked up three more hits. I was on a roll.

I was singing to myself as I shaved in the locker room after the loss. Just humming a tune, having a great time, feeling like a major-league ballplayer. Someone walked up behind me.

"Hey, Rook." It was Harry Dunlop, our bench coach. "We don't celebrate when we lose."

It crushed me.

Dunlop was looking out for me. He was a good influence—he had also been a catcher and really helped me out a lot when I first got to Kansas City. Dunlop didn't want me to make a fool of myself. It was an embarrassing moment, getting called out like that. But it was an important lesson.

Mind you, it wasn't a lesson that I learned easily.

Several of the older guys on that team looked out for me. I was

20 years old and had never even been to a big-league training camp before. And I had gone right from A-ball to the major leagues. I made a lot of mistakes. I was so naive. I did silly things, like cheering when we shouldn't be cheering, or basking in my own glory when we were getting beat. Veteran players like Dave Wickersham and relief pitcher Tom Burgmeier tried to show me the ropes. Wally Bunker, who was part of that great Orioles team in 1966, was another pitcher who really tried to help me make the transition to the big leagues. He'd pitched as a 19-year-old in the '66 World Series. He wasn't much older than I was, but he had already had success. He was a great pitcher.

So I had some great mentors on that team. But despite that, I still managed to make a fool of myself several times.

Shortly after the game in which I hit my first home run, one of our coaches, George Strickland, gave me some advice I'd never forget. He was a wise old guy and had been a pretty good player from New Orleans. In his southern drawl, he told me, "John, it is better to be silent and thought a fool than to open one's mouth and remove all doubt." Strickland then wrote it in marker on the pillar right in front of my locker.

In other words: Keep your mouth shut, you're making an idiot out of yourself.

The transition to the major leagues was difficult in many other ways. The most stressful part was trying to catch the pitchers, which didn't bode well considering that that's what I was there for. But when I first arrived there were guys on the mound for the Royals whom I simply couldn't catch. They were major-league pitchers and I was still a minor-league catcher. The first guy I had trouble with was Bill Butler. He was young like me, only 22, and he threw it hard and straight. During our first bullpen session, I couldn't keep the ball in my glove. Then I had to catch guys like Wally Bunker, Roger Nelson, Dick Drago and Jim Rooker. These guys were legitimate pros. I had never seen balls break like that. I'd never seen fastballs move like that. I'd just miss them; the balls would just zip past me. The Royals tried to figure out how they could get me into a game because I was so green.

As I mentioned earlier, I wasn't the only rookie on the Kansas City Royals during the 1969 season. A guy name Lou Piniella was in left field.

Piniella would stick with the Royals for five seasons before he was traded to the New York Yankees, where he played some of his most memorable baseball and finished his career. He was a lot of fun to play with, but also a lot of fun to play against. I remember chatting with him whenever he came up to bat and I was behind the plate.

"You're not going to get me out today, you little Mexican," he'd say.

"Yeah, we'll see," I'd say.

Then he would hit a home run. But we'd throw him the same pitch the next at-bat.

"You can't throw me that pitch—I just hit a home run," he'd say, after watching it go by.

"Strike one, Lou," I'd reply.

Piniella went on to play 11 seasons in New York, where he won two World Series. He went on to become a hitting coach and then the Yankees' manager and general manager, after which he became an announcer. He's done just about everything. Later, he was one of the best managers in the game, with the Cincinnati Reds, Seattle Mariners, Tampa Bay Devil Rays and Chicago Cubs.

THERE WAS A DRAFT LOTTERY at the time, and my number came up, so I was subjected to two years of military service. The Royals helped me sign up with the Missouri National Guard, which involved a six-year commitment but only six months of active duty. At the end of the season, I enlisted in the National Guard so that I could avoid going to war. This was at the height of the Vietnam War, and many major-league players were joining the national guard or army reserve so as to avoid losing two years of their career to service in the army. The national guard gave me its assurance that I wouldn't be called up for basic training until the fall of 1970, which wouldn't affect my career. But in March 1970, in the midst of spring training, I was notified that I needed to report to Fort Knox, Kentucky, on April 2. I would be going from major-league baseball to the army. It was a huge blow.

I remember when I got off the bus at the base at about two in the morning, the drill sergeant met me and screamed and hollered at me and told me to go up to my bunk. The barracks was lined with these uncomfortable bunk beds. I found mine, slunk into it and thought, "How in the world did I end up here?" I certainly wasn't in Kansas anymore. Right when I was thinking that, the whole building shook. "What in the hell is going on?" I thought, looking around as it shook again. It turns out that Fort Knox was a tank training center. At four in the morning the tanks would roll out for their morning drills. We'd all be shaking in our barracks. So things got off to a great start.

I was fortunate not to be going to Vietnam, but I still went through the same training as everybody else. And it was serious stuff. We had regular soldiers along with members of the national guard and army reserve all in the same barracks. Most of the guys were 17- and 18-year-old kids drafted right out of high school, and they were on their way to war. It was crazy. And here I was, a 21-year-old professional ballplayer—a distinction that held little sway with the sergeants.

I knew for sure that I wasn't going to be sent to war because I was in the national guard. They told me I was in for six months of basic training. The first eight weeks were basic training at Fort Knox. Then we would be moved into "AIT," or advanced individual training, at a different base.

It wasn't until about halfway through that it really hit me that the kids around me were going off to Vietnam, and they weren't remotely ready for what they were about to face. I mean, we were *young*. And some of these kids weren't coming back. I don't know if we fully understood the magnitude of what this was all about.

During the drills, there wasn't much time to think, anyway. In "basic" training we learned the fundamentals of being in the military. We learned how to be a team player, and they pushed us to get into great physical shape. So, really, you *could* say it was just like being a major-league baseball player. Except that it was much different.

A big part of military training is that they break you down— screaming at you, just like you see in movies—so that you understand you are part of a unit. It was the "team player" concept, taken to its ultimate level. They were trying to teach us discipline so that we understood we weren't going to succeed until we all worked together.

So, together, we got up at five in the morning. We pulled on our boots and put on our uniforms, and together, in the dark, we ran for five miles. And together we chanted and rooted for the others—"I want to be an airborne ranger! I want to go to Vietnam!"—all of those songs that build up anticipation that the routine is leading somewhere.

Our five-mile run would end at the mess hall. Breakfast was the same thing every day. We'd shuffle down in the line with our silver trays, and they would slop the stuff on our plates. It was always scrambled eggs and "shit on a shingle" (chipped beef on toast, the famous military dish). We'd get some coffee and milk and a glass of water.

And then we were running again. We ran everywhere. Everything was on a timeframe.

Then we'd go to marksmanship and learn how to fire weapons. We learned to march in sync. We learned how to bivouac and dig foxholes. We learned how to set up the tents for a base camp. We trained (it was called PT, or physical training). We did jumping jacks, push-ups, judo, all kinds of stuff.

Our drill sergeant's name was Smoky. He was a slim, athletic guy who looked exactly like a drill sergeant out of *An Officer and a Gentleman*. He'd holler at us. He'd get right up in our faces and shout, "I'm going to kick your ass!" In this strange way it was about pushing us to be part of the team, about working together, about surviving together.

I was named platoon leader. There were 135 guys in the company, broken into platoons. You'd probably have 20 guys in your platoon that you were responsible for.

Every night, we had to scrub the barracks. We quickly learned that if you organized a handful of guys, you could get more done than having everybody trip over everybody else. One time, they wanted us to paint the barracks. If we got the job done sufficiently, to army standards, the reward was a weekend pass to go into town.

So we gathered a handful of guys, maybe eight or ten, who we knew were relatively reliable, and said to the others, "You guys just get out of our way and we'll do it." Of course, after painting for ten hours, things started to get a bit goofy. It turned into a bit of a paint fight. Everyone was covered. As soon as one guy rolled paint on someone's back, the other guy had to get revenge. It was really kind of silly, these soldiers getting ready for war, laughing and tossing paint on each other. But it was great for team building. We were in charge and decided, well, that's what we had to do.

Over the course of two months, we were graded on our ability to shoot rifles. We had to pass ridiculous fitness tests. Everyone had to run a mile in under six minutes. You had to be able to carry another guy 300 yards while running.

I was never in better shape.

After eight weeks at Fort Knox in Kentucky, I was transferred to Fort Gordon, just outside of Augusta, Georgia, a military police and communications base. Of course, the drills became even more difficult. It was the middle of the summer in Georgia, so the heat was just sweltering. For some reason, our morning runs felt like they started even earlier than they had at Fort Knox. At the end of these grueling morning runs, we'd do exercises, using these large, heavy poles to do presses and curls together. We'd start with six guys and do the presses and curls together as a team, all holding on to the kind of pole they would hang telephone wire from. Then you'd go down to four guys, and then down to two guys. I had never experienced that kind of training before.

The one thing that Fort Gordon had over Fort Knox was that we had a baseball team. During our orientation, all of the soldiers sat in a big theater, and the captain of our company came out to introduce himself. It turned out he was a big baseball fan, and the company had a team that would play other military facilities in the area.

"We have a very competitive situation here," he said. "If you have played baseball, I want you to raise your hand. We're going to have tryouts for the team." The captain went down the row, asking the guys with their hands raised where they had played. There were several eager volunteers who had played in Little League or in high school. There were a few guys who had played at the college level. Eventually, he came to me.

"Where did you play, soldier?" he asked.

"The Kansas City Royals, sir," I said.

"Soldier, what kind of baseball was it?" he asked. "Was it high school baseball? Amateur baseball? Semi-pro baseball?"

"Sir," I said. "It was in the major leagues."

"You're not understanding me, soldier," he said.

"Sir," I said. "You know the Boston Red Sox and the New York Yankees?"

"Yes."

"I played *against* the Red Sox and the Yankees."

He paused for a moment.

"Soldier, get up here," he said.

And that's how I made the baseball team.

Now, much like the major leagues, there were certain perks that came with playing for the Fort Gordon baseball squad. In the middle of judo training in the hot August afternoon, in a sand pit in 100-degree weather and 200-percent humidity, a jeep would come and pick me up and take me back to the mess hall. I'd take a shower, eat and then go practice baseball. Of course, that kind of special treatment didn't go over well with the other trainees. But the captain was such a baseball guy that he made sure it wasn't a big deal. He was a good ally to have.

One of the guys who tried out for the team was a hotshot pitcher with kind of a big mouth. He started spouting off about how he had played Double A the year before and they didn't have anybody on the base that could catch for him.

"I think I can catch you," I told him.

His name was Leo Mazzone. He went on to become the Atlanta Braves' pitching coach for 25 years, all through the '80s and '90s, right up until 2005. All of those great years in Atlanta, with guys like Tom Glavine, Greg Maddux and John Smoltz. They all had Mazzone in the bullpen. He and I would end up together, years later, in Baltimore when I was the color analyst on the Orioles broadcasts and he had joined the team as its pitching coach in 2006. We laughed about our experiences all the time.

We played on a nice field in a decent facility. We would play night games, and the bleachers would be packed. A lot of people came out because there was nothing else to do. You could go watch a movie every night or you could go watch some live baseball. That was the extent of our extracurriculars. It was a tough time. In the back of everyone's mind, the grim reality of the Vietnam War was impossible to shake, so the sport was a nice distraction.

But the baseball was *awful*. There were a few guys who could play a little bit, but most had stopped playing in high school. Leo and I could hit pretty much anywhere we wanted on the field. It was no substitute for the real thing. It was depressing to know that, while I was getting yelled at by drill sergeants, the Kansas City Royals were out there playing without me, and eating much better food than shit on a shingle.

I SPENT ANOTHER EIGHT WEEKS at Fort Gordon. When my time was finally up, I faced one last scare. Instead of sending me home, they sent me to the Criminal Investigation Division. I wasn't eligible to serve in this agency because I was in the reserves and not a regular army guy, but just when I expected I'd be going home, I was given orders to report to this building. I tried to object, but no one would listen. I had already missed four months of the 1970 baseball season; now it looked like I was never going back. I worried that I had been wrong about what I had signed up for. I was panicking because I thought I was stuck in the regular army. *Would I be sent to Vietnam?* I sat in the orientation area and looked around the room. There were a bunch of foreign officers—

guys from Vietnam, Japan and other places. I was clearly in the wrong place. It turned out I had been sent to the Criminal Investigation Division by mistake. It took me two weeks to get transferred out.

Then, finally, after nearly five months of military training, I was sent back to Kansas City at the end of August. Excited to get back, I figured I could jump right back into baseball at the level I had played. After all, I was in the best shape of my life.

Boy, was I wrong.

I dropped my bags off back at my place in Kansas City, which I shared with relief pitcher Tom Burgmeier. Then I went to the stadium and met with the Royals' manager, Bob Lemon, who had taken over from Charlie Metro after the team started 19–35. Metro had taken over for Joe Gordon, who had stepped away from the job after one season. Lemon wanted to send me to San Jose to finish off the year in A-ball, but I didn't want to waste any more time. I just wanted to get back to playing major-league baseball.

"Oh no, I've been playing in the army," I said. "I don't think I need to go back to A-ball."

THAT WAS A HUGE MISTAKE. I played in a total of six games that season, mostly as a defensive replacement. I went 1-for-9 at the plate, for a batting average of .111. There is no question that I should have taken the demotion to Class A; it would have been the best thing for me. But I was only 21, and having played a year in the major leagues, I felt like any assignment to the minors, especially to A-ball, was a huge step backward. All I wanted to do was keep my place on the team.

Had I been older and wiser, I would have understood that it's always better to play than to sit. I would have understood that just because you're in great physical condition, it doesn't mean you're in great shape to actually play the game. There is a big difference between physical training and training for the game. There is no substitute for actually playing.

That's a lesson that is still applicable today. Many players who come back from injury feel a sense of urgency to get back with the big-league club as soon as possible. There are obvious economic incentives fueling that desire, and it's hard to argue with the desire to collect a major-league paycheck. But there has to be a process. The minors are designed to steadily work a player back into game-ready shape. I needed to go down, but my pride kept me up.

I wouldn't realize the value of actually playing until the end of the 1970 season, when the Royals sent me to Puerto Rico to get me back on track in winter ball, which is another valuable experience that is disappearing today.

8

WHAT WINTER BALL CAN TEACH YOU

The stadium pulsed with the beat of drums, a staccato of tin and bass, as wild, disjointed music swelled up into the dark San Juan sky. Fans danced in the aisles. Rum flowed like water. "This is more than just a baseball game," I thought, sitting in the dugout beneath it all. It was a carnival.

At the end of our bench sat the great Frank Robinson, then 35 years old, who had carved out his legendary status as an outfielder with the Cincinnati Reds and who had won the Triple Crown and the World Series Most Valuable Player Award in 1966 with the Baltimore Orioles. He had just helped the Orioles win a second World Series in the fall of 1970. Already, Robinson had pushed up against all of the game's great home-run hitters: Hank Aaron, Willie Mays, Babe Ruth.

Roberto Clemente was in the other dugout. The Puerto Rican god was already a ten-time Gold Glove winner, with four National League batting titles, a National League MVP Award and a World Series championship to his credit over his career with the Pittsburgh Pirates. At 36 Clemente was still a couple of Gold Gloves and another World Series championship—plus a Series MVP Award—from the end of his career, which would be cut tragically short in a fatal plane crash off the coast of Puerto Rico on New Year's Eve 1972, while he was delivering aid to earthquake victims in Nicaragua.

It was 1970, and I was 21 years old. It was my first season of winter ball, which is professional baseball played in leagues that operate during the major-league off-season, usually in Caribbean nations. In those countries the winter leagues are, really, the local version of big-league baseball.

I was about to make my first appearance for Cangrejeros de Santurce, the storied franchise from San Juan. Robinson was our manager.

We were playing our rivals, Senadores de San Juan. Clemente was their manager. Both clubs shared the 18,000-seat Hiram Bithorn Stadium in the Puerto Rican capital. But both teams had their own passionate fan bases. This was San Juan's enduring version of New York's historic Yankees–Giants rivalry. But *much* louder.

The Kansas City Royals had sent me to play winter ball to get back into playing form. I had missed most of the season because of my military commitment and had tried to return directly to pro ball having seen little actual game action in a year. My return to Kansas City was a disaster. I was in great physical condition from my time in the reserve, where we did intense drills every day, but that didn't mean I was in good playing condition. Physical training is no substitute for actually playing the game.

The winter assignment in Puerto Rico was the best move I made in my career.

This was serious baseball. The Puerto Rican Professional Baseball

League was no joke. There were fierce rivalries that reached back decades, and the island had a rich tradition of the game. The fans *knew* baseball, and they demanded *good* baseball. The teams demanded it too. If a player wasn't performing to expectations, the owners wouldn't hesitate to drop him from the roster, regardless of his major-league experience.

Along with Frank Robinson, our roster boasted some remarkable baseball talent. Sitting next to me on the bench, wearing the blue and gray Santurce jersey, was future Hall of Famer Tony Pérez, our third baseman. A young center fielder named Don Baylor was also on the team. He won the Puerto Rican League batting title that year, and in less than a decade he'd be the MVP of the American League. But at the time, Baylor was just a young prospect for the Baltimore Orioles. He'd been named minor-league player of the year, along with Roger Freed, who was also on our team. We had Rubén Gómez, another Puerto Rican legend, who pitched for the Giants through the 1950s. The bullpen also featured the Orioles' Dave Leonhard, an Ivy Leaguer who would write articles about his time in Puerto Rico. We even had characters like Yankees pitcher Mike Kekich, who'd become most famous for switching families—wives, kids, dogs, houses—with his teammate Fritz Peterson in 1973. Juan Pizarro, a tremendous pitcher with the White Sox, was also on our team. Our first baseman was Elrod Hendricks, from the Orioles. Rogelio Moret, a young Puerto Rican, was just beginning his major-league pitching career with the Boston Red Sox. Puerto Rico at that time was producing major-league players left and right.

On top of all that, we also had a guy named Reggie Jackson. Yes, *that* Reggie Jackson. He had hit 47 home runs for the Oakland Athletics in 1969, but he had an off-year the next season and only hit 23. So here he was in San Juan, working with Frank Robinson.

And there I was, in this sweltering Caribbean city, about to play the first game of the season in the biggest rivalry in Puerto Rican baseball. It was a tremendous atmosphere. The rum-fueled fans were wild before the game even started.

Then the lights went out. The stadium went completely dark. The power was gone. As the stadium workers scrambled to find out what had happened, the carnival started to get ugly. The mood went from celebratory to rage-filled very quickly. It looked like the season opener would be canceled, and that wasn't going to sit well with the 20,000 fans in the stadium. After several minutes of darkness a bank of lights on the first-base side of the stands of the field finally flashed on. It didn't light up the whole diamond, but it was just enough to allow us to make out the ball.

That's when Robinson and Clemente decided to take batting practice.

The two legends picked up bats and met at home plate. Under the shadowy light, they took turns hammering balls into the stands beyond the fence. The crowd went nuts. Each moon shot eclipsed the last, the light catching just one side of the balls as they arched through the dark sky before being swallowed by the booming mob. The sight of two of baseball's biggest stars taking swing after swing as drums pounded and the fans continued their dance party in the aisles is something I'll never forget. *Crack . . . crack . . . crack . . .* hit after hit, Robinson versus Clemente in a home-run derby for the ages.

When it became apparent that the one bank of lights was the only one that was going to come back on, Robinson came back to our dugout and told us to get ready to take the field. "We have to play this game," he said. "The fans will go nuts if we don't. They'll riot and they'll trash the place."

"Just be careful," he added, as we grabbed our mitts and pulled on our caps. "You can only see half the baseball out there."

We played the whole game under that one bank of lights. The imperfection of it was beautiful; the shadows created a need to adjust to the natural elements, just like when we were kids playing on a street or city diamond.

I don't remember who won the game, but I'll always remember that moment under a single slice of light playing baseball in San Juan. It was one of the most memorable experiences of my life. Decades later, I'd think back to that night when I was managing my first game in the major leagues in that very place, Bithorn Stadium, where the Blue Jays and Texas Rangers opened the 2001 season. It will always be a special place to me.

It wasn't just that I loved the unique experience of playing in the Caribbean. It was a necessity for me. For starters, it paid very well. Life in the majors was much different in the 1970s than it is today. I made about $3,000 a month down there at the time. That's about $18,000 today. It was *a lot* of money to me. It still is a lot of money, but obviously it's dwarfed by what the guys pull in these days.

The economics of the game have changed dramatically over the course of my career, thanks to the efforts of my late friend Marvin Miller and the Major League Baseball Players Association. I remember I had been in the major leagues for six years in 1976, and I was making $16,000 a season. I played winter ball for four seasons over those six years because I loved it *and* because it supplemented my income. When free agency came in, my salary jumped from $16,000 to $60,000, and I felt like a millionaire.

UNFORTUNATELY, THE PROMINENCE OF winter ball has diminished over the past couple of decades. The leagues still exist, and they still have a passionate local following. But you don't see established major leaguers spending their off-seasons playing for a team in the Dominican or in Venezuela, which both have popular leagues. The Caribbean Series, the championship of all the Caribbean leagues, is still a big deal. We played in it when I was in San Juan, against the Tigres del Licey from the Dominican Republic.

Today, players will spend a fortune developing their own training facilities and will work out on their own over the off-season. They will hire the best personal trainers money can buy and attempt to tailor their training to aspects of the game that will increase their value when it comes time to negotiate contracts or go through arbitration hearings. They will work on skills that get them paid, not necessarily those that will make them better baseball players.

Back then, it wasn't odd to see established major leaguers spend a few months in winter ball in the off-season. Some of these teams were stacked with talent. Our San Juan rivals had Manny Sanguillén, Milt May, Al Oliver, Mike Jorgensen, Freddie Patek, Coco Laboy and Ken Singleton. They also had Boston's Jim Lonborg on the mound, the hero of the Red Sox' 1967 American League pennant run. Ken Brett and José Santiago were in the rotation. It was a terrific team.

But there were major-league players everywhere. Criollos de Caguas had Félix Millan, Willie Montañez, Jim Rooker and Bob Oliver. Leones de Ponce had José Cruz, Luis Melendez and Jorge Roque, three rookies with the St. Louis Cardinals who could compare favorably to what the Toronto Blue Jays would one day have in the outfield in George Bell, Jesse Barfield and Lloyd Moseby.

As I mentioned, winter ball was the best thing that happened in my career. I went from the dumbest move—returning too soon—to the smartest. Kansas City had insisted that I go that first year—it wasn't really up to me—but the benefits were enormous.

I went back to play for Santurce in San Juan the following year. I played in Maracaibo in Venezuela in 1972 and 1973, and then returned to Puerto Rico to play for Arecibo on the northern coast in '74.

Later, I found myself back in winter ball under unforeseen circumstances.

In 1976 the Royals had a fantastic season, going 90–72 and winning the American League West for the first time. It was probably one of my best seasons. We went all the way to the American League Championship Series, but we lost to the Yankees.

It's funny how, just when things seem to be going well, life throws another challenge at you. In my case it was a gunshot.

I've always loved hunting and used to go almost every day in the off-season. In the fall of 1976, after the playoffs, I took one of my teammates, Doug Bird, out bird hunting. He didn't have any experience with a gun, but he wanted to give it a try. Unfortunately for me, he got spooked by a bird and fired without realizing that I was standing in front of him, about sixty yards away. The blast knocked me over. Stunned, I put my hand on my eye, and it was covered in blood. A piece of the buckshot had entered the soft tissue of my eye and moved to the back of it. I was rushed to the hospital and saw three specialists who tried to figure out what to do. They kept passing me off to the next guy. I worried that I was going to lose my eye. Finally, the third doctor laid me on my back and shone a bright light in my face. "You're going to need surgery," he said, in an urgent tone.

"When?" I asked.

"In ten minutes," he said.

My wife wasn't aware yet of what had happened, so I told my

friend to call her: "Tell my wife I'm having surgery. I've been shot, and I'm at Baptist Hospital." In retrospect it wasn't the best way to relay the news.

Meanwhile, Arlene had been to the hospital that day already. As luck would have it she had a doctor's appointment, at which she found out she was pregnant. She was waiting at home for me with a bottle of champagne at 11 p.m. that night, wondering where the hell I was, when she found out that I'd been shot.

The surgeon had to pull my eye out to remove the BB. In the end, I had a detached retina, and I had to lie on my back in the dark for two weeks. Every time my good eye moved, the injured one would hurt. It was hell. Just a terrible time. Arlene started to feel sick from the pregnancy, so she was laid up in bed beside me. During that time, someone kicked our dog, Tammy Lee. She was seriously injured and died as a result of the assault.

I got shot, my wife was pregnant and our dog died—it was like I was living in a country-and-western song.

My vision would never be the same. In fact, I played the rest of my career with a contact lens in one eye so I could see.

I spent the entire 1976–77 off-season recovering from the accident and played in only 29 games the following summer. My injury had limited my ability to play, and the Royals had traded for catcher Darrell Porter, who became the clear starter.

If I wanted my career to continue, I had to get myself back into playing condition. So after the 1977 season, I packed my bags and went back to winter ball. This time, I returned to Puerto Rico to play for Mayagüez, a smaller town on the west coast of the island. My son, Casey, was only a few months old then, which was a unique experience for Arlene and me. The next couple of off-seasons I would play in

Caracas, the capital of Venezuela, so Casey had quite the international experience through the first years of his life.

IN THE END, WINTER BALL was an essential part of my development as a catcher over the first decade of my major-league career, just as it was for many other major-league players. But winter ball wasn't a vacation. It was hard, demanding baseball. The only way to keep playing winter ball was to win. If you didn't win, you were sent home. So not only did it cost you economically, it was also a matter of pride.

Players came and went all the time. The competitive reality of winter ball stoked the will to win in many players. There was no time off from competition—you couldn't afford to take it easy. If a pitcher showed up and put together a couple of bad starts, there were repercussions all over the place. The teams had affiliations with major-league organizations, which often had staff at the games. If a player wasn't showing any promise, the major-league team was very well aware of it. And if you were sent home from winter league, you had much bigger problems to deal with.

John McLaren was the third-base coach when I managed Team USA in the 2006 World Baseball Classic. He started out as a coach in the Toronto Blue Jays' minor-league system, and he has seen more international baseball than anyone I know. He has been involved with baseball everywhere, from Italy to Belarus. But he first got involved internationally when he started out as a minor-league coach with the Blue Jays in the late '70 and through the '80s.

With the Jays, McLaren spent two off-seasons in Colombia and seven in Venezuela. Under general manager Pat Gillick, the Blue Jays used winter ball as a key component in the franchise's player-development program. It wasn't that crazy a concept just a couple of decades ago. If a player didn't have a good season at the plate, winter ball was an obvious chance for him to correct that. Gillick was resourceful in that regard: He used the off-season to his advantage. He wanted his guys to play winter ball so they would get better. He wanted them to learn how to compete.

"It was the Pat Gillick and the Toronto Way," says McLaren. "We sent all our guys down there."

Kelly Gruber spent time in Venezuela. So did Willie Upshaw, Todd Stottlemyre and Pat Borders. Lloyd Moseby was there too. Jesse Barfield's son was born in Venezuela. "That was part of how you graduated to the big leagues," says McLaren. "You went to winter ball."

One year, in Venezuela, McLaren had David Justice, Rob Ducey and Glenallen Hill in the outfield. During a game in Caracas, the fans started throwing batteries at the players. Hill, who was just starting out his career in the Blue Jays system, came into the dugout and said, "Mac, they threw a battery at me!"

"Great," McLaren said. "Get used to it, because they're going to do that in New York too. It's just a little part of your schooling here, brother."

IT'S HARD TO IMAGINE a team sending a major-league player to winter ball these days. Think about having an outfield like the Jays had, all taking an assignment to Venezuela. Or imagine guys like Mike Trout or Bryce Harper working on their swing in Puerto Rico. These guys are superstars. But so was Reggie Jackson. So were Frank Robinson and Roberto Clemente.

For some reason, the concept of winter ball sounds outrageous to most players today. I imagine that the reaction many players would have if their team asked them to report to a Caribbean league in November would be something like, "You want me to do *what*?" It would be viewed as a demotion, even though it's really more of an opportunity than anything else. Instead, players will say that they are going to stay home and do some work in the batting cage. They are going to lift weights and put themselves through a new, cutting-edge training regimen. The game will come to them. But really, what does that accomplish? Instead of putting themselves in real game situations that actually matter—situations where you have to react and keep your mind and body in top form—the idea is to put themselves in a series of static exercises, without experiencing the game. It lacks the practical experience of actually playing the game. Training is important. Branch Rickey established that. But even he knew there was no substitute for the experience of playing a real game.

"Don Zimmer used to tell me stories about playing [winter ball]," recalls McLaren. "I'm talking about major-league players that have played the whole year in the big leagues [who] would go down there and get at-bats because they maybe didn't get enough at-bats [in the regular] season . . . and now guys, they train year-round because if they make the money, they don't want to sacrifice some of their off-season for whatever reason. And I understand it, I get it, but I know that winter ball has helped so many players over the years and it's been a great stepping-stone."

It certainly was for me. I used to come to spring training head and shoulders ahead of other players because I played winter ball. My arm was in great shape, and I was able to step right into the first game in spring training because I'd been playing right up to March. Because of that, my performance would earn me a spot on the team. That's how I stayed in the major leagues.

It's no wonder that players who come from Latin countries and have played in places like the Dominican Republic, Puerto Rico, Venezuela or Mexico seem to have an extra step each spring. They've been playing all winter long! They never went into off-season mode. It's constant competition.

These aren't polite prospect games in a quiet ballpark in the Arizona Fall League. These are wild, energized atmospheres in which winning is the only thing that matters. If you think fans in Boston or New York can be demanding, just visit Puerto Rico. There is no quantifiable measure for the benefit of a player batting in front of 20,000 venomous fans in an opponent's park in winter league. But as I've said, baseball is not simply a game of quantifiable measures. The intangibles matter. A lot.

During the 2014 off-season, Blue Jays reliever Liam Hendriks, who had finished the season with Kansas City, went to the Dominican to fine-tune his game in winter ball. He went with Royals catcher Francisco Peña. The Royals had come within a game of winning the World Series, but at the time, Hendriks wasn't sure where he was going to land for the 2015 season. (The Royals had received him in a trade that sent Danny Valencia to the Blue Jays. Toronto would end up reacquiring him through a trade.) Hendriks was looking for any extra edge he could find to find success in the majors.

Hendriks felt that the excitement during games in the Dominican rivaled anything he had seen playing baseball in the major leagues, which means a lot considering he had just been through a seven-game World Series. He played for Águilas Cibaeñas, which is the team Edwin Encarnación played for before his major-league days. Hendriks pitched a game against the rival Tigres del Licey, which was the team José Bautista had played for. "It was insane," says Hendriks. The atmosphere offered so much more than a typical spring-training game. You can't simulate an experience like that.

The learning opportunities were key for Hendriks. The Águilas roster had both Miguel Tejada and Manny Ramírez on it. Hendriks had the chance to sit around with Ramírez, talking about what one of the game's great hitters would look for from inside the batter's box. "The experience you can get from some of the guys you play with is invaluable," he says. He also sat down with Tony Peña, Francisco's dad, who had a 17-year career in the majors. Peña told Hendriks not to worry about trying to throw the ball as hard as he can. Instead, he told him to paint his spots and then, on the last couple of pitches, to let it go a little bit. That helped Hendriks's command immensely. Coming out of the bullpen, he'd been trying to throw as hard as he could right away, only to find he was tiring himself out. Now, he had learned to get into a rhythm to get ready for a game.

When he returned to spring training, Hendriks was a step ahead of where he had left off with the Royals. He felt great in camp, throwing harder and with better command on his pitches. The success carried into his season, where he appeared in 58 games as a reliever for the Jays, posting a career-best 2.92 ERA and becoming a key weapon in the Toronto bullpen.

If baseball players want to get the most out of their off-season, they need to start looking south each November. It may not be a matter of finances anymore—at least not in the short term. But in the long term the developmental possibilities are enormous. There is nothing like playing the game. It's the best training any player can have, regardless of whether he is an established star or just trying to break into the big leagues.

9

WHY ATTITUDE IS SO IMPORTANT

When we watch players like Troy Tulowitzki, Josh Donaldson and Mike Trout play the game today, we often see the kind of generational players that harken back to the all-time greats. They are supremely talented players. But I also see traits beyond their natural ability. I see an approach to the game that brings out the best in the players around them.

What's so incredible about these kinds of players is that, even when they are the best in the league, they play like rookies just trying to stick around. Every play matters, regardless of how insignificant it might seem. I believe that's really what sets these guys apart.

When I played for Kansas City, we had a guy I think of whenever I see players today who have that intangible factor that brings out the winner in his teammates. His name was Hal McRae, and I have never seen anybody play the game with the kind of passion and intensity he had.

I would take a player like McRae over so many of the most talented in the game today. If a scout can detect McRae's approach to the game in a young prospect today, I'd suggest they do everything they can to lock that player down. Hal McRae is the one who showed us in Kansas City how you win. *You don't accept anything. The other team is the enemy.* He played hard. He ran his ass off. He was known as the most aggressive baserunner in the 1970s. They changed the rule about trying to break up plays at second base, making it mandatory for players to slide, because McRae was so intense, he'd just run straight at the man on the bag.

But above all, he was a tremendous teammate.

McRae was a product of Cincinnati's Big Red Machine. He learned from the example of Pete Rose and Johnny Bench. I remember when he showed up on the first day of spring training in 1973, having been traded to the Royals the previous November. He came into my room at the Sheraton Hotel. He didn't really know me at all, but I had been sent down to the minors. "I don't know who you are, I don't know what the deal is, but you're getting screwed," he said. "You're the best catcher we got." He felt I wasn't getting my fair share of playing time. Obviously, I liked him after that.

But all kidding aside, McRae changed the culture of our team. That's what is so important about character guys who have nothing but winning on their minds. They can actually change the mentality of a team. He was the guy that made us a winner.

When he first came over, he brushed off Charley Lau because he thought he knew everything there was to know about hitting. But after a rough start, when he was hitting a paltry .161, he tore off his uniform and went over to Lau. "I'm all yours," he said. Lau turned him into a hitter. He finished off that season hitting .234 for us. After that first season, he hit above .300 for three straight years. His willingness to learn set a precedent on the ballclub.

His intensity, though, is what rubbed off on the field. He was all about playing rough. "When I can't be good, I've got to be rough," he'd say. He was the kind of player you couldn't shut up. He'd be in the dugout saying, "You got to get in position for the RBIs. I'm driving them in. You just get in position." He was always talking like that.

McRae's philosophy of the game was simple: Whatever it takes to win, you do. You get yourself in position to win. You go from first to third if you have to. You take out a guy at second base. You block the plate. McRae was the kind of player who would trash-talk our opponents during batting practice. He was always on.

During a game on May 17, 1974, in the second inning, McRae was hit in the head by a pitch from Jim Bibby, who was a big son of a gun. He was 6-5 and weighed 235, in an era where big guys were about six feet tall. Bibby threw hard. The pitch broke McRae's helmet and it shattered into pieces. But McRae just picked up the helmet as if to say, "You can't hurt me." He picked up the pieces and went to first base.

Charlie Lau helped him get back into the box the next night. "I got to get back on the horse," he said. The biggest hurdle an athlete confronts is fear—the fear of not being able to get back into the batter's box after taking a 98-mile-an-hour fastball to the helmet; of not being able to hang in there on a tough down-and-away slider. After McRae was beaned he and Charlie sat in the locker room for hours that night, talking about getting back up on that horse. Charlie knew Mac had to get right back in the box the next night to make sure his fear didn't take over.

The next night, Steve Hargan was on the mound for Texas. Charlie had convinced McRae that the only way this was going to work was for him to take the first pitch like a statue. Don't move a muscle, don't blink, don't flinch. Take it all the way. Show everybody in the park that you can handle being in the batter's box. McRae did just that. Hargan fired the first pitch right down the middle, and Hal took it like he knew what was coming. He had met the challenge. He was back in the box. What he did after that pitch is what made him the player he was for the rest of his career. He finished up 3-for-3 that night and let the world know you couldn't intimidate Hal McRae.

That was just one of the many ways he taught us how to play the game. Play it as if you might never get another at-bat, as if you might never get a chance to beat out another infield hit, as if this could be the last time you have a chance to break up a double play.

That was the first year Mac hit .300.

The Royals learned from Hal McRae. There are others in the game today who play with the same passion, the same intensity and the same will to win. Just not as many.

Josh Donaldson has the burning desire to beat you any way he can. José Bautista never backs down from a challenge, as we have seen over the years with his battle with Darren O'Day and the Baltimore Orioles. You have to be good to be in the position to compete, but then you have to go the extra mile and produce under pressure to earn the title of "winning player."

To me, McRae is the gold standard for how players should approach the game: all out, all the time. It's the stuff true leaders are made of.

And he was psychologically intimidating. He didn't cozy up to our opponents the way some players do today. I remember in 1977, we were playing the White Sox in Chicago, who were in first place at the time. During the White Sox' batting practice, Hal walked up to the cage while Ralph Garr was batting. He got down on all fours and put his ear to the ground. Then he said, "The cavalry's coming! The cavalry's coming!"

It pissed Garr right off.

"What are you doing, McRae? What are you doing?" he shouted from the batter's box. "Get up! You're crazy!" But McRae was just intimidating an opponent. He was always in their heads.

Later, he started the game in left field by straddling the foul line. I was catching that game, and I remember Garr coming up to bat and seeing McRae out there on the line. He tried to get the umpire to get him to move. "He can't do that!" he shouted. But McRae was in his head. That was just part of his game. He got to our opponents.

McRae ran hard and broke up more double plays than anyone else I watched. There was one play, in the 1977 American League Championship Series against the New York Yankees, where he crushed Willie Randolph in probably the most famous takeout slide in baseball history. The story came up again during the 2015 National League Division Series, when the Dodgers' Chase Utley slid hard into Mets second baseman Rubén Tejada and was suspended for two games. The McRae hit on Randolph was immediately cued up on broadcast for comparison's sake.

It was the second game of the ALCS, which was already a heated affair because it was the second straight time the Royals and Yankees had met in the series, and frankly, we hated each other. This was an era in which these kinds of collisions happened much more frequently. The game was much more physical than it is now. It was just accepted that contact was going to happen. On the play, our shortstop, Freddie Patek, was on second base and McRae was on first. Yankees manager Billy Martin went to the mound to speak with his pitcher before George Brett came up to bat. During the stop in play, McRae got Patek's attention and told him that if Brett made contact on the ground, Patek was to run all the way around third to home; McRae would take care of the rest. Sure enough, Brett slapped a groundball to third and the ball was thrown to Randolph at second. But just as he caught it, McRae went barreling into him. McRae and Randolph ended up in a mangled pile about ten feet from second base. Meanwhile, Patek ran in and tied the game.

"I wanted to get him in; I knew I could get him in," says McRae. "That was the plan. I threw a cross-body block on [Randolph]; it was a football play, just to make sure that I'd knocked him down and he couldn't throw the ball."

The Yankees were furious. They took it personally. Randolph actually threw the ball at McRae as he trotted into our dugout. The next day, New York's designated hitter, Cliff Johnson, wanted to fight McRae, but he didn't get the chance. During the game, our second baseman, Frank White, had to keep his head on a swivel. But there was no retaliation. The Yankees just went on to beat us three games to two, and then beat the Dodgers to win the World Series. That was enough revenge.

You can see the same kind of intensity in the game today, but not to the same extent that it once existed. The culture has changed.

Richie Hebner, who played third base for a great Pittsburgh Pirates team in the '70s and is now the Triple-A hitting coach in the Jays organization, puts it well. "I see big-league guys go around the cage, talking to other guys. [The Pirates] didn't talk to anybody," he says. "Now, it's a friendly game. Everybody's making $10 million, let's play for three hours and let's not get hurt—and let's meet somewhere after the game. Really?"

I think the best players today show their intensity. I'm not talking about going out there and hurting an opponent. But showing the kind of grit and competitiveness that Hal McRae did goes a long way. It was just the mentality in the '70s. We've seen that kind of attitude in flashes throughout the league. The Jays have several players like that. Josh Donaldson and José Bautista come to mind. Neither are dirty players, and they don't actively try to get under anyone's skin. But they play *hard*. Watch Donaldson run from first to third and you'll see what I mean. He isn't stopping for anything. Watch the way he slides—he is getting to that bag no matter what. Bautista shows the same kind of attitude at the plate and in the field. He is one of the most dangerous batters in the league, and it gets to the pitchers facing him.

During a game in 2013, Orioles pitcher Darren O'Day drew the ire of Bautista's competitive side when he struck him out to end an inning. O'Day was jacked up and said something to Bautista as he walked off the mound. Bautista asked him what he said, and the two exchanged some heated words. The next day, with the game tied at two in the bottom of the ninth, Bautista hit a two-run home run off O'Day. He ran around the bases with a stern look on his face, and as he went from third to home, he made a talking gesture with his hands at O'Day. It was Bautista's kind of revenge.

The battle between the two continued a year later, in a late-season game, when the Orioles were about to clinch the AL East. Marcus Stroman threw a ball over the head of catcher Caleb Joseph, who had gotten caught up with Jays shortstop José Reyes earlier. When Bautista came up to bat, O'Day drilled him in the kidney. And on it went. Early in the spring of 2015, O'Day threw behind Bautista in the eighth inning of a game in Baltimore. Bautista simply stared down O'Day. Then, on a full count, he hit a two-run home run and ran around the bases without saying a word to the pitcher.

Once again, it was Bautista's kind of revenge. That's the kind of competitive spirit you want leading your baseball team.

10

WHY QUALITY COACHES ARE
SO IMPORTANT

There's a sense today that there isn't much left to teach to ballplayers once they've made it to the big leagues. After all, they've *made it*, right? What more can they possibly learn?

This is one of the most damaging mentalities in the sport today. In most professions the most talented people rarely stop learning. They improve in their area of expertise, constantly looking for new ways to become better at what they do. At least that's what the most successful people do.

It's no different in baseball. The best players in the game are always working to become even better. The smartest ones know that they can't do it on their own, and that the best teams make sure to hire coaches who know how to bring the most out of their players.

But the culture of learning has changed. Walk into a clubhouse today and you rarely see the kind of engagement among players and the coaching staff that fosters real improvement on the field or at the plate. This is detrimental to the players. And it's detrimental to the team.

I would say that the coach who had the most impact on me as a player was Charley Lau. Earlier, I mentioned how effective Lau was as a hitting instructor at the Royals Baseball Academy. In fact, today, Lau is remembered as one of the best batting coaches the game has ever known.

You might know some of Charley's best students from his time with the Royals in the 1970s: five-time All-Star Amos Otis; career .290 hitter Hal McRae; and George Brett, who won three American League batting titles, finished his career with 3,154 hits and remains one of the best to ever swing a bat.

But Charley wasn't just a great hitting coach. He was just a great coach, period. When I was a young catcher with the Royals, Charley taught me everything. He taught me how to catch at the major-league level—remember, I couldn't even get a glove on some of the pitches when I first showed up as a rookie in 1969. I first had the privilege of working with Lau in 1971, when he officially joined the Royals as a hitting coach after working with the Baseball Academy. Before his career as a coach, Charley had been a catcher with the Detroit Tigers, Milwaukee Braves, Baltimore Orioles and Kansas City Athletics. He had an average career as a ballplayer. But Charley was one of those guys who excelled as a coach. He taught me how to call a game from behind the plate and helped me better understand pitchers. He was more influential on me in those areas than probably any other coach I had while playing in the majors. But as good a hitting coach as he was, Lau couldn't do a thing to help me at the plate!

The thing about Charley was that he never stopped teaching.

As the Royals' batting coach he would sit with me every day and go over the lineup of the team we were about to face. Charley studied every hitter in the league. He'd run down the list and tell me exactly what I needed to know: what pitches to call, where to set up my mitt. He was always thinking about the game. We'd literally go from one through nine and talk about the strategy for each batter. And we'd talk about the pitcher on the mound—what he could throw well, what pitches it was better to avoid, and if he didn't have a weapon to attack with, or if there was a clear weakness, we had to come up with something else.

"Now, this is Reggie . . . he likes the ball here and you can't throw him that," Charley would say. "You have to remember that. And Al Fitzmorris can't throw a curveball, so, you know, you have to think of something else. Here are your options . . ."

Just like that. Always thinking about the game. Always teaching. I used that kind of analysis throughout my career. Later on, when I was playing with the Toronto Blue Jays, I'd chat with Ernie Whitt, our younger catcher, about how to call the game for each pitcher. Jim Clancy could never pitch inside—he just *couldn't* do it—but Whitt would try to get him to. "Ernie, he can't pitch inside! He's tentative. He makes mistakes," I'd say. "Just stay away. That's where he's the strongest." A catcher has to be able to see those weaknesses, understand the patterns a pitcher goes through and call the game accordingly. You can't force something that just isn't working.

Certain guys just can't do that. But a catcher has to be able to make those calls and to control the plan of attack. It's what makes a catcher like Russell Martin so valuable to the Blue Jays today. He does things that most fans can't see. He studies the game. He knows his opponents. No matter which Jays pitcher is on the mound, he has absolute confidence in the pitches Martin is calling. Dioner Navarro had the same results with Mark Buehrle and Marco Estrada with the Jays. Navarro had such a dramatic impact on Estrada, who parlayed his fine 2015 season into a beautiful multi-year contract.

Lau and I would communicate between at-bats. We'd talk between innings. And after each game, we would sit down in the clubhouse and have a couple of beers while going over every inning that we just played. Sometimes my wife would have to sit in the car for two hours after a game. But those clubhouse beer sessions were invaluable to our game plan, and also to my development as a catcher.

And it wasn't just me. I know that Charley had a big influence on Lou Piniella as well. Lou was one of the first that Charley worked with. They would sit and talk hitting all the time. And they would argue about it. Lou was very intense. He could speak Spanish, so when he would throw a tantrum he'd do it in English and then throw one in Spanish too. But the arguments were fueled by their passion for hitting. It channeled into something positive. You could just see it when Lou played. He had real passion every time he stepped on the field.

But that was the benefit of having a guy like Charley Lau around. He could work with fiery guys like Piniella and help them get even better. He would talk to great hitters like Piniella, George Brett and Hal McRae and walk them through the pitchers they had just faced, or pitchers they would be facing in an upcoming game. Charley would explain why George got three hits and why McRae got three hits. They'd talk about what they saw compared to what he saw from his perspective. Charley had no problem calling us out when we didn't play great. "Buckshot," he'd call me, "you made some bad calls tonight. You shouldn't have thrown *this* guy *that* pitch in *that* inning."

We would sit and talk about the previous game for hours. It was like that every day. We just loved to talk ball. It was pure baseball immersion.

It was the same way when I played for the Milwaukee Brewers, where I was traded after the 1977 season.

It was a scary time. It took a while for my vision to come back, and I wasn't sure if I'd be able to play again. I had played in only 29 games in 1977, after playing 100 the season before. The Royals had picked up catcher Darrell Porter from Milwaukee, so I knew my time with the Royals was coming to a close. The end of the 1977 playoffs was very difficult for me. We had made it to the American League Championship Series for the second straight season, and for the second straight season we lost to the Yankees in five games. Afterward, I sat in the Royals locker room with a bunch of guys I had played a long time with. I knew it was my last game with the team. It was very emotional. Not only had the Yankees beaten us for the second straight season, but it was clear that I wasn't going to get the chance to put on the Royals jersey again.

My son, Casey, had been born in August, so there was a lot to be excited about. But time was moving on and change was pushing me toward something new. That fall, my wife and I packed up and moved to Puerto Rico with our newborn son so I could play winter ball and try to make up for the time I had missed with my eye injury. That winter, while in Puerto Rico, I got a call from the Royals' travel coordinator, who told me that I'd been traded to the Milwaukee Brewers. It was a disappointing way to be told, after having spent nearly a decade with the organization.

IN NEARLY A DECADE since the 1969 expansion, the Milwaukee Brewers had never posted a winning record (including the first season in Seattle, when the team started as the Pilots). But after the 1977 season Harry Dalton took over as general manager. Dalton, of course, was the man who helped bring glory to Baltimore. And just as he had with the Orioles, Dalton went to work building a winner from the foundation up. To do so, he brought together the best staff he could. First, he brought in George Bamberger to be manager.

Bamberger had spent his pitching days in the minors, making a few appearances with the New York Giants and then with the Orioles, but he never recorded a decision in the majors. Still, he knew the game and could teach it. He proved it when he became a player/coach in the Orioles' minor-league system, earning a spot as the organization's roving pitching coach when he retired. He helped develop the young arms that would carry the Orioles to the World Series in 1966. He became the Orioles' major-league pitching coach in 1967, when Earl Weaver took over as manager. Baltimore went on to win three American League pennants, and the World Series in 1970.

Bamberger was a tough-as-nails manager in Milwaukee. He was from Staten Island and was a rough, New York kind of guy. He'd always take bubble gum out of his mouth and put it on the top of his cap, and then go out and start yelling at the umpires. He had a tendency to use adjectives that can't be printed today. It was a habit that got him tossed out of many games. He was fiery, and we loved that about him.

Bamberger was all about pitching and defense. He told the pitching staff that we were going to cut our walks in half. He wanted us to pretty much eliminate them. He was adamant that when we had a guy with two strikes, I was to call a pitch down and away because it's the hardest pitch in baseball to hit. He knew what he was talking about. After all, this was the guy who helped produce Jim Palmer, Mike Cuellar, Pat Dobson, and Dave McNally.

The first season the Brewers had under Dalton and Bamberger turned out to be a remarkable success. We became good right away. Milwaukee had won 67 games in 1977, scoring 639 runs and allowing 765. A year later, with Dalton as general manager, the Brewers won 93 games and finished third in the American League Eastern Division, scoring an American League–leading 804 runs and allowing just 650. That's a serious turnaround.

Under Dalton and Bamberger, the Brewers adopted an unconventional approach to the locker room. It was the most dynamic locker room I had the privilege of being a part of.

Instead of having the coaching staff in a separate room, they were right there with the players. They had lockers like everybody else on the team. Cal McLish was the pitching coach, Harvey Kuenn was the batting coach, Larry Haney was the bullpen coach, Frank Howard was the first-base coach and the third-base coach was Buck Rodgers. They were just a great group of coaches.

They all sat next to the rest of us, as though they were players. Everybody was on the same page; everybody was equal. The coaches were fighting just as hard to win as the players were. That's the feeling it built. It was a great relationship.

We would all come in before a game and get ready, putting on our uniforms as a team—players, coaches and manager. I sat next to Rodgers. He had been a catcher in his playing days, so he was invaluable to me. Just like Charley Lau, Rodgers would chat about how to work with whoever was on the mound for us that day. Buck had been a great catcher with the Angels in the franchise's early years. He was only about 40 years old when he was coaching in Milwaukee. He was a very handsome, stylish guy. He'd push his sleeves up on his uniform during games so he looked like a baseball coach in a film. We called him "Hollywood" because he looked like a movie star.

And Hollywood knew the script on every team that came into town. With all of his experience, he had incredible insight into how a catcher should strategize when calling a game. He'd offer up advice like "These sons of bitches run a lot. You've got to be ready to throw." Or "You know, they're going to bunt and they're going to play hit and run."

Rodgers also had a plan for every pitcher who was on the mound. He was always trying to help me out with catching and calling games. For example, one of our pitchers was Moose Haas, who had a four-pitch mix and a good curveball. Rodgers told me to think about calling that curveball on the first pitch because Haas would make a point of throwing it for a strike. He wouldn't try to overthrow it, Rodgers said; he'd try to slow down and drop it in there for a first-pitch strike. Everybody in the game is paying attention to the first pitch of the game. It sets the tone. You throw a first-pitch curveball and the other team's going, "Oh, my God, he's got his curveball tonight." But he had only thrown one pitch. And it might have been his fourth-best pitch, but we had established that he could throw it and we had gotten him into the flow of the game. It was all psychological.

We'd chat about those kinds of things before every game. Meanwhile, our bench coach, Frank Howard, would be sitting with our center fielder, Gorman Thomas, reminding him which players to keep an eye on when they were on base because they'd be likely to make a break for home on contact, so he'd have to charge for any balls that reached the outfield.

The conversation was always about baseball. That's what we lived for. It was the same after the game. We'd sit in the locker room with the coaches and chat, just like I had done with Charley Lau in Kansas City. We'd talk about what happened in the game, why we won, why we didn't, and what we could do differently.

A major-league coaching staff needs guys like Buck Rodgers and Charley Lau: wise and experienced, with a knack for teaching and a clear passion for the game. But a team would also benefit from a guy like Frank Howard, our first-base coach, who was one of the biggest personalities in the Brewers locker room. We called him Hondo. And Hondo was a monster of a man. He was about 6 foot 8 and well over 250 pounds—just enormous. He had played for the Los Angeles Dodgers and the Washington Senators and had been one of the big sluggers of his generation, hitting 382 career home runs. He once hit a ball on top of the roof at Tiger Stadium, just like that. He's one of four players to have done that, along with Harmon Killebrew, Cecil Fielder and Mark McGwire. He was also reportedly the only player to hit a fair ball out of Yankee Stadium. It was ruled a foul ball, but the umpire called it fair. During a game at Robert F. Kennedy Stadium in Washington, Hondo hit a ball 500 feet into left center. They painted the seat the ball landed on white. "That's where the big boys go," Hondo always said when he told the story of the hit and the seat marked at RFK Stadium in Washington.

Hondo was just a fun-loving guy, the kind of personality you want to have in a locker room. He could certainly be serious, but he knew how to lighten the mood. Hondo would always stroll around wearing nothing but his jock, with a big cigar in one hand and a beer in the other. We'd all yell at him, "Hondo, cover up that body!" He didn't care. "Oh, man," he'd laugh. "You're just jealous."

He was just a beauty. Everyone loved to play for him. Hondo was one of those guys who would walk off the field and chat with fans.

"Hey, great to have you here today!" he'd say. "Welcome to County Stadium. Hope you enjoy the game." He was always talking to the fans.

Once, when we'd just come off the field and I was about to go out and hit, Hondo came up to me and said, "John, you have any hits yet?" He knew I didn't have any so far in the game.

"No. No, I don't," I said.

"Yeah? Well, I'm booing your ass next time they introduce you," he said.

"You're not gonna boo me," I laughed.

"No. I'm booing your ass," he said. "You don't have any hits yet."

And sure enough, as soon as the stadium announcer said, "And now batting, Buck Martinez," I looked down the first-base line, and there was big old Hondo with his hands cupped around his mouth, booing as loudly as he could. That's my favorite memory of Hondo. He just knew how to make you smile and make you relax. When a guy is having trouble at the plate, sometimes the best thing to do is to get him out of his own head and loosen things up.

The one thing that Hondo was terrible at, however, was throwing batting practice. I mean, he was just *awful*. But he always threw. And every day he'd hit our young catcher, Jamie Quirk, with a pitch. Every time. He'd pretend it was an accident.

"Hondo, you suck!" Quirk would yell. "Come on now, we gotta go to work."

"Stick with me, boys!" Hondo would shout back. "I gotta get my release point."

When the Brewers played a road game in spring training, not all of the players would make every trip. Hondo would always stay back with the players who didn't travel and run the workout. He'd hit "fungoes"— fly balls hit for fielding practice—and run infield drills, over and over, before ending with a marathon session of batting practice. Robin Yount was then a young star on the team, and Hondo would always chirp at him when he took to field for a drill. "Who signed you, kid? You can't play!" Hondo would shout, with his big booming voice. "He must have been drunk when he signed you!" And he'd keep going— "I'm a hard-working coach!" he'd shout. "I don't have time to waste on you."

Near the end of a day of drills, Hondo would take a grocery basket and fill it right to the top with baseballs. Normally on a day like that, you'd do your groundballs, your running and other exercises. At the end of the day, you'd do a round of batting practice, starting off with a few bunts and then take maybe eight swings. But Hondo worked guys hard. One day, Robin asked him what was on the agenda for the day.

"Oh, let's start out with two bunts and 50 swings," Hondo said.

Afterward, Yount went to George Bamberger, our manager, and jokingly asked that he not be subjected to the rigors of a workout with Hondo again.

"Bambi, don't ever leave me back with Hondo," he said. "He kills us!"

And, of course, Yount became a Hall of Famer. Hondo knew Yount was a great player. But he was always working everybody hard, regardless of who they were. We would be exhausted by the end of practice. He took baseball so seriously, but he was also so upbeat. He always made it fun and he made everybody enjoy the game. He was kind of like a favorite uncle or grandfather. Everybody loved Hondo. If you are standing around any batting cage in the major leagues today, I'm sure someone will have a story about him. (Especially in Toronto. Jays manager John Gibbons had Hondo as a coach when he played for the Mets.)

MY POINT, THOUGH, IS that even at the major-league level, coaching matters. Just because someone has made it to the pros doesn't mean they stop learning. The Milwaukee Brewers created an environment where the interaction between coaches and players felt natural. It encouraged communication. It encouraged learning. And it built camaraderie among us.

The best coaches are always looking for ways to improve their players, whether with specific mechanics or with a better understanding of how to approach an opponent. Likewise, the best players are always looking to coaches for insights on how to improve, game in and game out. That's what we had in Kansas City, and it's also what I experienced in Milwaukee.

I came to the Brewers at the same time as Cecil Cooper, who had come up in the Boston organization, where he played regularly for three seasons. Cooper was a very talented hitter. At first, his swing was a lot like that of his Red Sox teammate, the great Carl Yastrzemski—everybody wanted to copy Yaz. But Cooper struggled at first in Milwaukee. He had been a career .280 hitter up to that point, so it wasn't as though he didn't know what he was doing. But Cooper asked me one day if I could put him in touch with Charley Lau, who was still with the Royals. Everybody knew about Charley's reputation by then, and even a great hitter like Cooper believed he could still learn something. He asked me if I thought that Lau would be willing to give him some advice. And, of course, he would. Lau was kind enough to help anyone looking to improve, even if he was on a different team. I called Lau and he said he'd be happy to chat with Cooper.

Something had changed with Cooper's swing over time. He had a long swing, which means there is a windup to the swing and the bat takes a longer path to the ball. Charlie always made a point of watching the end of the bat, which indicated the length of the path to the ball. It was a subtle change, and only a coach like Lau could work him out of it. Under Lau's guidance, Cooper altered his stance and his approach. Lau had him stand back and hit the ball where it was pitched instead of trying to direct the ball to the pull side all the time. After they met, Cooper really blossomed. He hit above .300 for the next seven seasons and finished with a .298 average through his career, with almost 2,200 hits. He became a five-time all star with the Brewers.

ONE OF THE THINGS that has really changed in the game today is that coaches have begun to do most of the thinking for the players. Coaches stand in the dugout and wave guys around, making all of the calls on defensive positioning from the bench. But the players haven't had the conversations necessary for them to really know where they need to be, or why they need to be there. They just respond to instructions. Everything is a mechanical reaction.

You can see it on the mound. Pitchers are pulled out when their pinch count reaches a predetermined number, regardless of what is happening in the game. The *feel* of the game is gone. Everything is controlled to the point that the pitcher doesn't have the instinctive ability to react to what he's seeing on the field. We have taken that away from them. So when they see that a batter has fouled the ball over the dugout, many don't have the instinct to make a change. Instead of thinking, "He's not getting around on the ball. He can't pull. I've got to play him opposite," they stick to a predetermined plan. Years ago, I used to point at my eye when I was catching. I'd make a motion as if to say, "Did you see that? He's moving his feet now. He's making a change."

And the pitcher would know that the batter was thinking about the next pitch, so he'd react to stay a step ahead of him. This is the subtle skill, bolstered by attentive catchers, that helps separate good pitchers from great pitchers who can read bats and make adjustments from what they see.

It's the instinct of how to read the game and how to react.

The best coaches show players how to do that. Not only do they show them how to study their opponents before the game, they teach them how to read them during the game. This is what Charley Lau was so good at. It's what Buck Rodgers and Frank Howard were so good at. The Blue Jays have a couple of coaches who are real good at reading players. Luis Rivera, the third-base and infield coach, and Tim Leiper, the first-base and infield coach, both pick up things many players and coaches never even notice.

Guys like these can be as valuable to your team as anyone on the roster, because they know how to make ballplayers better.

11

HOW TO GET TEAM CHEMISTRY RIGHT

Team chemistry is a concept that is often dismissed today. Many pundits continue to think of the game more as a series of mathematical equations and less as a sport where a unified team can actually make a difference.

But it's cynical to think that team chemistry doesn't matter. You can tell when a team is on the same page. You can tell when the players are excited to battle together. Baseball is not a game of individuals. The best teams understand that.

Over the decades, the emphasis on team building has been diminished. To be honest, I feel bad for this generation of players. They don't sit around and enjoy each other's company the way we used to. There are so many distractions. And there is often little incentive to work on being a part of a united team.

Players still arrive at the ballpark early, several hours before game time. But they don't communicate. The Blue Jays clubhouse is enormous and immaculate. It looks like an executive lounge at a high-end social club. There are TVs everywhere. Players sit in their cubbies, typing on their phones or staring up at whatever baseball or soccer game happens to be on that afternoon. They sit in their stalls listening to their iPods or staring at their iPads. It's as quiet as a library.

It's great that the facilities are so nice. But this does nothing to build team chemistry. The players hardly talk to each other. This was something that the Blue Jays improved upon dramatically with the addition of key character guys in 2015. In particular, Russell Martin was a natural leader. Often, through the season, you'd see several of the players kicking around a soccer ball together, which is something that started with Martin and backup catcher Dioner Navarro during spring training. It became a very popular part of the Jays' preparation for each game; they all bought jerseys of their favorite players and wore them during each kick-around.

Across the major leagues, though, teams don't seem to spend as much time together as in the past. Much of that is because of the economics of the game. Players used to carpool to the park and live in the same apartment complexes. Wives would lean on each other when the team traveled out of town. Now, because they can afford it, players have several cars and live in different parts of town, and when they leave for road trips, their families may return to their off-season residences until the club returns.

One of the first things Buck Showalter did as manager in Baltimore was to make the clubhouse smaller. He felt it was too spacious, and as a result the players never had to visit or interact with each other. He saw that his players weren't communicating, so in 2010 he had the clubhouse condensed to force them to interact more. The bigger the room, the easier it is for players to isolate themselves. He also added a Ping-Pong table.

Ironically, players today spend much more time in the locker room than they used to. Most teams provide three meals a day in the locker room, although the postgame meal is usually taken home in a takeout container. (That's much different from when I played, when we'd eat lunch, then play the game, and afterward have a beer and bag of chips.)

Joe Maddon, now the manager of the Chicago Cubs, found an interesting solution to this problem. When he was managing the Tampa Bay Rays, he actually locked the clubhouse until 3:00 p.m. He didn't want the guys hanging around, wasting their time. They weren't communicating, so there was no point. Letting the team in later actually had the effect of bringing his players together at a more focused point in the pregame routine. With less free time to kill, the moments the players spent together would actually be geared toward playing the game. It was an interesting concept that may seem somewhat counterintuitive, but Maddon is one of the best managers in the game today for a reason. He understands the dynamics of his team. His instincts told him that he needed to make a change.

There is always a lot more communication on the field when a top team is playing than when a middle-of-the-pack team is playing. It's difficult to see, but it's there. Catchers like Matt Wieters, Yadier Molina, Sal Pérez, Russell Martin and Dioner Navarro are great at this. Teams that win are in constant communication with each other. The infielders watch the catcher, whose signs help inform them where they should set up. They should know what pitch is coming. And the catcher makes adjustments, moving them into position based on the next pitch. A slight head nod or tap on the right thigh can say, "We're pitching him this way. You can't play him over there . . . shift." The small details make a big difference. Everyone on the field sees the catcher on every pitch. They pick up on his focus, his energy—or lack of it. It doesn't take something dramatic, like waving a flag. It just takes players who are in tune with one another, watching each other and always communicating.

Think of some of the teams that have had success in recent years: the St. Louis Cardinals, the San Francisco Giants, the Kansas City Royals, the 2015 Blue Jays. You could see how much these teams enjoyed being in the dugout together. Especially with the Blue Jays. They had strong central leadership and a cohesive core. And it's not just winning that creates that environment. I'd argue that it's the opposite. That kind of environment is an essential foundation for building a winner.

THE BEST PLACE TO START developing team chemistry is from day one, at spring training. The environment is perfect for getting the players to ease into the season while developing camaraderie. Spring training is different for players at all points along the spectrum, of course. Many are just trying to prove they belong in the big leagues. Established vets are trying to work off the rust so they can stay in the show a little longer. The circumstances are different for every player.

But because the culture of the game has changed today, so has the nature of spring training. In the Branch Rickey era, spring training was used to get players back in baseball shape after a long winter layoff. Many teams would travel to hot-spring spas to start their conditioning programs. Now, a player comes into camp in tip-top physical shape after spending weeks with a training guru at a state-of-the-art conditioning center. Despite this apparent head start it's evident that spring training today is a shadow of what it once was. The main change has been the extent to which baseball fundamentals are being taught. They've essentially been discarded. Even the daily routine of taking infield and throwing from the outfield has, for the most part, been sidelined. This lack of repetition has dramatically diluted the arm strength and accuracy of catchers and outfielders.

When I played for the Royals in the '70s, we conducted spring training in Fort Myers, Florida. All the players lived near the training facility. Nobody had two cars, so if a guy had his family with him, he'd have to figure out a way to get to the park and leave the car with his wife and kids. We'd all live at the same place and carpool to the park. There would be five or six guys riding into the ballpark together every day. They'd become friends. People would have to lean on each other. Even the players' wives would have to lean on each other. Nobody had nannies, and nobody could afford to go out to dinner every night. We would have potluck dinners on the beach in Fort Myers, just because that was the only way we could all survive. We'd have barbecues three or four times a week. The guys would bring hot dogs and hamburgers, or stop and buy some fresh shrimp, and we'd hang out all night. It was a wonderful time because teams got to be teams and families got to be families.

It's almost impossible to imagine something like that happening today. Obviously, I don't begrudge players the money they make these days, but I feel bad that they don't have the same environment in which to develop the relationships that we did. There were fewer distractions before—less celebrity. Fewer outside pressures. Less concern about individual brands. The culture that players exist in today is much different. My point is that the kind of collective experiences we had when I played built connections among the players on the team.

Those opportunities have decreased. And that matters. Anyone who says team camaraderie doesn't matter is either being grossly cynical or terribly naive.

Today, almost every player travels to the baseball park by himself. Players' families travel with them, so their partners and kids are on the road, which is certainly a good thing for the families, but it doesn't allow the players to bond with their teammates as much as we did when I played. The team-building element isn't the same.

We had roommates on the road, and we'd spend pretty much all of our time together. I remember you would actually have to negotiate a private room into your contract as a perk—it was a privilege! Having players double up on rooms wasn't just an attempt to cut costs. Management wanted us to bond. They wanted us to learn about our teammates. They wanted us to understand that if we were going to succeed, we would have to do things as a team.

It's a hard thing to do now. As part of the collective bargaining agreement, all players now have single rooms. To some, it would almost seem like an insult if they were told to bunk up. But beyond the hurt egos it's a team policy that should definitely be reintroduced.

I can tell when a team is in tune (and when it isn't). Most often, it's the teams that are clearly—almost exuberantly—on the same page, like the Toronto Blue Jays during the pennant race in 2015. They have fun coming to the park. They have fun cheering for each other. They don't look bored or disinterested in what the team is trying to accomplish. They are in it *together*.

That was the feeling in Milwaukee when I arrived for the 1978 season. Bud Selig was the team's owner. He was a Milwaukee native, and he wanted to bring back the glory the city had felt when it had the Milwaukee Braves, of which he'd been a minority owner. The Braves won the World Series in 1957 and the National League pennant in 1958, but left for Atlanta in 1966. The Brewers had never enjoyed a winning season since moving from Seattle in 1970, and Selig wanted to change that. He wanted the Brewers to become a big-time team. After nearly a decade of losing, he hired Harry Dalton to take over as the Brewers' general manager in 1978. Suddenly, there was a sense that something new and exciting was happening with the franchise. I was lucky to be part of it.

It was exciting to be a part of the rebuilding process in Milwaukee. It was also exciting that it didn't look like the rebuilding was going to take very long. The Brewers had a stable crop of emerging talent in Robin Yount, Paul Molitor and Cecil Cooper. They had a foundation of veterans that could support the rising talent. Don Money was an experienced second baseman who could fill the gap while Molitor and Yount developed into everyday players. Third baseman Sal Bando came over from the Oakland A's with three World Series titles in his back pocket. They brought in Larry Hisle from the Minnesota Twins, who would have been one of the best hitters of the era if not for his trouble with injuries. (Hisle was the Jays' hitting coach in 1992 and 1993, when they won back-to-back World Series championships and John Olerud, Paul Molitor and Roberto Alomar finished 1–2–3 in the batting race in 1993.)

The team brought me in to share catching duties with Charlie Moore, who was several years younger than I was. Dalton wanted to improve the team's pitching, and I had great experience with that from my days with the Royals, so my job was to help build up a foundation on the mound. At first, I would catch three of the starters and Moore would catch a couple. But he was a much better hitter than I was, so eventually he'd ease into playing more and then catching the majority of the games.

One of my most memorable experiences with that team was playing against the Royals for the first time. It went well. I caught my old
teammates Frank White, Willie Wilson, U.L. Washington and Freddie
Patek stealing. They kept running and I kept throwing them out. And
we kept hanging in there. But the Royals were leading, 3–0, going into
the bottom of the ninth. That's when Sal Bando hit a three-run home
run and Gorman Thomas took a walk with the bases loaded to end the
game. It was a four-run walk-off with a walk, one of the most unlikely
comebacks I've ever been a part of. It felt great because my defense had
played such a big role in the win over my former team. Not only that,
but I had thrown out four of the best baserunners in the game. After
that, Harry Dalton came down to congratulate me. "Man, that ought
to feel good playing against your old team and having a game like that,"
he said. "That really had to be something special for you."

It's funny, the moments we hang on to. That's one of the games I can
close my eyes and think about like it was just yesterday. I can remember
each toss. This was one of those games where everything just works
and you know that *this* is what you were meant to do.

It was just my 17th game with the Brewers.

There were a lot of great moments that season in 1978. I remember
that, near the end of the season, we were about seven and a half games
back of the New York Yankees for first place in the American League
East, and a few games back from the Boston Red Sox for second. But
in a late-September game against Oakland, our final Saturday home
game, we clinched third in the division. We had a six-run fourth inning
against Mike Norris, and then Larry Hisle hit a three-run homer in
the fifth to blow the game wide open. The team celebrated like we had
just won the pennant. At first, I didn't know what was happening, but
then I realized that the Brewers hadn't finished as high as third in their
history. After the game the fans were standing and cheering, and Bud

Selig wanted Hisle to come back onto the field for a curtain call. He reluctantly obliged.

I was used to Kansas City, where we had been a dominant team. Celebrating a third-place finish was so foreign to me. This was certainly something new, but it felt great to be a part of. It set the tone for what was being built there, which would ultimately lead to a trip to the World Series in 1982, where the Brewers would put up a good fight but would lose to St. Louis in seven games.

THERE WAS SOMETHING ABOUT that team that was different from the other teams I played for. I don't think I really understood it until spring training before my second season with the Brewers. That was an incredible illustration of what team chemistry is all about.

Well, at least it turned out to be one. At first, it seemed like a nightmare.

The Brewers had spring training in Sun City, Arizona. For me, it was a dramatic change from the beaches of Fort Myers to the desert of Sun City, which was basically a seniors' community. Everybody had golf carts, and kids weren't exactly welcome. So here were all of these young ballplayers, with their families and a bunch of kids, taking over the town. My wife hated it. She was a beach person and we were stuck in the middle of Arizona. It wasn't good.

But Arizona did provide me with one of my most memorable spring-training experiences, one that really emphasized the value of building team chemistry. In 1979 the Brewers switched to a new workout facility closer to the riverbed that ran through the area, which was prone to flash flooding. It started raining one day early in camp, before we had even played a game, and it wouldn't let up. We went back to our clubhouse to put all of our stuff on top of the lockers and make sure there wouldn't be much damage if the water flooded in. But the clubhouse was completely wiped out by a flash flood. We lost everything.

That was the bad news. We had no field. No clubhouse. Nothing.

It couldn't have been more out of whack. But it turned out to be the best thing that could have happened to us. The loss of our spring-training facility turned into a rallying point for our team.

That spring, the team rode buses everywhere. We were the homeless baseball team of spring training. We'd just show up at the location of the washed-away training facility and climb on the bus to our next practice or game, wherever that was. We had to get dressed for games and practices at home. We even had to take our own uniforms home to wash them, which didn't work out very well for me. My wife accidently put my white, pinstriped Brewers uniform in the wash with my blue sweatshirt, so it became a baby blue uniform. She and my mom stayed up all night with toothbrushes and bleach and tried to whiten it, without much luck. I ended up having the only baby blue uniform on the team.

One day, we would be at the Giants' facility, the next day we'd be at the Athletics', and the next we'd be at the Mariners'. We had to beg and borrow playing time. When we arrived at the other team's complex, we had to wait—sometimes up to two hours—until they finished practicing before we could borrow the field for our own practices. And of course, we didn't get a real locker room. We'd basically get a spare bathroom to use. It was just like when we were kids playing in high school. There was a small area to put your cleats on, and that was it. After each practice or game, we'd climb back on that bus again and head home.

The entire time, it was just the players on the bus. There were no distractions beyond building stronger connections, in the tried-and-true traditions of ballplayers. And that meant a *lot* of ribbing each other. Outfielders Gorman Thomas and Jim Wohlford were always at it. "You're the worst ballplayer." "You can't hit, you can't play." *Stuff* like that. In fact, Thomas got on pretty much everybody. He was a terrific teammate that way (counterintuitive as it may sound). He loved to get on his teammates and chirp at them for their weak swings or to question whether they deserved to be in the big leagues. It was just a constant rib fest.

But we grew so close because of those road trips. We just spent so much time together, not playing the game. I don't ever remember there being any tension or any bad blood. It was as if everybody just said, "Well, this is what we've been dealt, and we've got to make the best of it."

The Brewers had a fantastic roster in 1979. Consider the talent we boasted: Cecil Cooper, Paul Molitor, Robin Yount, Sal Bando. Our other catcher was Charlie Moore, and he was a great guy who hit .300. But we also had character. We had the kind of players who just draw everyone together. You can call them the "glue guys." They unified the team. Bando, Gorman Thomas and Don Money played that role on our team.

I *hated* Bando when he starred with the Oakland A's in the early 1970s, when they won three straight World Series championships. He was short and stumpy and he always figured out a way to beat us. They were the Oakland A's, after all—*everyone* hated them. They were brash and cocky, and they were always kicking our ass in Kansas City. So we hated them. Remember, this was a time when you didn't really know your opponents the same way you do now. There were no 24-hour sports channels and everything else that provides a constant stream of information on your opponents. You played for your team, they played for their team, and for the most part that was pretty much it. But of course, Bando was a terrific teammate. He couldn't have been a better guy to play with. He was in his early 30s when he joined the Brewers and fit into the role as a pseudo big brother for everyone on the team. He was the leader. Everyone looked up to him. And everyone listened to him. We called him Captain Sal. (It was a nickname he picked up when he was captain of the A's, and it carried over to his being captain of the Brewers. Unlike hockey, not every baseball team designates a captain. In fact, they are a rarity.)

He knew how to keep us in line, how to keep things focused, but also how to keep it light and relaxed. Bando was funny. He was always talking during practice.

I'd take infield practice, bounce a few throws to second, and the captain picked right up on it. "Hey, Buck," he'd yell. "They're running this year. They're not crawling!"

And then I would throw one over the second baseman's head into center field. "Hey, Buck. They're running this year. They're not flying."

It was always like that. The whole team had that kind of atmosphere. It was fun and relaxed, and in so many ways Bando set the tone.

That Brewers team was a veteran team, and it had incredible communication during the game. It was the best team I played on when it came to relaying signals and pitch location. Everybody wanted to know the pitches that were coming. When a guy got to second base, he'd signal to the batter, "I got 'em," tipping off the pitch, the location—whatever intelligence he managed to pick up. One game, I was at second base and screwed up the sign when Bando was at bat. I signaled fastball to him at the plate, but they threw him a breaking ball and he hit a weak grounder to short to end the inning. I sat next to him, putting on my shin guards, before we went out for the next inning. "Captain, I'm sorry, man," I said. "I screwed you up. I gave you the wrong sign." I thought he'd be upset.

"Kid, don't worry about it," he said. "I'd rather have you guessing at second than me guessing at home." Bando was a terrific hitter when he knew what was coming. Stealing signs was part of the game, and part of his approach at the plate. He could wear a pitcher out, just having that slight edge in knowing what was coming next. We got really good at that in Milwaukee, probably the best I've ever seen.

But honestly, it's because we were a team. Everybody wanted everybody else to succeed. We were constantly trying to find whatever edge we could to help the next guy along.

One of the routines we had that really brought us together was an old game called "flip," and it was a passionate priority for our team. Before each game, at around 2 p.m., Gorman Thomas would call the team together on the field. "Okay, come on, guys!" he'd shout. "We gotta play." We'd have 22 to 25 guys gather on the field, playing flip together. Everybody would stand in a semicircle and a batter would hit a ball into the group. Whoever it came to would use his glove to smack the ball to another guy, who would slap it with his glove to someone else. The object was that you had to hit it to the next guy, who couldn't let it hit the ground or he'd be knocked out of the game. It was an elimination thing, and so naturally it got very competitive. Everybody thought they were the best—Charlie Moore, Jim Gantner, Robin Yount, Bob McClure and Gorman were all particularly prone to declaring their expert ability at the game. We'd play the game for a couple of hours sometimes.

The goal was just to get loose before we started going to work. But it got so serious that actual fights would break out. Dust and dirt would be flying everywhere. We hit the baseball at each other as hard as we could, because if it hit a player's glove and then hit the ground, he'd be out. The batter was the judge. So if the batter called it on you, you were out of the game. And then you had to stand around and wait until everybody was out to play the next game.

One time, before a game in Toronto at the old Exhibition Stadium, Sal Bando was the judge and he called Jim Wohlford out. Wohlford didn't like it and charged at Bando. Bando, a fireplug of a guy, just grabbed Wohlford and flipped him on the ground. Another time, Bob McClure was the judge and he called me out. I threw the ball right at him and hit him right on the wrist of his pitching hand. I immediately snapped to my senses. "Bobby," I said, "I'm sorry." But he was okay and he admitted it was a bad call. It always got so intense, but we were such good teammates, it didn't really cause problems beyond the game. It was just something we loved to do.

It was an old tradition. Some people called it "pepper." You see highlights of guys playing similar games in old highlight clips. Originally, guys would catch it in their glove and flip it to the next guy. We took it to the next level by actively trying to knock it to the next guy. You don't see it as often in the game today, but the Blue Jays actually broke out the soccer ball in spring training. For the most part, though, it doesn't happen. For starters, it would seem like an unnecessary waste of energy and a potential injury hazard. Today, all you'll see is group batting practice. There will be three or four guys lined up to hit while the infielders line up on their spots on the field. They'll keep the infielders together so that they can work on turning double plays and everything else. Meanwhile, the outfielders will be grouped together, so they all field and bat at the same time. They like to hit with each other so they can all bullshit and banter with each other. Sometimes a guy will ask to be part of a different hitting group because he doesn't like the one he's in.

They can be equally picky about which coach is throwing them batting practice. There really isn't the same sense of simple unity that we used to have. Now it's all about being part of a clique. Bringing back team games like that—flip or any other—is a great way to counteract that.

The Yankees did something similar to what we did at the time. I remember seeing Mel Stottlemyre, Mike Kekich, Fritz Peterson and some of the other Yankees playing a game one time on the field. They would divide into two teams, each having two fielders and a batter. They counted two points for every line drive caught and a single point for every one-hopper. They would play to 21. It was a combination of fielding practice and batting practice for them, and it was intense as hell.

PLAYING IN MILWAUKEE WAS a great time in my life. It was a blue-collar town, and the atmosphere was great for baseball. People were so down to earth. And they just loved the Brewers. Before every game, fans would tailgate in the parking lot. They would barbecue bratwurst, and smoke would drift in from the parking lot into County Stadium. We could smell it during batting practice. After the game we could wander around to any of the tailgate parties and the fans would offer us a brat and a beer and talk about the game. They were terrific fans.

But the best part was that I enjoyed the team so much. We were always together. And together, we were always fighting to win. With the roster we had, we were always in a position to do just that.

There was no question that Larry Hisle was our star player. In 1978, at the age of 31, he hit 34 home runs, drove in 115 runs and batted .290. A season earlier, Hisle had led the American League with 119

RBIs. He was a terrific player, but he suffered injuries throughout his career and didn't play as many games as he might have been able to. Hisle really knew how to hit. As I mentioned, he'd later become the Blue Jays' hitting coach.

Our other heavy hitter was Gorman Thomas, who had slugged 32 home runs and 86 RBIs in 1978, his first season as the Brewers' everyday center fielder. Thomas was the first player drafted by the Seattle Pilots in 1969, but he bounced around in the minors until his career took off when he reached his late 20s.

That was when the team first became known as "Bambi's Bombers," a reference to our power hitting and to manager George Bamberger. As I mentioned earlier, the Brewers took off under the acumen of Harry Dalton and Bamberger, jumping from 63 wins before they arrived to 93 when they took over in 1978. That wasn't just a flash in the pan.

The team grew even closer the following season. Everybody had a nickname on that team. Robin Yount was "Chisel Chin," because of his protruding jaw. Paul Molitor was known as "Dr. Molitor" because he wore white buck shoes that Bando wrote "doctor" on. Bando was "Captain Sal." Larry Hisle was "Boomer" (and we would also tease him that he was George Scott, because he looked a lot like the Brewers' old first baseman). We called Gorman Thomas "Chewie," after the *Star Wars* character Chewbacca. Cecil Cooper was "Black Magic." Charlie Moore was "Charlie Chinker," because of all the bloop hits he got! We also had Lenny Sakata on our team; we called him "Sammy Sock a Single."

My nickname was "Tour Guide" because I'd arrange sightseeing trips, golf games and team dinners in every town we went to. We always did stuff like that as a group with that team. I honestly believe it had an impact on how we played together on the field.

After our spring-training facility was washed away, we went on another tear through the 1979 season. We won 95 games but finished second in the American League East behind Earl Weaver's outstanding Baltimore Orioles. (They would reach the World Series but lose to the Pittsburgh Pirates.)

That season, the Brewers hit 185 home runs. Stormin' Gorman hit 45 of them and tallied 123 RBIs. Ben Oglivie hit 29 home runs, Sixto Lezcano hit 28 (and batted .321 with a .987 OPS) and Cecil Cooper had 24. Hisle suffered a debilitating rotator cuff injury that season and didn't play much. You can imagine how good we'd have been if he had. On top of that, Paul Molitor was only 22 years old that year, Robin Yount was 23, and they were both on their way to Hall of Fame careers. The two of them, along with Jim Gantner, would end up playing together for 15 years.

I PLAYED ANOTHER SEASON with the Brewers in 1980, but my playing time diminished each year. Charlie Moore was emerging as a solid catcher who was very good at the plate. I still played in 76 games, but it was clear that Moore was set to be the main man in Milwaukee. Early in the 1980 season, George Bamberger had heart trouble and was briefly replaced as manager by Buck Rodgers, one of the Brewers' excellent coaches. Bambi returned, but the team took a slight dip compared to the success we had had the two previous seasons. He resigned in September.

Still, the key pieces of that Brewers team were performing. We had three guys with more than 100 RBIs. Thomas had another big year, with 38 home runs and 105 RBIs. Ben Oglivie emerged as a big-time power hitter, launching a career-high 41 home runs and adding 118 RBIs. Meanwhile, Cecil Cooper hit .352 with 120 RBIs. He was outstanding that season, knocking out 219 hits, but was eclipsed by my old teammate George Brett, who hit .390 after flirting with .400 all season.

I was in Milwaukee at a time when everything was swinging upward for the Brewers. That team was my favorite group of guys to play with. They taught me everything I needed to know about chemistry. The locker room has to have the right mix of like-minded, competitive people who understand that the game is about more than building a personal brand. You need a mix of veterans and youth. And you need to know how to have fun. Those are the ingredients in success. The Brewers understood that better than any team I've seen.

Unfortunately, I wasn't around when Milwaukee finally reached the pinnacle, making it to the World Series in 1982 with the team Harry Dalton built.

As happens with most players in major-league baseball, there comes a time when you are the extra man. Throughout my playing career, I was always the extra man.

Leaving a team is never easy. With the Royals, I had grown up with the team, with guys such as George Brett, Amos Otis, John Mayberry and Hal McRae. Basically, I was always a backup catcher, but I became a prominent part of the team in 1975 and 1976, when we won the Western Division crown and met the Yankees in the American League Championship Series. But then they traded for catcher Darrell Porter the following year and once again I became a spare part. It was time for me to go. I knew that. But it's always difficult when you leave your first team. You grow up with them, you make your debut with them, you win for the first time with them. And suddenly it's all over.

When I got to Milwaukee, I just knew that it would never be as good as Kansas City, because the Royals were the best team I had ever played for. But to my surprise I learned more about what it means to be part of a team. And I learned how much being on the same page with your teammates can lead to success. Playing for a team run by Bud Selig was exciting. It had energy. Working for Harry Dalton and George Bamberger—and learning from Buck Rodgers, Harvey Kuenn and Hondo—it renewed my passion for the game.

But of course, I was on the move again. Charlie Moore became a better catcher, and then they traded for Ted Simmons from the Cardinals in December 1980. The Brewers also had a young catcher named Ned Yost coming up. Teddy was the star, and he looked like the final piece in the world championship puzzle. So heading into the 1981 season, I was fourth on the depth chart. I was 32 years old, and it was clear that my future with the Brewers had an expiry date.

All through spring training in 1981, Charlie Moore and I both thought we were going to get traded. We were good friends, so we talked about it all the time. Our wives talked about it too. We were *hoping* to get traded, because we knew that Teddy was going to play. In the end, Charlie became the Brewers' right fielder. Meanwhile, I heard that I was going to be traded to the New York Yankees. That was my hope, no question about it. My wife is from New Jersey, and her family was there as well. It would have been a thrill to play for the Yankees, so I really hoped the rumors that I had heard were right. I just kept saying, "Well, you guys have got to trade me. Obviously, there's no value for me here—I'm the fourth-string catcher!"

But the season started and there was no trade. I didn't play at all. I must have been a miserable bastard that month. Then, on April 30, during a road trip in Anaheim, Buck Rodgers called me into his office. He had taken over as manager after George Bamberger resigned the previous September. Buck sat across from me and told me the team needed my roster spot. Paul Molitor had been injured and they needed to fill his position. "We're going to designate you for assignment," Rodgers told me.

It's a gut-wrenching feeling to be designated for assignment. It's difficult to describe. For four seasons, I had been part of a team that was clearly headed in the right direction. I had grown close to my teammates. I had come to love the city I played for. And suddenly, I was done. I was in limbo.

It was 6:30, a half-hour before our game. I called up my wife. "Don't come to the ballpark," I told her. "I'm coming home. We've just been let go."

The Brewers had a ten-day period during which they could find a resolution to my contract. They could trade me or let me pass through waivers. And if nobody wanted me, I'd have the option of going to the minors. With my service time, I would have had to agree to the demotion or become a free agent and forfeit my contract.

So I was in limbo for ten days, not knowing which way my career was heading.

We went back home to Sacramento, where my family still lived. We had sold our house in the fall of 1980, so we were in between places. Through those uncertain ten days, we stayed with my mom and dad. I kept working out while we were there, hoping to be ready for whatever came next. When I got back from one of my runs, there was a bottle of champagne on the table.

"The Toronto Blue Jays called," Arlene said. "You've been traded to Toronto."

WHENEVER I THINK ABOUT team chemistry, I think of that team we had in Milwaukee. Whenever I see a team that seems to have *it*, I can see the same kind of connection I had with that Brewers team. In particular, I saw it with the Blue Jays through the 2015 season. It wasn't just the fun that came with winning. The additions of guys like Josh Donaldson and Russell Martin before the season injected a new attitude, which added to the approach that guys like José Bautista had exemplified for several years. The culture of the team changed. It was a culture of expectation, even before the trade-deadline deals that made the Jays' run to the postseason possible. After a frustrating early loss to Houston, Donaldson set the standard for the season. "This isn't the try league," he told reporters. "It's the get-it-done league. And eventually they're going to find people who can get it done."

Donaldson didn't call specific players out with his statement. He called the whole team out. The essence of what he was saying was, "This isn't good enough for us. We can do better. And we *will* do better." On some rosters it might have been a divisive moment. But the rest of the Jays were with him. It was a difficult first half of the season, but the precedent was set early on. Even though most will look to the trade deadline as the moment that everything changed for the Jays in 2015—and rightly so—it's important not to forget that the clubhouse culture was set early on. Guys like Donaldson, Martin, Bautista and Mark Buehrle were leaders in that locker room. They understood what it took to win, and the attitude necessary to do so. Young players like Devon Travis, Ryan Goins and Kevin Pillar lifted their games to meet the expectations the others had set.

They genuinely wanted to play together, and to win together, and that meant everything. That's what it takes to build a winning team. Talent is essential, but there's more to it than that. You can have a team of All-Stars and still make it to the postseason because they don't connect. You might scoff at the notion, but it's true. Character played a key part in the players that general manager Alex Anthopoulos added to his lineup in 2015. He dramatically changed the way he viewed the makeup of a team, learning key lessons throughout his tenure with Toronto. How a team connected off the field, the identity they developed together, had a direct correlation to the output on the field. He finally found the right mix. The shift in philosophy worked.

It always does.

12

HOW PAT GILLICK BUILT THE BLUE JAYS

When Pat Gillick accepted the job to become the Toronto Blue Jays' general manager in 1978, he had a clear vision of how he wanted to build the franchise: the Dodgers Way.

Long before Gillick began his Hall of Fame career as a baseball executive, he was a player chasing a dream like the rest of us. He was born into a baseball family, the son of minor-league pitcher Larry Gillick and actress Thelma Daniels. Gillick grew up in the Los Angeles area and followed his father into the game. He became a talented southpaw pitcher and earned a spot on the team at the University of Southern California, which won the College World Series in 1958.

It was the same year that Walter O'Malley, Brooklyn's biggest villain and baseball's most forward-thinking profit seeker, moved his storied franchise to the West Coast. Los Angeles had become the second-largest metropolis in the United States. O'Malley, the Dodgers' owner, saw a lucrative business opportunity in moving his famed Boys of Summer from the sacred but outdated Ebbets Field to a giant parcel of open land next to the converging freeways of L.A.

O'Malley didn't see only expanded profits at the gate, he also sought the potential gold mine that was broadcast television at a time when most major-league owners were reluctant to embrace the medium. The move left a giant scar in Brooklyn, while it reminded the romantics that baseball was, above all else, an entertainment business. Loyalty would always be overshadowed by dollar signs.

But prescient as he might have been in making his team a cash cow, O'Malley was much less knowledgeable about how to build a winner on the field. That was Branch Rickey's area of expertise.

From the mid-1920s through the early '40s, the Dodgers were owned by a group made up of the heirs of former owners Charles Ebbets and Edward McKeever. The two factions each owned half of the team and couldn't agree on anything, so to keep the franchise from falling into total chaos, a tiebreaker vote was added to the board of directors: George McLaughlin, president of the team's primary lender, the Brooklyn Trust Company. In 1938 McLaughlin brought former Cincinnati Reds executive Larry MacPhail to Brooklyn, and as president and general manager, he set the Dodgers' financial house in order and overhauled their lineup. In 1941 they won their first pennant in over 20 years.

The following year, MacPhail departed to accept a commission in the U.S. Army, and his on-again, off-again friend Branch Rickey took his place. The Dodgers needed new legal counsel, so at McLaughlin's recommendation, Rickey hired O'Malley, then a New York bankruptcy lawyer. After the 1944 season 25 percent of the Dodgers' stock was sold to four people: O'Malley, Rickey, John L. Smith (president of the Brooklyn-based Charles Pfizer chemical company) and Andrew

Another summer learning to love the game of baseball, with my friends on the Redding Redlegs Little League team in 1958. That's me, top row, second from the left. I didn't always smile like that, but I always loved the game. —Courtesy Buck Martinez

My team photo with the Cangrejeros de Santurce in 1970. I played winter ball (middle row, far right) alongside stars such as Reggie Jackson, Juan Pizarro, Don Baylor and Tony Pérez. —Courtesy Buck Martinez

A young George Bamberger (left) and Harry Dalton survey the scene before an Orioles game. In the late 1970s, both men would repeat the success they had in Baltimore with the Milwaukee Brewers. —Baltimore Orioles

Don Baylor was a homegrown guy for the Baltimore Orioles, one who has spent decades extolling the virtues of the Orioles Way. After his playing days, Don became a major-league manager with the Colorado Rockies and the Chicago Cubs. —Baltimore Orioles

Jim Palmer learned the Orioles Way from Bamberger, Dalton and Paul Richards. He became one of the best pitchers in the history of the game, winning three Cy Young Awards and three World Series championships, all with Baltimore.
—BALTIMORE ORIOLES

Paul Richards was a mentor in Baltimore to guys like Harry Dalton and Lou Gorman. Later, with the Houston Astros, he found an eager pupil in a young Pat Gillick.
—BALTIMORE ORIOLES

The Reds thought 30-year-old Frank Robinson was over the hill when they traded him to Baltimore in 1966. He won the Triple Crown and led Baltimore to the World Series that year. Robinson was a consummate leader. Everyone followed his example. —Baltimore Orioles

Ewing Kauffman takes the mic, with his wife, Muriel, right beside him. They were the innovative owners of the Kansas City Royals. Ewing laid the foundations for the most successful expansion team in the game. (Note the gentleman on the left, wearing the Royal Lancer blazer. He was from a group of local businessmen Kauffman recruited to build the brand of the team in the community.) —Kansas City Royals

Frank White, the most famous graduate of the Kansas City Royals Baseball Academy, was an eight-time Gold Glove Award winner and was named an All-Star five times with the Royals. Early on, teammates tagged him "Academy Frank," a handle that stuck with him through much of his career. —Kansas City Royals

Charley Lau (right) with relief pitcher Al Hrabosky. Lau may have been the hitting coach, but pitchers flocked to him for ideas on retiring opposing hitters. A former catcher, Charley was the most influential coach I had in my development as a major-league catcher. (Unfortunately, he didn't have much of an impact on my hitting.) —Kansas City Royals

This is an interesting picture! It was spring training in Fort Myers, Florida, in the late '70s. The player under the hood is working with a visual-training aid that the organization tried for a while. Outfielder Steve Braun, team doctor Paul Meyers and GM John Schuerholz are looking on. (We're not sure who the player under the hood is.) —Kansas City Royals

A very young George Brett on his way to the Hall of Fame. A Royals draft pick, Brett made his home in Kansas City early in his career and is still a big part of the organization and the community. —Kansas City Royals

The three-man brain trust of the Royals' first AL West Division championship team in 1976. From left, pitching coach Galen Cisco, hitting coach Charley Lau, Hall of Fame manager Whitey Herzog. —Kansas City Royals

Three-time batting champ George Brett learned how to hit under Charley Lau. Brett was the youngest of four brothers who played pro ball. He was a naturally great athlete. But when he became a pro ballplayer, Lau and his Royals teammate Hal McRae had a tremendous impact on his ability.
—Kansas City Royals

Sporting my moustache with the Milwaukee Brewers after my early years in the Royals system.

—Milwaukee Brewers

Frank Howard was our first-base coach in Milwaukee. I wish everyone loved the game as much as Frank does. In his prime, "Hondo" was one of the most powerful hitters in baseball history. He hit two home runs longer than 500 feet.

—Milwaukee Brewers

Schmitz, who quickly sold his shares to the other three. Within less than a year, the trio had also bought out the Ebbets heirs, giving them overwhelming control over the franchise.

By the time Rickey joined the Dodgers at the age of 61, he was already one of the most revered men in the game, following his success with the St. Louis Cardinals, where he had pioneered the farm system, spring training and the use of scouts. Because of his elevated status, many in the game simply called him Mr. Rickey. He was also a very rich man, having purchased several minor-league teams and selling the players his teams produced. For all his important innovations, Rickey was also a shrewd and stubborn negotiator who was notorious for making money off the backs of players he grossly underpaid. One sportswriter gave him the nickname El Cheapo. Rickey's contract with St. Louis gave him a 10 percent cut of player sales.

O'Malley and Rickey clashed immediately. As general manager and president of the Dodgers, Rickey was paid a handsome salary of $50,000 a year and, as in St. Louis, his contract stipulated that he keep 10 percent of the proceeds of player sales. Rickey also made regular use of the team's private airplane and embarked on costly endeavors to scout potential talent. Perhaps his most radical idea was his new approach to spring training: Rickey wanted to bring every major- and minor-league player from across the Dodgers system to a single location, to undergo evaluations and be trained together in a uniform way. Rickey built a full-time spring-training facility in Vero Beach, Florida, on the site of an old naval base.

Rickey opened Dodgertown in 1948 and a year later brought all of the players in the Dodgers system to train together for the first time. During spring training, the American flag was raised every morning at dawn, and the camp mailman and night watchman, Herman Levy, would recite the Pledge of Allegiance. The players then had a communal breakfast, and at 8:30 a.m. Rickey addressed the group of about 500 players with a lecture on baseball.

After breakfast the players would do calisthenics en masse before splitting off into groups. Pitchers worked on throwing techniques, often using a contraption Rickey had devised that outlined the strike zone using string and poles set up at home plate. When taking a break from throwing, the pitchers were sent to the sliding pits to work on their base-running technique. Hitters practiced their swings on batting tees or against a pitching machine. Later, all of the players gathered in the outfield to run through defensive drills. After lunch there was more instruction and drills in the infield and outfield, followed by an intrasquad game. All of the players would then eat dinner together, after which Rickey would meet with his coaches and scouts to discuss and evaluate what they had seen on the field that day. In the evening, Rickey would conduct lectures on baseball in the dining hall.

The instruction Rickey oversaw during spring training became known as the Dodgers Way. Al Campanis, the Dodgers' director of player personnel, even wrote a book called *The Dodgers' Way to Play Baseball*, which outlined the club's fundamental principles and instructional techniques and was handed out to all of the players at the camp.

In 1947 Jackie Robinson broke the color barrier as the Dodgers' second baseman. Brooklyn won the pennant that year but lost the World Series in seven games to the New York Yankees. Two years later, the rivals met again in the World Series, and again the Yankees prevailed. Despite losing to the Yankees, the Dodgers had emerged as America's team in the 1950s, on the strength of a lineup of beloved stars such as Robinson, Gil Hodges, Roy Campanella, Don Newcombe, Duke Snider and Pee Wee Reese.

When John L. Smith of Pfizer passed away in 1950, the Brooklyn Trust became co-executor of his estate and aligned itself with O'Malley. It was an untenable situation for Rickey, whose contract as president expired the same year. If Rickey were to continue as the Dodgers' president, O'Malley had decided that he would have less control over the team. At the same time the Pittsburgh Pirates offered Rickey a job as their team president, which he saw as a much better option than being controlled by O'Malley. But to take it he'd have to sell his share of the Dodgers. O'Malley offered $346,667, the same price Rickey had paid for it. However, a friend offered Rickey a million dollars for his stake in the franchise—significantly upping the asking price. O'Malley was stuck. He relented and paid a little more than a million to take controlling interest in the Dodgers—and sealing the team's fate in Brooklyn.

WHEN THE DODGERS MOVED to Los Angeles in 1958, a young Pat Gillick was pitching for the University of Southern California. (Before attending college Gillick had played in the Foothills-Wheatbelt League in Western Canada on a team in Vulcan, Alberta, having hitchhiked there from California. It was his first taste of baseball north of the border.) The team's scouts and directors, among them Al Campanis, often came out to USC games and practices to watch the players work out. In the winter the Dodgers had a team in a weekend league in the L.A. area. Thus, Gillick experienced the Dodgers Way firsthand. Even though he was still a player, Gillick saw the value in the way the Dodgers approached the game. They were built on pure athleticism. And they understood the value of versatile players who could be trained to play the game the way the Dodgers wanted them to. He believed it was the right approach to building a baseball club.

After university Gillick became a pitcher in the Orioles system for five years between 1959 and 1963. There, he was immersed in the system that Orioles general manager and bench manager Paul Richards was implementing across the franchise, and which would soon be inherited by Harry Dalton. As mentioned earlier, Richards believed in building a lineup that emphasized athletic, defensive players as the backbone of the team. He believed that good pitching was paramount. And he implemented an offense that relied on speed and basestealing, commonly referred to as "small ball."

Richards left the Orioles to accept the position of general manager with the expansion Houston Colt .45s in 1962. With him, he brought along Eddie Robinson, who had won the World Series as a first baseman with the Cleveland Indians in 1948 and had had success with the Washington Senators and Chicago White Sox. After he retired Robinson became a coach with the Orioles before moving into the team's player-development department. In Houston, Richards made Robinson his assistant general manager and the director of the farm system. He was heavily involved in Houston's expansion draft.

Meanwhile, Gillick's playing career was cut short because of trouble with his arm. In 1963, when he was just 26 years old, Gillick joined Richards in Houston as the team's assistant farm director. "He had one of the best minds in baseball—one of the most fertile minds," says Gillick of Richards. "He was an imaginative type of guy."

Gillick worked under both Richards and Robinson through those early years, watching as they built the franchise from the ground up. (The Colt .45s were renamed the Astros after the 1964 season.) In Branch Rickey fashion they stocked the farm system with young, athletic talent. They signed players such as Joe Morgan, Jimmy Wynn, Mike Cuellar, Don Wilson and Rusty Staub, all of whom went on to have great major-league careers.

But when the Astros didn't enjoy immediate success, owner Roy Hofheinz fired Richards after the 1965 season. Robinson left Houston to become assistant general manager of the Kansas City Athletics in 1966, a year before they moved to Oakland. Gillick remained with the Astros for 11 years, spending his later time with the team as a scout, but he remembers those early seasons under his two mentors as having an enormous impact on his philosophy of how to build a franchise. He saw Richards and Robinson as the kind of guys who could see things in a player that others simply couldn't. They had a unique eye for potential, Gillick says, and it had a huge influence on his career.

In turn I was impacted by Gillick's presence in Houston in December of 1968, when I was taken by the Astros from the Phillies in the Rule 5 draft. Gillick had seen me play during my time with the Phillies and thought I would be worth taking a shot on, although the Astros traded me to Kansas City two weeks later.

After leaving Houston in 1973 Gillick became the New York Yankees' scouting director. With these experiences, Gillick had developed an outlook on the game that was founded on innovative ideas and focused on building a team on athleticism and speed. He had also developed a sharp eye for talent.

When Toronto was granted a major-league franchise in the 1977 expansion, Peter Bavasi was named the team's first general manager. Gillick was hired as his assistant.

Bavasi was a Rickey man. It was in his DNA—he was the son of Buzzie Bavasi, who had risen through the ranks as an executive in the Dodgers' minor-league system in the 1940s, where he was known for helping to break the color barrier by adding Roy Campanella and Don Newcombe to his club in Nashua, New Hampshire, shortly after Jackie Robinson had joined the Montreal Royals, the Dodgers' top farm team. After Rickey's departure from the organization, Buzzie Bavasi became the Dodgers' general manager, a role he held for 18 seasons, during which time the team won eight National League pennants and four World Series championships. In 1968 Buzzie left the Dodgers to become part-owner and president of the expansion San Diego Padres.

Because of his father, Peter Bavasi grew up with a front-row seat from which to watch the dealings of Rickey, O'Malley and MacPhail. After graduating from college he became business manager of the Albuquerque Dukes, a Dodgers farm team in New Mexico, in time for the 1965 season. While there, he met Roy Hartsfield, who had played outfield for the Boston Braves for two seasons before being traded to the Dodgers in 1953. Hartsfield never played for the Dodgers but spent two years in the system with the team's Triple-A affiliate, the Montreal Royals. In 1956 he began a nearly two-decade career coaching and managing in the Dodgers' farm system. While coaching in Albuquerque, Hartsfield impressed Peter Bavasi so much that he promised that if he ever took over a major-league team, he would make Hartsfield his manager.

In 1969 Peter Bavasi followed his father to the Padres, where he ran the farm system before taking over as general manager a few years later. He had Hartsfield manage the Padres' Triple-A affiliate in Hawaii. Then, in 1976, Bavasi was hired as the Toronto Blue Jays' first GM. (The job had been offered to Frank Cashen of the Baltimore Orioles, who declined the position.)

As GM, Bavasi made good on his promise to Hartsfield, hiring him as the Jays' first manager. Pat Gillick was hired away from the Yankees to be Bavasi's assistant GM.

When they set out to build the team, all three men agreed that they intended to create something akin to the team they all had in common. "The Dodgers were kind of the people that we wanted to follow," says Gillick. "That style."

Paul Beeston, who was vice-president of business operations and was famously the Jays' first employee, distinctly remembers the vision the front office laid out for the franchise right from the start. And they had every intention of imitating one of the most successful franchises in the game.

"We wanted to become a brand," Beeston says. "We knew it was going to take time—you can't become a brand overnight. That takes 25, 35, 40 or 50 years, because you have to have history to become a brand. But the Dodgers had it. The way they put their players together, they put their teams together, was based on players that they signed, players that they developed, players they brought to the major leagues. They expose them a little by little each year—bring two guys up, three guys up."

Beeston added one more point about the Dodgers that Toronto wanted to emulate: They had swagger. And the Jays were going to have some of that too.

THE BLUE JAYS' FIRST game was a memorable affair, with more than 44,000 people packing Exhibition Stadium and snow covering the field. Toronto beat the Chicago White Sox, 9–5, but the success was short-lived. The Blue Jays posted the worst record in the major leagues that first season, winning just 54 games. Toronto would finish at the bottom of the standings for each of its first five seasons.

But at the same time, the Jays front office was busy building a team that would one day be a winner. Gillick ascended to the GM position after that first season, while Bavasi served as the team president—a position he was pushed into after his micromanagement irked enough of the Jays brass, and because it was clear that Gillick was operating as the GM anyhow.

Gillick knew that if the Blue Jays were going to be successful, they needed a core of homegrown players. They needed a strong farm system that would consistently develop talent and they needed to find that talent in places where others weren't looking. Under Gillick, the Blue Jays invested in one of the most robust coaching and scouting staffs in the major leagues.

Gillick relied on Al LaMacchia and Bobby Mattick, two men with a remarkable ability to judge talent who would be integral to the future success of the organization. Bob Engle joined the original staff in 1976 as the team's eastern scouting supervisor after several years spent scouting for Harry Dalton's Baltimore Orioles. He would remain with the Blue Jays for nearly 25 years.

Mattick was a baseball savant. He played a couple years of major-league ball with the Chicago Cubs and Cincinnati Reds, but his legacy in the game began off the field. Between 1946 and 1976 Mattick became one of the most respected scouts and player-development minds in the game, working for several teams, including the Reds, Astros, Montreal Expos and Milwaukee Brewers. Along the way he was credited with signing such players as Frank Robinson, Rusty Staub, Curt Flood and Gary Carter. He signed on as one of the Blue Jays' original employees in 1976, as the team's scouting supervisor, and he helped with the expansion draft.

LaMacchia was another career minor-leaguer who excelled as a coach and scout. He was a scout in the Braves organization from 1961 to 1976. Gillick hired him as the Blue Jays' scouting coordinator in 1977. Both Mattick and LaMacchia would become essential figures in building the franchise into a winner. Along with them, the Blue Jays hired a stable of scouts to hunt for talent as they built a minor-league system that was arranged specifically to address the needs of the major-league team.

"Pat was very dedicated to the draft, scouting, player development and building your own core and then supplementing your core with either trades and/or free agency," says Gord Ash, who joined the Blue Jays in the ticket department in 1979 and worked his way up to becoming Gillick's right-hand man. "I think primarily the focus was on building the core, utilizing the Rule 5 draft to secure talent and building the club from within. Free agency was available, but it wasn't something that our club really could get into until we were a proven winner, and then it became a lot easier to attract players."

In those lean years the Blue Jays' brain trust was particularly adept at making use of the Rule 5 draft, in which players who weren't listed on an organization's 40-man roster within three to four years of signing were made available to other teams for $50,000. Using the Rule 5 draft, the Jays managed to pick up key players like Willie Upshaw in 1977 and George Bell in 1980.

The Jays picked up Bell on the recommendation of Dominican scout Epy Guerrero, who became the team's chief Latin American scout in 1978. Guerrero would become the most influential scout the organization has ever had. It was Guerrero who convinced the Blue Jays to trade for Alfredo Griffin, co-winner of the American League Rookie of the Year Award in 1979. He then urged the Jays to take Bell from the Philadelphia Phillies in 1980, having scouted the future American League MVP in the Dominican.

Like LaMacchia and Mattick, Guerrero had a sharp eye for talent. Gillick had first hired him in 1965, when he was running the Houston Astros' farm system. A couple of years later, Guerrero signed a speedy 16-year-old prospect from Santo Domingo who was being compared to Willie Mays. César Cedeño went on to have a 17-year major-league career, most of it with the Astros, in which he batted .285 and stole 550 bases. After Houston, Gillick and Guerrero moved to the Yankees organization together, before having their greatest success with the Blue Jays. Guerrero was able to understand the different levels a player needs to operate on. He saw talent and potential as well as the best scouts did, but he also had a unique ability to assess how well a Latin American player would be able to adjust to life in North America.

Guerrero created a valuable link between the Blue Jays and the remarkable talent in the Dominican and across Latin America. He traveled far and wide searching for prospects and was known to trek up mountains and ride donkeys to get to them. Legend has it that he once dressed like a soldier to sneak a player out of Nicaragua. One story that is certainly true was the potential Guerrero saw in a young boy who walked with a limp and played with a milk carton around his hand to soften the pain of groundballs because he couldn't afford a glove. Guerrero arranged for the boy to undergo surgery to fix a bone chip in his right knee, which fixed the hobble in the boy's step. Then he signed him to the Toronto Blue Jays. The kid's name was Tony Fernandez, and he went on to become one of the best shortstops in the game. A five-time All-Star with Toronto and San Diego, and a four-time Gold Glove winner, he helped Toronto win the World Series in 1993.

Understanding the value of fundamental skill development, Guerrero also created the Blue Jays' Dominican baseball academy, which stood on an isolated farm, where he provided young hopefuls with the opportunity to learn the game properly and develop their talent while remaining under the radar of scouts from other major-league teams. The Los Angeles Dodgers were the only other franchise running a similar program at the time. Guerrero brought equipment and professional instruction to isolated locations across his homeland, setting up the infrastructure that would make the Dominican Republic the second-largest producer of professional baseball talent today, after the United States.

Guerrero's impact on the Blue Jays franchise reverberated through the team's glory years. In 1987 he convinced the team to trade for ace pitcher Juan Guzmán. And his impact would continue well beyond the World Series championships—he recruited and signed a 16-year-old kid named Carlos Delgado, who went on to be the best hitter in the team's history, launching a franchise-record 336 home runs and posting a .949 OPS in 12 seasons.

Part of Gillick's initial strategy in building the Blue Jays was to tap into the talent that Epy Guerrero knew how to uncover. It was that focus on the Latin American market, and the team's unique approach to scouting, that set the franchise apart.

John McLaren, who was a minor-league catcher in the Astros system in the early 1970s while Gillick was running Houston's farm teams, became a scout, coach and manager in the Blue Jays' farm system in 1978. McLaren started out managing the Jays' Rookie-league affiliate in Medicine Hat, Alberta, moving up to Short Season Class A (Utica, New York), Single A (Kinston, North Carolina) and Double A (Knoxville, Tennessee). Over the course of those eight years, he saw how Gillick and company rapidly transformed the Blue Jays from a weak team struggling with the challenges of expansion into a perennial contender in the American League.

It started with a simple philosophy, based on years of wisdom collected through decades of experience in the game, reaching all the way back to Branch Rickey. While other teams would see players as possible extra outfielders or extra infielders, Gillick wanted all of his players to be the complete package. That required remarkable scouting and impactful coaching at all levels of the organization.

"If you look back over the history of the game, the Brooklyn Dodgers and the St. Louis Cardinals and Branch Rickey, that's what they were all about," says McLaren. "Toronto always believed in scouting and development. . . . They draft good talent; they know what they're doing. And they have good people in the minor leagues to help shape and form these players and teach them how to play the game. And it's always been a Toronto philosophy, and it goes back to Pat Gillick."

BUT IF SCOUTING AND DEVELOPMENT were going to be two of the key ingredients to success for the Blue Jays, Gillick knew a third element would be needed to bring the team identity together. The organization set out to treat players differently than teams had done traditionally. By the late 1970s, labor disputes were rife in the major leagues, as players came together to fight for additional rights after decades of exploitation at the hands of greedy owners. (Branch Rickey included. On this matter the Blue Jays diverged from the Dodgers Way.)

The Blue Jays' ownership and executives wanted to create an open environment that treated its employees like family. They wanted everything to be done face to face. That meant Gillick would fly to meet players and agents in person for contract negotiations. At one point, when they were negotiating with free-agent reliever Goose Gossage, the Jays had to alter their offer three times, and each time they flew to San Diego to present it. Nothing official was done by phone.

Every year, the team's chairman, Peter Hardy, would meet with the players to discuss the team's finances and let them know if the franchise was making money or losing money. In the off-season, while McLaren was managing winter ball in Venezuela, Gillick would always come out to visit with and to scout players. Often, Peter Hardy and Peter Widdrington, the club's chairmen, would also make the trip. They played a big part in building the team's favorable reputation. "Their support and their interest was enormous," says McLaren.

During those winter months, the team would have regular conference calls, involving every scout and coach in the system. "One thing about Pat Gillick: There was never a pecking order for him," says McLaren. "He valued the small guy as much as the big guy." On a team that employed such scouting and player-development giants as Guerrero, Engle, LaMacchia and Mattick, everyone had an opportunity to chime in and share their thoughts—as long as they spoke with conviction and knew what they were talking about. Otherwise, their colleagues would take them apart. This approach fostered the idea that everyone in the organization was playing an important part in building the identity and success of the Jays franchise.

It resulted in something unique, something special. The Blue Jays didn't have the history that other franchises could cling to for their identity. They didn't have pennant races or World Series championships. They didn't have legends like Mays or Mantle. They didn't carry the lore of the Dodgers or Cardinals. The team was simply a product of the expanding business of Major League Baseball. And in that sense, the franchise could have become a soulless expansion club without a real sense of connection to its fans or to baseball. But from the start the

Blue Jays sought to create their own identity, building their team with a clear vision and a vanguard approach to scouting and development, well schooled in models that had worked in the past. And they sought to build pride throughout the far reaches of the organization. A sense of unity and family. They worked to create the feeling that being a Blue Jay—and being in the city of Toronto—was truly something to be proud of.

WHEN MY WIFE, ARLENE, answered the phone at my parents' house in the spring of 1981, we didn't know anything about what was being built in Toronto. The good news was that I'd be staying in the big leagues. But to be honest, I had mixed emotions. *Okay, I got a job—but it's Toronto.* I imagined it as a freezing, backwater city north of the border. They were an expansion team and they had a *terrible* ballpark. At the time, no one realized that the organization was going to be something special. I didn't really want to go, but I figured I'd only be there for a year, tops.

The Blue Jays had traded me for minor-league outfielder Gil Kubski. They sent Wayne Morgan, one of the team's scouts, out to Sacramento to bring me the contract. I signed down at the Nut Tree restaurant.

We flew to Toronto within a few days. I was greeted by Rick Amos, who was a gofer for the Blue Jays at the time but would go on to become a major-league executive in Canada.

Amos ushered me to a white van parked out front. It was a gray, rainy day. Only one thought came to mind.

"What the hell have I gotten myself into?"

13

WHAT I LEARNED AS THE JAYS TURNED INTO A WINNER

The first person I met when I arrived at Exhibition Stadium was Pat Gillick.

"Great to have you here," he said. "We've got some good young pitchers and we think you'll help us become better. You're here to help the pitchers, and help Ernie Whitt be a catcher."

Whitt had been with the organization since the inaugural season in 1977, but he had seen limited playing time. The Blue Jays saw potential in him, but they needed a veteran to help him out and to build a connection with the pitchers. That was what my role would be. It wasn't perfect, but it was better than being the fourth-string guy in Milwaukee.

We played the Baltimore Orioles in my first game behind the plate for the Blue Jays. Jim Palmer was on the mound for the Orioles—not the kind of pitcher you want to face during your first game with a new team. In the bottom of the fifth, I was given my first real opportunity to make an impression on my new team. We were down, 2–0, to start the inning. Our right fielder, Barry Bonnell, took a walk to start the inning. Then our second baseman, Garth Iorg, slapped a single to right field. Danny Ainge, our third baseman, was up next. He laid down a bunt that led to a force out of Bonnell at third.

(This was Ainge's third and final season with the Blue Jays. Gillick had picked him up in the 1977 amateur draft, and he's the perfect example of the team's quest for players who were both athletic and versatile. Ainge switched over to his other love, basketball, at the end of the season and went on to win two NBA championships during a long career with the Boston Celtics, a team he later became president of.)

Batting ninth, it was my turn. I came up to the plate with one out and runners at first and second, facing Palmer, a three-time Cy Young Award winner. The odds were against me. But thankfully, the baseball gods smiled down on Exhibition Stadium while I stood at the plate. I made solid contact and whacked the ball into the gap between center field and right field. Iorg and Ainge both charged around to score, while I slid safely into second base for my first hit as a Blue Jay. The runs I drove in tied the score at two.

Palmer threw a wild pitch to our leadoff hitter, Alfredo Griffin, during the next at-bat, and I went to third. Then Griffin cracked a double to center field, which sent me home as we took the lead. Palmer was yanked, but that didn't stop our momentum. By the end of the fifth inning, we led 5–2, which wound up being the final score. My double had broken the shutout and tied the game. My run gave us the lead and knocked a six-time All-Star off the mound. And it all sparked a rally that gave us a comfortable cushion. Meanwhile, Dave Stieb tossed a complete game for the Jays with me behind the plate. (The entire game took two hours and ten minutes—games today average roughly three hours.)

Both the fans and my teammates were thrilled. Suddenly, I wasn't a cast-off spare part. I wasn't just a third-string catcher. I couldn't think of a better way to start with a new team, even if it *was* Toronto. "Maybe this place isn't going to be so bad after all," I thought.

THE JAYS WERE a very young team at the time. But if you look at the roster, you can see how Gillick was already piecing together the elements that contributed to the team's future success. I didn't know it when I first arrived, but once you started to look around, you could see that the Jays were building something special.

Center fielder Lloyd Moseby was 21 years old. He had been drafted second overall in the 1978 amateur draft. Left fielder George Bell and right fielder Jesse Barfield were also both 21. As I mentioned earlier, Bell had been picked up from the Phillies in the Rule 5 draft in 1980, thanks to the insistence of Epy Guerrero. Barfield was taken in the ninth round of the 1977 amateur draft and would come up to the Jays at the end of the '81 season. Eventually, he would display one of the strongest outfield arms in the game. The trio would become the Jays' "Killer Bs" outfield, widely viewed as the best defensive outfield in the game through the 1980s.

It was clear that the Blue Jays were going to be built on pitching and defense. The pitching staff also had lots of young talent. Dave Stieb was only 23 years old, and he was already as good as anybody I'd ever seen.

Al LaMacchia and Bobby Mattick had scouted him as an outfielder at Southern University but were unimpressed until he was pressed into service in the game as a relief pitcher. It's just one example of their incredible scouting ability. Stieb was taken in the fifth round of the 1978 amateur draft. By 1980, he was already an All-Star. He pitched 242 innings in 1980. He was head and shoulders above anybody else. He was just a very talented guy and easily the Blue Jays' biggest star.

The rest of the pitching staff was very good too. Luis Leal, just 24 years old, had been signed as an amateur free agent in 1979. The Jays picked Jim Clancy, 25, in the expansion draft from the Texas Rangers. In December of '81 Gillick would again take advantage of the Rule 5 draft, taking 22-year-old righty Jim Gott from the St. Louis Cardinals.

TORONTO WAS A UNIQUE place for baseball. Exhibition Stadium was both a terrible and ideal home all at once. To me, it was the incubator for baseball in the city. It was perfect for Torontonians—it was cold, it was outdoors, but the fans were tough. They sat on aluminum benches! The fans were great, but at the time they were also relatively new to the game. My wife was used to the fans in Milwaukee, where there is tailgating with brats and beer in the parking lot. During the games in Milwaukee, there were people standing up and yelling and screaming and having a great time. But when we first arrived in Toronto, Arlene sat among the fans and everyone was so quiet and calm, it seemed like they were watching a play. They hadn't gotten into the spirit of the game yet. Arlene would stand up and try to get them going. "Come on, you guys, cheer!"

But to be fair to the fans, there really wasn't much to cheer about in those early days. That era was on its way out.

The Ex was an odd place. The dugouts were level with the ground, so not really "dug out" at all. And the playing surface was made for football, as the Toronto Argonauts of the CFL played there. It sloped upward in the middle; it was highest in the center of the football field and sloped to the sidelines for drainage purposes. You couldn't see the center fielder's legs when you squatted down to catch. The football field ran from the left-field foul line out to center field, so the crown ran from that left-field line right along the middle of the field. If you got a ball in the alley in left-center, it would roll downhill and go all the way to the fence.

It was nothing like you would see in the big leagues today. Our locker room was Spartan. We had a little lounge where they had beer and potato chips, and there was pizza once in a while after the game, but that was about it.

But it was a uniquely Canadian atmosphere. The north grandstand was jam-packed. There were always kids there. In the early stages they wanted to fill the stands with as many kids as possible because they brought life to the park. While others sat politely, the kids were always having fun. We'd throw balls up to them. It turned into such a great atmosphere. It was cold and it was outdoors, but it was *our* ballpark. I think the unique nature of it brought the team together.

During one of my first games, I ran down from the dugout to the bullpen and I heard somebody holler at me, "Are you the new bad catcher?"

"What?" I thought. "The new *bad* catcher? No, I'm a pretty good catcher, actually."

I went down to the bullpen and forgot about it. When I sat down, the same kid came over and asked, "Can I see your decker?"

"What?" I said.

It took me a moment, but then I realized he was talking about my catcher's mitt. I had never heard it referred to as a decker before. When I figured that out, the rest of it suddenly made sense. The kid had been asking if I was the Jays' new *back* catcher! I had never heard that phrase before either! Nobody I knew had ever called a catcher a "back catcher." So these were the first of many Canadian phrases that I would eventually become familiar with. ("Toque" was another. I remember they told us that the team was going to have a toque giveaway night. "What the hell's a toque?" I thought.)

The Jays were unique in other ways. One of the perks of playing for Toronto was that the team gave each of the players a car—a powder blue Honda Civic with Blue Jays emblems on the doors. It's how we got around town. Most of us lived at the Palace Pier condominium complex on the west side of town next to Lake Ontario. It was a quick drive down Lake Shore Boulevard in our little Hondas. There was a great group of guys living there—I think about 15 of the players lived there with their families: Alfredo Griffin, Rance Mulliniks, Garth Iorg, Willie Upshaw. The Palace Pier was Blue Jays Central in the early '80s.

THAT SEASON, BOBBY MATTICK took over from Roy Hartsfield as manager. Managing wasn't really what Mattick loved doing, but he was a valuable guy to have in that role with a team so young and raw. He was a remarkable instructor. He's the reason George Bell was able to refine his talent. I've heard great baseball minds describe Mattick as the best judge of free-agent talent in the game, but as great as he was at seeing the potential in ballplayers, he was even better on the development side of the game. It's part of the reason why, to this day, Mattick, who passed away at the age of 89 in 2004, is still revered as one of the most important and influential figures in the history of the Jays franchise. He could be stubborn and difficult, and he had his share of demons, but Bobby Mattick was a baseball genius.

"I would say he was the foundation, when it comes to scouting and development," says Paul Beeston of Mattick's influence on the Blue Jays' blueprint. He basically ran the minor leagues for the organization. He made it his business to know everything he could about each prospect at every level.

A good development guy is a rare gem in baseball, says Paul Beeston. You can get a good scout, but a guy who really understands development is hard to find. Mattick worked constantly with the team's prospects, preaching repetition, repetition, repetition. Beeston remembers watching Mattick in action, coaching during spring training and in the instruction league. When a player made a glaring mistake, he'd address the problem immediately. "Stop!" Mattick would shout, throwing down his hat, even if a game was going on. "You'll be here later on," he'd say. "We're going to work on this after!"

"If a guy missed a pop-up or didn't go to the fence, he brought that guy out there, even after a game," says Beeston. "You don't see that anymore."

The result was that players actually learned from Mattick. He knew the game and he knew how to *teach* the game. "More importantly," says Beeston, "he knew how to motivate. He knew the guys that needed a kick in the ass and the guys that needed a pat on the bum."

When Mattick took over as manager of the Blue Jays that year, a lot of the players who came with him from the minors had been developed by him. In fact, they were still being developed. Mattick didn't really care about winning; it was about using the season to show the players what the game was all about. On the road, at home—it didn't matter. Mattick thought of the manager's role as a teaching position. "As long as they were prepared to put in the time, he was prepared to put in the time," says Beeston. "He never bullshitted."

His goal was always to improve the player he was working with. If it was a player in A-ball, he wanted to move him up to Double A, or from Double A to Triple A. He wanted to help get his guys to the next level. But he was tough too. He worked his players hard. He exhausted them. But if he knew that other teams were having their prospects take 5,000 groundballs before going to the major leagues, Mattick made sure his prospects fielded 10,000. That was the way he was. He did things differently, but it always came back to the fundamentals.

If the player he was working with refused to learn, Mattick knew when to cut him loose. "Release him," he's said more than once. "You're not helping us, we're not helping you."

Mattick was old-school, like Charley Lau, Buck Rodgers and Hondo, in that he just loved to talk and talk and talk about the game. I remember in Toronto, he'd sit around and talk about baseball for hours before and after the game. He was always instructing. And he was always learning. That's one of the key traits a coach can have: He watched the game and learned the game constantly, no matter how much he already knew about it. One of Mattick's mentors was Paul Richards, with whom he'd worked in Houston. Mattick used to just dive into Richards's mind with questions. Good questions. And they were always questions about the game, not the players. They were about how to play the game the right way. Mattick was an encyclopedia of useful, practical baseball knowledge. Just as he gleaned that wisdom from the great minds in the game, he was always passing it on to any of the coaches he brought in or any of the players who were willing to listen.

"You go to anybody. Go to anybody that was around back then," says Beeston. "They rave about the guy."

The other coach who stood out in my days with the Jays was Jimy Williams. In fact, I believe that Jimy was the best coach I ever worked with. He studied every pitch in a ballgame. He knew why pitchers did certain things, and he was incredible at knowing which pitch would be most effective in specific situations.

He also worked hard with Bell, Moseby and Barfield, turning them into the incredible outfield they would eventually become. He even taught me about catching. Williams was just a natural teacher.

DESPITE BEING IMPORTANT TO the development of the Jays, the 1981 season was a bit of a bust. A labor dispute canceled much of the season. We played our last game on June 11 and didn't return for exactly two months, on August 11.

I had been involved in the players association in Kansas City and Milwaukee, so I was nudged into the role of player rep in Toronto too. I spent a lot of time flying to New York to be part of the negotiations.

The owners had lost the free-agency battle but now were demanding compensation for players who signed with other teams. They wanted to be able to select a player from the roster of the team that their player signed with. We argued that punishing a team for signing a free agent would undermine the very concept of free agency.

Today, it seems ridiculous that we even had to go through it. But the strike wiped out 56 games over two months, which was 38 percent of the entire season. When I wasn't a part of negotiations in New York, Arlene and I were stranded in a city we barely knew. Because we had sold our home in Kansas City, we lived in Toronto full time. It was a city that we still knew next to nothing about. And if we were going to get to know Toronto, we'd have to walk—the team took back all of the players' Hondas during the strike. These were much different times, when salaries were far lower than they are today. There were guys on our team who took on construction jobs during the strike, just trying to survive. It was just a matter of doing whatever you had to do to get by while the money wasn't coming in. The strike was hitting a lot of guys hard.

I was probably making $120,000, maybe. When the money stops coming in, you're going to worry. Guys were very concerned about the labor stoppage. We knew it was going to happen, we knew it was a possibility, and some of us had a few bucks saved up. But a lot of guys weren't able to. I was in New York at different times during the strike and I'd get phone calls from guys pleading with me to end it. "You've got to get this over with. I'm running out of money!" Guys were really concerned. This wasn't a bunch of millionaires taking extended vacations. This was really about labor. Guys were stuck. While I was visiting New York, I would stay with Arlene's mother in New Jersey. Here I was, a major-league veteran, and I was living with my mother-in-law!

When I was back in Toronto, Arlene and I took the bus and the streetcar to get around the city. I remember strolling through the park along the Humber River. We realized how beautiful a city Toronto really was. It was just too bad we weren't able to play baseball there at the time.

As the strike stretched on, we worried that it was going to keep going, so we flew to California and stayed with my mom and dad. While we were there, I received a call to meet with the players at a hotel near the L.A. airport to discuss the next step. There were more than 300 players in a conference room at the airport. The meeting was run by Marvin Miller and Don Fehr, then the players association's general counsel. I remember that it got very contentious, because at that time there were players who had stipulations in their contracts that they would be paid during a strike. I remember players getting up and saying, "These assholes that are getting paid, you know, they shouldn't be getting paid. They're not suffering!"

It was a very heated meeting. The money was running thin for far too many of us. We were about to break.

But really, in the end, it was a unifying situation for us. It was us against them. And again, the players were sticking by their guns. The negotiations were very intense.

The strike finally ended in early August. The players ceded a small victory to the owners. The agreement allowed for teams to be compensated for losing "premium players" to free agency, by selecting another player from a list of unprotected players pooled from all major-league teams, not just the team that had signed the "premium player."

That's how screwed up things were. Teams that lost a player to free agency by not signing him could be compensated for failing to secure their player. The issues between the union and the league were far from resolved, even though the league returned with the festivities of the All-Star Game in Cleveland on August 9. The owners' negotiator, Ray Grebey, and the players association rep, Marvin Miller, wouldn't even take a picture together at the peace ceremony.

IT FIRST BECAME APPARENT just how important the Jays' scouting and development philosophy was to the team when I arrived at spring training in 1982. There were players everywhere. "Who the hell are all these guys?" I thought.

With Bobby Mattick's guidance, the Jays had built a robust minor-league system, paying attention to every detail, regardless of the level. Paul Beeston and Peter Hardy made two trips to every minor-league team in the system each year. Every player knew that they were there from the major-league club. The intent was to develop a culture across the entire system. It didn't matter if you were in A-ball—you were part of the Toronto Blue Jays organization. And it was an organization that was always watching and always developing players. It built a sense of pride in being there. Mattick hired minor-league coaches that had all been major-league players: Duane Larson, Denis Menke, Al Widmar, Mel Queen, Vern Benson, Larry Hardy, John McLaren, Bob Humphreys and Jim Beauchamp.

He wanted coaches who could teach the minor leaguers not only how to play the game like a major leaguer but also how to act like one. The Blue Jays taught how to prepare like pros. "You want your best teachers in kindergarten," Beeston says of the approach.

It was all about giving confidence to the players, inspiring them and preparing them. The end game was the major leagues, and anyone in the Blue Jays system would have confidence in knowing that the organization was giving them the tools they needed to get there. It pushed the players to give back what the Jays were investing in them. Nothing would be given to them, but if they worked hard they'd have every opportunity to make it.

"We were a draft-and-development team," says Beeston. "All of our players had basically come through the system. That was the key—that became the philosophy." There was another new face in the spring of '82. Bobby Cox had taken over for Mattick as our manager. His arrival was a turning point for the Blue Jays.

To be honest, we didn't really know much about Bobby Cox when he first arrived. He was a young guy, only 41 when he arrived in Toronto. He'd been manager of the Atlanta Braves from 1978 through 1981, but was fired by Braves owner Ted Turner at the end of the strike-affected season. (Joe Torre took his place in Atlanta.) For most of his playing days, Cox had been a minor leaguer in the Los Angeles Dodgers system, but he did play two seasons with the Yankees, in 1968 and 1969. His was another mind that understood the game better than he could play it.

Cox knew as little about us and we knew about him when he took over the team. But he went straight to work in spring training. He told us right away that he intended to personally evaluate every player, and he would consult the coaching staff about each of us. He also intended to make us work. Cox threw batting practice himself. He hit the groundballs and fly balls during fielding practice.

He spoke to each one of us individually before our first game of the season, explaining what each guy's role on the team would be. He told us what he expected from us, and what we should expect from him. This was something I had never seen before. He was always available to talk if you didn't agree with a decision he made. You knew he was going to be frank about how he felt. He didn't hold back. Cox earned our respect that way.

In my mind, Cox is an example of the kind of manager you need to have running a team. Obviously, he went on to have so much success in his career. A major part of that success was that he knew how to get the most out of his players. It's a unique skill, the kind you see in the best managers in the game today, like Buck Showalter, Joe Maddon, Mike Scioscia—all old-school baseball guys who earned the loyalty and respect of their players. Their players know that their manager has their back. They also know that he won't be afraid to tell them when they've messed up, and will demand that they fix it.

Tom Kelly was a lot like that in Minnesota in the late '80s and through the '90s. He would actually take his players out onto the field after games to show them what they had done wrong. He'd yell at them on the field when they messed up, in a way that many players would be insulted by today. But he got the best out of them because of it. He was always teaching them. Today, veteran players like LaTroy Hawkins and Torii Hunter credit Kelly with teaching them how to become successful professionals. He could be hard on them. All of these guys can be hard on their players. But it works because they have earned their players' respect.

Today, we often underestimate the role of a manager. But the position requires so much more than deciding the batting order and pitching rotation. A good manager sets the tone for a team. A good manager is a clear leader in the locker room, and he demands the best out of his players. Look at the success Maddon had with the Tampa Bay Rays and has had more recently with the Chicago Cubs. A good manager can be the difference between a winning and losing team, because they play such an important role in how the team approaches the game.

Managing is a role that can't be quantified with numbers. John Gibbons in Toronto is a great example of that. He has a laid-back persona, especially in the media, which sometimes makes it difficult on the surface to see how he impacts the team. Every manager has a different style, and any one of many different approaches may be the right one. In Toronto, the players know and trust Gibby. He's a great guy, and he has their respect.

There are some managers who know when to push and when to back off better than others do. There are managers who push a good team to become a great one. That's exactly what Bobby Cox did for us. It was Cox who really turned the Blue Jays' fortunes around. Under

Cox, we became a platoon outfit. He had meetings with us right away. After spring training he met with everybody. He told Ernie Whitt, a left-handed batter, that he was going to play against right-handed pitchers, and he told me, a right-handed batter, that I was going to play against left-handed pitchers. "I don't see much difference between either one of you," he said. He was just going to use each of us based on the circumstances of the game. That Jays team didn't just platoon behind the plate. We also did it at third base, in right field and in left field. But no one on the team felt like they were viewed as just an extra man. This was the strategy—no one went more than a week without making an appearance in a game, whether at the plate or in the field. Cox knew how to keep his players focused and ready to play.

Cox was the kind of manager who creates success. He was consistent and calculating. He knew the other teams well and had a plan for every hitter. With the platoon system, he used his players like pieces on a chessboard. And he stuck with the system he implemented through the inevitable ups and downs of a game. He didn't panic. He did his research and managed with confidence. Because of that, we had confidence too. We had confidence in him as our leader, which is really what a manager needs.

Cox would show up to the evening games at one in the afternoon. He would chat with visiting managers and coaches about teams they had played recently, trying to get information on how he should prepare to play them. Cox wanted to know anything he could about the other team's defense, pitching and hitting. He'd take any edge that could help us win.

If someone wasn't playing his best, or if it appeared that a player's focus was elsewhere, Cox would speak to the player right away, in private, and put things back on track. And he was clear—things would be done *his* way. This was not a debate. There were no illusions about whose team this was. Cox was the manager. The manager was in charge.

As I mentioned already, that's how a baseball team should be run.

What the Blue Jays also understood in the mid-1980s is that a good manager is only as good as his pitching coach, first-base coach, third-base coach, batting coach and bullpen coach. And in turn, a franchise is only as good as the coaches and managers throughout its minor-league system. And the quality of players they get is only as good as the team's scouting staff. Every part of building a franchise is connected. It requires foresight and investment. And it requires a united philosophy on the game.

Pat Gillick's Blue Jays were built on those principles.

WE ONLY WON 78 games in Cox's first season with the team in 1982, but we could tell that things were changing. Our attitude was different. We went from a team that expected to lose to a team that expected to win. That was what Bobby Cox brought us. And that mentality means everything.

These days, you'll hear a lot of talking heads saying that every player wants to win, and that attitude really doesn't play a role in winning. They assume that all players are created equal—that they all care about winning as much as the next guy. That just isn't true. You can tell the difference between a team that wants to win and a team that is simply showing up at the ballpark and going through the motions.

And that starts at the top. With Cox, there was no way to just go through the motions. We expected to win. We were building a team that was *going to* win. That was it, plain and simple. Bobby Cox was one of the main factors in the Blue Jays' success in the mid-1980s. We just got better and better.

It all started to come together in 1983 and 1984.

In 1983 we won 89 games but still finished fourth in the AL East. We posted the exact same record in 1984 but finished second in the division, 15 games behind the powerhouse Detroit Tigers, managed by the great Sparky Anderson and starring Jack Morris, who pitched a no-hitter early that spring. The Tigers started the season with an astonishing 35–5 record. It was an incredible team. Meanwhile, although our record was the same as the previous season, we were getting better. We tied for second in the league that season with a .980 fielding percentage, which measures the rate at which fielders handle batted or thrown balls without making an error. All of that fielding work with Jimy Williams was paying off.

One of the things that stands out about the 1984 season was our unconventional approach to the pitching rotation. We basically went with a four-man staff. It was pretty much unheard of at the time, and probably one of the last times we've seen something like that. Dave Stieb, Doyle Alexander, Luis Leal and Jim Clancy carried the load, combining for 141 starts. The remaining 21 were split among four other guys. But our weakness that season was the bullpen. We didn't have a real closer. Roy Lee Jackson filled the role, but it wasn't really the right place for him. Dennis Lamp managed to save a few games and was solid. The real spark in the pen came from 23-year-old Jimmy Key, who earned ten saves as a rookie. Gillick had drafted him in the third round of the 1982 draft.

The Jays had gone from a lowly expansion team in 1977 to having the second-best team in the American League (behind only an epic Detroit Tigers team) in just its eighth season. It was a remarkable turnaround, one that the Jays' executives themselves didn't expect to see happen so quickly. Consider the team that Gillick and company had pieced together. It was built entirely on the Blue Jays' stated philosophy of building through the draft, developing a core group of players and then supplementing that core through trades or free agency.

"If you look at that team, the first team to go to the playoffs, there were some traded players in there, there were some Rule 5 players in there, but a good hunk of the team was developed from within," says Gord Ash, who started working as the Jays' administrator of player personnel at the time. It's worth noting that the Seattle Mariners, who joined the league the same year as the Jays, routinely floundered through those early years and wouldn't finish first in their division until 1995.

The Jays' infield in 1985 consisted of Willie Upshaw at first base (taken from the Yankees in the 1977 Rule 5 draft); Dámaso García at second base (picked up in a trade with the Yankees in 1978); Tony Fernandez at shortstop (scouted and signed by Epy Guerrero); and Rance Mulliniks and Garth Iorg at third base. The left-hitting Mulliniks was a fantastic hitter who was brought over in a trade in 1982 with the Kansas City Royals, where he learned his batting prowess from Hal McRae, George Brett and Amos Otis. The right-hitting Iorg was picked up by Toronto from the Yankees in the expansion draft. We called the third-base platoon "Mullinorg" because we thought of them as one player.

Our outfield was made up of George Bell in left, Lloyd Moseby in center and Jesse Barfield in right. Behind them we had reliable talent in Ronnie Shepherd, Mitch Webster and Lou Thornton.

That season would mark the appearance of two other names that would soon be well known across the league. A young Cecil Fielder broke into the big leagues with the Jays in 1985. So did a kid named Kelly Gruber, who came from the Indians in the Rule 5 draft in 1983.

Ernie Whitt and I were behind the plate, with us still platooning, but Whitt caught more games.

Our rotation was bolstered by the addition of Jimmy Key as a regular starter. He carried the load with Dave Stieb, Doyle Alexander and Jim Clancy. Luis Leal and Tom Filer would also pick up some starts. To bolster the bullpen, the Jays brought in Bill Caudill and Gary Lavelle, hoping one would be a reliable closer, but neither was really healthy. Jim Acker also filled in as closer. But the bullpen would be bolstered by the addition of Tom Henke, picked up as a free-agent compensation pick from the Texas Rangers in January 1985. Henke would spend his early months with the organization in the minor leagues, and after he was promoted to the majors partway through the season, he never looked back. Henke recorded 13 saves after coming up from Triple A and took us to the next level. He was the piece that would spark the first great moment in Toronto Blue Jays history: the drive of '85.

The 1985 Blue Jays brought playoff baseball to Toronto for the first time. And when you look at that team, you can see the culmination of the Blue Jays' philosophy of building a franchise through savvy drafting and player development. One that was built on athleticism and skill and had a homegrown core. The Blue Jays emphasized scouting and quality coaching throughout the organization. In less than a decade the organization had developed a Blue Jays Way rooted in an old-fashioned approach to building a long-lasting winner. An approach that would work just as well today as it did back then.

14

WHAT 1985 MEANT TO ME

The 1985 season was one of the most memorable of my career, for good reasons and bad. It was also, in retrospect, my last real year behind the plate.

The season started off great. By early June, we had a decent lead in the American League East, with a 35–16 record. We faced the Detroit Tigers, our division rivals, who were a few games behind us, on June 6. I remember that my wife, Arlene, drove me to the ballpark that day. Our seven-year-old son, Casey, was in the backseat. I gave Arlene a kiss goodbye.

"Hit a home run tonight," she said. I laughed—I wasn't even supposed to play. At the time, Ernie Whitt and I were still operating in Bobby Cox's platoon system, but Ernie was getting more playing time than I was. The only way I was going to get into the game was as a pinch-hitter against a lefty, I reminded her. And Detroit only had one left-handed reliever. "Well, I just feel you're going to hit a home run today," she said.

We both laughed. I'd been struggling at the plate and had been working with our hitting coach, Cito Gaston, to help get me out of my slump. At the time, I was batting .134.

Jimmy Key was on the mound for us that night, in front of 36,000 fans at Exhibition Stadium, a good number of them dressed in black and orange and supporting the Tigers. Key was only 24 years old, and he was doing a great job for us as a starter. He was hot again that night, carrying a no-hitter into the top of the ninth inning. Unfortunately, his no-hit bid was broken up when Tom Brookens lined a leadoff single into left field.

The game went into extra innings, with the fans on the edge of their seats. In the tenth inning Manny Lee came in to pinch-run for Ernie Whitt, so I was in to catch in the 11th. The game remained scoreless as we entered the 12th inning. The Tigers had Aurelio López on the mound. I came up to bat with George Bell on first and one out. López, known as Señor Smoke, was a righty with a very good fastball. I had actually caught him when we both played in Kansas City. I knew the odds were stacked against me.

I guessed correctly on the first pitch and fouled a fastball behind me. The next pitch was outside, followed by another fastball that I caught up with and fouled back. Behind in the count, I shortened up my stroke, planning to hit a line drive and avoid a double play.

López threw a breaking ball—a bad one. It hung over the plate and didn't break at all. I swung and made contact. The ball jumped off my bat, and I felt the rush of excitement that surges when you know it's going deep. The ball flew into left field as I ran toward first. I didn't see where it landed, but the crowd told me all I needed to know. It was a two-run walk-off home run. I didn't even know what to do! I just ran around the bases, as ecstatic as I had ever been in a baseball game. When I got to home plate, I was greeted by Bell and Willie Upshaw, who was on deck. We were the only Jays on the field. Everyone else stayed in the dugout—quite a contrast to what happens whenever there is a walk-off in the game today.

The best feeling came later that night, when I found out my son Casey had been listening to the game on the radio.

"Mom," he said to Arlene, "how did you know?"

THAT SEASON, ERNIE WHITT really came into his own as a catcher. He had grown so much as a player in the few years we had been together. When he first started in Toronto, the team wasn't sure of what kind of a catcher he'd become. That got him down on himself. But he learned to have confidence in himself regardless, which is important because a catcher's confidence is essential to a pitcher. A catcher has to know that he is making the right call on a pitch, and the pitcher has to trust him. In 1985 Ernie Whitt would be named an All-Star and carried a .300 batting average well into June, which was a testament to how far he had come as a player. Whitt's excellent play also meant that my opportunities behind the plate were diminishing.

By July, Toronto had the best record in baseball. The team was on to something huge. We were in the midst of a grueling West Coast road trip, which started off with a four-game series in Oakland that we split. Then we traveled up to Seattle on July 8. Dave Stieb beat Mike Moore, 4–0, in a very good game. Whitt was supposed to catch the second game of the series in Seattle on July 9, but before the game Cox came up to me at two in the afternoon when I arrived at the ballpark and told me *I* was catching that night.

"We're bringing up Tom Filer and he's gonna make his Blue Jays debut," Cox told me. "I want you to catch him."

That sealed my fate.

In the bottom of the second, Jim Presley and Bob Kearney got two base hits in a row for the Mariners, and then moved to second and third on a sacrifice bunt by Spike Owen. The next batter, Harold Reynolds, hit a fly ball to right field. Jesse Barfield made the catch and threw a bullet to me at the plate. The ball was on the first-base side of the plate, so I had to reach over to snare it and then dive back to catch Jim Presley as he was sliding into home. It was a great double play. Everyone was high-fiving in the dugout afterward. When Barfield came into the dugout, I said, "Jesse, great throw! But next time throw it on the other side of home plate."

Unfortunately, he took my advice.

The very next inning, with the game still scoreless, Phil Bradley hit a single and then got to second on a balk. Alvin Davis popped out, bringing up my old teammate Gorman Thomas.

I signaled Filer to try to get an outside fastball past Gorman. Big mistake. I should have known better. Gorman smacked a hit through second base and into right field for a single. Bradley sprinted around third and barreled his way toward the plate. Barfield fired a bullet from right field toward the third-base side of the plate, just as I had asked him to. It was a perfect throw. Just as it hit my glove, I could see Bradley out of the corner of my eye. He ran through me like a freight train, hitting me on the left side of my shoulder. The collision bent me back straight, but my foot stuck in the dirt. I dislocated my ankle and broke my fibula up by my knee. Still, I held on to the ball to secure the out.

Everyone in the Kingdome that night knew something was seriously wrong with my leg. The umpire, Larry Young, stood over me, shouting, "Show me the ball! Show me the ball!" I showed him, and he called the out.

But from the ground, I saw Gorman making a break for third. I threw the ball from my butt toward third, but it sailed past the third baseman, down the left-field line toward their bullpen.

I knew Gorman would be coming home. I scooted around to get into position to take the throw. Thankfully, Gorman is a good man and a friend. Knowing I was hurt, he tried to tiptoe around me instead of barreling straight through me. The ball hit the dirt and hopped into my glove just before Gorman stepped around me.

It was the only 9–2–7–2 double play in the history of the game. It was also the last play I made that season.

All of my teammates crowded around me as I collapsed in a heap, but I didn't feel any pain yet. I was probably in shock. I was just numb. "Don't worry, don't worry," Bobby Cox kept saying. "You'll be all right. It looks like it's just dislocated.

"And if you can stand the pain," he continued, "you can probably play tomorrow, because it's not going to hurt your speed." He had a good sense of humor.

"I don't know how you did it, Buck," said Jimy Williams, "but that was the greatest play I've ever seen."

George Bell grabbed one end of the stretcher when they came to get me, insisting that he carry "Bookie," as he called me in the locker room, from the field. As he grabbed the stretcher, he jammed my foot into his back. "George! George!" I shouted. But he was just trying to help. He was a terrific friend and a great teammate.

While the play was stopped, Gorman Thomas came over to see how

I was. "Nice going, Martinez," he said. "They're booing me cause I didn't slide!"

He sat with me until the ambulance arrived.

I was still wearing my uniform when they rushed me into the emergency room at the hospital. Seattle's team doctor came in, accompanied by a young intern. The doctor picked up my foot and cupped my heel in the palm of his hand. "When you have something like this, you stabilize the foot," he said. "You put your hand on the instep and pull it like that." The doctor pulled down and popped my ankle back into the socket, and I must have gone white as a sheet. I nearly passed out. It hurt so much, I couldn't believe it. It also didn't help that he didn't know that my fibula was broken.

Meanwhile, back at the stadium, the game had gone into extra innings. George Bell hit a thrilling grand slam off Ed Vande Berg in the 13th inning, and the Jays went on to win, 9–4. It had been a four-and-a-half-hour battle. I was the only casualty.

After the game a bunch of the coaches came to visit me in the hospital—Bobby Cox, Jimy Williams, Bobby Mattick, Galen Cisco and John Sullivan. It must have been two in the morning. Mattick told me he had never seen a play like that at the plate. He doubted that he'd ever see one like it again. (I didn't point out that, in my very first game in the major leagues, there was a similar incident, when I was crushed by 225-pound Bob Allison at home plate.) I remember being touched that they came to visit me. When they left, I shifted in my bed to get comfortable, and the weight holding my foot up got caught on the end of the bed, forcing my leg up toward the ceiling. It had pulled me down far enough that I couldn't reach the button to call the nurses. I was stuck. I couldn't go anywhere. I just lay back and laughed. "What else can happen?" I thought.

NEEDLESS TO SAY, it was going to take a long time for my leg to heal. In the end, the fracture in my fibula—it was up near my knee—only required a cast and some time to heal. But my ankle was going to need a screw to keep the broken bones in place.

It was terribly disappointing. We had started the season so well and were likely to be in a pennant race. Now it looked like I was going to be out for most of the regular season.

The injury came at a difficult time in my career as well. I was 36 years old. My career was winding down and I had been struggling to give the team everything I could.

I was in a cast for eight weeks. I watched the rest of the season from the discomfort of my crutches, while the Blue Jays surged toward the playoffs and secured the team's first division title. Dave Stieb was unbelievable on the mound with 2.48 ERA, at one point pitching 26 consecutive scoreless innings. Jimmy Key was also sensational with a 3.00 ERA. The outfield of Bell, Moseby and Barfield was probably the best in the game.

I hoped that I'd be able to make it back in time for the postseason and did everything I could to be ready. I started squeezing newspapers and picking up marbles with my toes to get the movement back. I remember thinking, "I can do this, I can do this," and working out like crazy. But in reality, it was never going to happen. Ken Carson, the trainer, had a machine with a big leg sleeve, and it would pump ice-cold water and apply pressure at the same time to reduce the swelling. So after each workout, he would put my leg in the contraption. I did that for the rest of the season. It really helped. But still, there was no chance that I was going to get back into playing condition.

Meanwhile, excitement for baseball in the city reached a peak that had never been experienced before. Toronto fans were completely behind the team through the "Drive of '85." It was a level of enthusiasm that wouldn't be surpassed until the early '90s, and then wouldn't return for another two decades.

In early October we were a game away from clinching the pennant. All we had to do was beat the Yankees. The buzz in the city was amazing. Everyone in the clubhouse could feel the celebration coming on. Before the first game of the three-game series, Bobby Cox gave a speech in the locker room.

"Don't worry about a thing," he told us. "You guys are playing well. We're proud of you. The organization is proud of you. The City of Toronto is behind you 100 percent. Just go out there and have a good series. Go out there and play. Everybody's free-swinging. Turn the bats loose!" Right before he dismissed the meeting, he made one final request. "Pitchers report tomorrow at 4:30 . . ." And everyone laughed. Perhaps the nerves were getting to Bobby too. Saturday was a day game, and by the afternoon we'd be in the middle of a battle with the Yankees.

The fans at that game were rabid. I remember sitting in the dugout and listening to them. They had come a long way from the tame crowd that Arlene had urged to cheer when we first arrived a few years earlier. Now they booed every Yankee they could. It seemed like they wanted the pennant as much as we did. We led, 3–2, in the top of the ninth, and we felt like we were about to explode in excitement. Tom Henke got the first batter, Mike Pagliarulo, to pop up. Then he struck out Willie Randolph. We were one out away. Butch Wynegar came up to bat. We were practically popping the champagne corks already. Wynegar, a switch-hitter, was batting left against the right-handed Henke. The count quickly went to 3–2. We were a strike away! Henke wound up and threw his pitch, and Wynegar connected. The ball sailed over the wall. Tie game. A few plays later, Moseby dropped a fly ball hit by Don Mattingly, and Bobby Meacham scored from second base. Suddenly we were down, 4–3. Exhibition Stadium was dead quiet. All 47,000 fans were stunned, feeling the same disappointment we did. We were unable to get a run in the bottom of the ninth. Our big opportunity had been squandered.

The next day, we took a different approach. We were good, but we were still learning what it meant to win. In particular, we were learning not to get ahead of ourselves. I sat in the dugout as the Jays carried a 5–1 lead into the top of the ninth. But no one celebrated all game. This was business, and we weren't going to let the lead slip away again. And once again, we were three outs away in the top of the ninth. Our excitement built, but it was more controlled this time, even though we had a relatively secure four-run lead. No one said anything about winning until two outs were posted on the board. It was then that someone suggested we carry Doyle Alexander off the field when he got the final out. He had pitched great and was about to pick up a complete game. That's when I knew it was real.

The crowd knew it too. You could see them already inching toward the field. It was clear that the Ex was about to explode. Doyle pitched to Ron Hassey, who connected and popped up to left field. George Bell squared himself under the ball. He made the catch and fell to his knees with his arms up in the air—yielding one of the most famous pictures in Blue Jays history.

As everyone rushed the field, I hobbled after them. When I reached the mob, there were tears in my eyes. We had won the division! I'd been through this before with the Royals, but for some reason I hadn't appreciated the moment the way I did this time. This had been such a journey, from last place in the league to first. It was special. It meant so much to me at that moment, even though I wasn't playing. Maybe it was my age. Maybe it was because I knew how rare this was, and how fleeting the moment would be. Maybe, deep down, I knew it was over.

I watched as my teammates carried Doyle around the field, and as the fans surged around us, I thought of what Toronto had meant to me over the past few seasons. It was the place that had given me a second chance when it looked like my career was done. It was such a strange, new place when I arrived. Now it felt like home.

I looked for Arlene in the chaos after the win, but I couldn't find her until I finally spotted her standing in the stands at the edge of the dugout. I climbed up on top of the dugout and went over and gave her a big kiss. "We did it!" I said. I handed her a bottle of champagne, and she sprayed everyone around her. Later, Arlene led the wives down to the locker room. She walked up to Paul Beeston as we were celebrating inside and said, "We're going in. We deserve to go in there."

"You're right," he said, handing her a cigar. "You do. Come on in!"

It was pandemonium inside the locker room. All of the players and their families were celebrating together. Beeston was there. Mattick, Gillick—everyone. It had been such a journey, and here we were.

The Jays had finally won the American League East.

The postseason, however, would be a disappointment. In the American League Championship Series, we faced my old team, the Kansas City Royals—starring Frank White and George Brett. We took a commanding three-games-to-one lead in the series, and it looked like Toronto was heading to its first World Series. The city was ecstatic. But as every Blue Jays fan knows, the dream quickly fell apart. We lost game five in Kansas City and returned to Exhibition Stadium with two chances to eliminate the Royals.

It was a miracle year for Kansas. The Royals beat us, 5–3, in game six to force a seventh game. They had all the momentum in the final game of the series, and we fell, 6–2.

Remarkably, the Royals fell behind three games to one against the St. Louis Cardinals in the World Series and again managed to come back. This time, they were world champions.

We were devastated by the loss. But despite the agony of defeat, the Jays' core remained in place. This was a team that had been built to win, and the foundation for success had been laid.

It was only a matter of time.

I TRIED TO COME BACK the following season. I rehabbed all winter, worked my ass off. In spring training I was hitting off my front foot and not putting any pressure on my right ankle at all. Everything I did was off that back leg. I managed to get back on the roster, but I wasn't myself. I played, but I didn't play very well. And I didn't play very long. It was a difficult year.

Bobby Cox had returned to Atlanta in the off-season, taking over as the Braves' general manager. Jimy Williams, one of the best coaches I ever had, took over as the Jays' manager.

We had a decent season in 1986, but not quite as good as we hoped. Perhaps it was a hangover from our success a season earlier. But we went 86–76 and finished fourth in the American League East, which was a powerhouse division at the time with the Yankees, Orioles and Tigers all among the best in the game. I believe we expected that year to be just a walk-through for us to get to the World Series, but it would take seven more tries before the Jays made it.

Meanwhile, I knew it was over for me, but I still didn't want to accept it. I mean, nobody ever wants to think that their career is over. But that's what I learned more than anything by being part of the Jays' win in 1985: Everything ends, bittersweet as that may be. The Jays were building something great in Toronto, and I was there for the start of it. It was clear, though, that I wouldn't be part of wherever this team was heading.

On the final day of the season, Jimy pulled me aside. Usually, players don't hang around at the end of the season. When they know the season is over, they make plans to get out of there right away.

"Can you come in tomorrow?" Jimy asked me.

I knew what was coming.

"Yeah, I can come in tomorrow," I said.

When I arrived the next day, Pat Gillick, Paul Beeston and Jimy Williams were all in the office. Pat and Jimy were wringing their hands.

"You've had a tough year, but boy, you're a great player for us," said Gillick. "You know, we don't know how to tell you this."

I stopped him.

"Fellas, listen," I said. "I came here in '81. I thought I was going to be here for a year. I ended up playing six years here. It was a great time. I was very lucky to be here. I want to thank you for everything."

Beeston spoke up next.

"Do you want to do television, Albert?" he asked. (Beeston always called me by my middle name.)

"What do you mean?" I said.

"We'd like to talk to you about doing the television for the Blue Jays next year," he said. TSN—like the Blue Jays, owned by Labatt Breweries—was broadcasting Jays games, and they wanted to talk to me about covering the games. I had done some broadcast work in the playoffs, and I'd done a regular radio interview segment where I talked about the game from an insider's perspective, but I hadn't considered making a career out of it. To be honest, I really didn't want to at the time.

"I don't think so," I said. "I think I want to play. I'm going to go out and see if I can find a job and play another year or two."

When I got home that afternoon, Arlene asked me what they had said. I told her that I was going to be released from the Jays, but that I was being offered the TV job. I told her that I had said no.

"Call him back up and tell him yes," she said, without hesitation. "You can't play anymore."

And just like that, I was retired.

It was hard to leave the game. It's always difficult to see players approaching the end of their careers, facing the end of the most vibrant, exciting time of their lives. It's a unique experience for an athlete, when your body can no longer keep up with the demands of the one thing that you've dedicated every day of your life to. It's why everyone roots so hard for the guys at the end of a great run, like Mark Buehrle chasing those last few innings late in 2015 to keep up his streak of 200-inning seasons. He had the chance, but he just couldn't do it. Still, he walked away from the mound with his head held high.

Like him, I walked away from my playing days feeling grateful for everything I had been a part of. I had felt what it was like to be a winner, with both the Royals and the Jays. But I had never gotten all the way. I had never felt the rush of winning a World Series as a player. Still, my entire career seemed like a map of how to get there. Every step along the way had revealed a new aspect of how to build a winner. From Kansas City to Milwaukee to Toronto, I had witnessed what winning teams looked like and how they were constructed.

It turned out that I was doubly lucky, because the game I loved would always be part of my life, and it had so much more to teach me.

15

WHY THE BLUE JAYS HAD THE PERFECT BLUEPRINT

W AMCO is one of the greatest acronyms that Toronto fans have ever known. Do you remember it?

Devon White, Roberto Alomar, Paul Molitor, Joe Carter and John Olerud—leadoff through fifth, the most dominant top of the order in Blue Jays history. In the fall of 1993, as the city was on the verge of its second straight World Series championship, WAMCO took over.

Consider this:

- Devon White had a .341 on-base percentage, 42 doubles and 34 stolen bases as the Jays' switch-hitting leadoff hitter. He also had 6 triples and 15 home runs.
- Roberto Alomar had a .408 on-base percentage, 35 doubles and 55 stolen bases.

- Paul Molitor had a .408 on-base percentage and 22 stolen bases, along with 47 doubles and 6 triples. He could run like a deer.
- Joe Carter had 33 doubles and 33 home runs.
- John Olerud had 54 doubles with a .473 on-base percentage and a team-leading 1.072 OPS.
- Olerud, Molitor and Alomar finished first, second and third in batting average among American League hitters.

That was WAMCO.

But the Blue Jays in the early '90s were more than those five hitters. In 1993, returning to Toronto after being shipped to the Padres in the trade that brought Roberto Alomar and Joe Carter to the Jays, shortstop Tony Fernandez hit .306 with 9 triples. In fact, eight of the Jays' nine regular batters combined to hit 35 triples. That certainly had something to do with the artificial-turf field at the SkyDome, but it also had to do with their attitude. The Jays had that swagger that Gillick, Beeston and company had once admired in the Dodgers and wanted to instill in the franchise.

Three key things stand out about WAMCO and the 1993 Blue Jays: They could hit; they could run; and they were athletic. Alomar, Olerud, and Molitor all posted on-base percentages higher than .400. In 2015 there were only six guys in all of Major League Baseball who posted on-base percentages higher than .400: Bryce Harper (.460), Joey Votto (.459), Miguel Cabrera (.440), Paul Goldschmidt (.435), Mike Trout (.402) and Andrew McCutchen (.401). Think about that.

The summer of 1993 was the height of Blue Jays mania in Toronto. A year earlier, the club had posted a record of 96 wins and 66 losses. More than four million fans had packed into the state-of-the-art SkyDome. The Jays beat the Oakland Athletics in the American League Championship Series, finally winning the pennant on their fourth try. Then they beat the Atlanta Braves to win the World Series.

In the year of WAMCO the Jays dominated again, with 95 wins and 67 losses. Alomar, Molitor, Carter and Olerud were named starters on the American League All-Star team. White was a reserve, along with pitchers Pat Hentgen and Duane Ward. Toronto won its second American League pennant, beating the Chicago White Sox in the ALCS, then beat the Philadelphia Phillies in the World Series on Joe Carter's three-run walk-off home run in the bottom of the ninth in game six, one of the most exciting moments in baseball history.

I had a front-row seat for it all, working as a broadcaster with TSN.

The Blue Jays of the early '90s were the culmination of years of work by Pat Gillick and his front-office team. They started collecting the pieces to the puzzle way back in the early 1980s. The outcome looked a lot like the vision they had started with. It was a team built on a homegrown core that relied heavily on one of the most effective and robust scouting and development systems in the game. And despite the fanfare that WAMCO garnered for their prowess at the plate, they were only part of what set the Blue Jays apart. The old adage was as true as ever in the early '90s: Pitching and defense win championships.

After our appearance in the ALCS in 1985, the Jays returned to the brink of winning the pennant two more times—in 1989, losing to the Oakland A's, and in 1991, losing to the Minnesota Twins. It was clear that the franchise had passed through the challenging expansion-team phase and had evolved into a legitimate contender. There is no question that this success was rooted in the team's scouting department. The 1980s were the golden age of scouting for the Blue Jays, and the prime example of the team's ability to find talent and potential was John Olerud.

Andy Pienovi, a Jays scout in the Pacific Northwest, found Olerud, and he let the team know that there was a bright star rising on the campus of Washington State University. That information was backed up by Joe Ford, the Jays' man in the Midwest, based in Oklahoma, who saw the 6-foot-5 first baseman and pitcher have an outstanding tournament in Wichita, Kansas. Gillick then sent scout Don Welke out to Pullman, Washington, to get another pair of eyes on Olerud.

Soon, Bobby Mattick made the trip west. He was big on Olerud right away. Al LaMacchia went to see him too—he was also a fan. Finally, Pat Gillick and Moose Johnson flew to Washington and watched Olerud play in a doubleheader against Gonzaga. He pitched one game and was the designated hitter in the other. Gillick went back six more times to watch Olerud play in summer league games. When Olerud's team was scheduled to go on a 12-game road trip, Gillick asked Welke to go along. "Take him out to dinner," Gillick said. "Get to know him." Welke did. And on that trip, he watched Olerud take 48 at-bats without missing a pitch. He didn't swing at and miss one pitch in nearly 50 at-bats!

But Olerud was also an incredible fielder. He had great hands and a long reach as a first baseman, so he saved a lot of errors in the infield, which was something that people in the game tend to overlook. It's not something that shows up on the stat sheet.

"We thought he could probably make it in the big leagues," says Gillick, stating the obvious.

The problem was that so did everyone else.

As a freshman with Washington State, Olerud was an All-American, hitting .414. (He also pitched, with a 3.00 ERA.) He improved in his second season, hitting .464 and posting a 2.49 ERA on the mound with 113 strikeouts. *Baseball America* named Olerud its College Player of the Year. The Jays' gem had become a consensus first-round major-league draft pick.

But in 1989, when he was just 20 years old, Olerud suffered a brain aneurysm. While he was recovering in the hospital, Gillick wrote him a get-well card. They had never met, but the Jays' scouting staff had been following Olerud so closely that Gillick had learned all about him, and news of something so terrifying happening to someone so young was very upsetting.

Thankfully, Olerud recovered. He returned to Washington State for part of the 1989 season. But his draft stock had fallen. Understandably, Olerud's numbers weren't as good on his return, and most scouts seemed to think his potential to make it in the major leagues was diminished. However, the Jays' faith in him didn't waver.

Toronto stole Olerud—there is no other way to put it now—in the third round of the 1989 amateur draft. (They took Eddie Zosky, Mike Moore and Brent Bowers before him, none of whom had much of a major-league career.)

Olerud played his first season with the Jays in 1990 as a platoon player, regularly appearing as the designated hitter. He stepped right into a roster that had made it to the American League Championship Series the year before. He hit .265 and had 15 doubles in 111 games as a 21-year-old rookie. He was one of the few players to go straight from college to the majors without playing a major-league game, along with Dave Winfield, Bob Horner and Dave Roberts. The team around him was almost entirely homegrown, developed through a minor-league system that was full of talented coaches with major-league experience and consistent emphasis on the fundamentals of baseball. It was now the Blue Jays Way. Of the Jays' starting lineup, all but Fred McGriff and Manuel Lee had been developed by the Jays, either as amateur draft picks (Pat Borders, sixth round in 1982), through the Rule 5 draft (George Bell, lifted from the Phillies in 1980) or through amateur free agency (Tony Fernandez, signed in 1979). The starting rotation was entirely homegrown, made up of Dave Stieb, Todd Stottlemyre, David Wells, Jimmy Key and John Cerutti.

"The core was there through development or trades," says Gord Ash, who had risen to the position of assistant general manager in 1989. The team was in a position to make necessary improvements through intelligent free-agent signings or trades for big-name prospects.

The Jays won 86 games and lost 76 in 1990, finishing second in the American League East. Toronto was almost there but just didn't have what it took to get them into the World Series. So with a roster stacked with homegrown talent, Pat Gillick set out to make a trade that would finally put the Jays over the top.

I WAS DRIVING WITH my 13-year-old son, Casey, to go see *Home Alone* in Mission Viejo when we heard the news over the radio that the Blue Jays had just traded Tony Fernandez and Fred McGriff to the San Diego Padres. It was December 4, 1990. Joe Carter and a kid named Roberto Alomar were coming the other way. Everyone knew who Joe Carter was, but I had no clue about Alomar. I had played against his father, Sandy Alomar, when he was with the Yankees, but I had never seen the younger Alomar play the game.

It was a blockbuster deal. Fernandez had spent his entire career with the Blue Jays, after Epy Guerrero discovered him and signed him. The Toronto fans loved Tony. He was still a fantastic shortstop and was only 28 years old. He was a three-time All-Star and a four-time Gold

Glove winner, but his average had dropped from .322 in 1987 to .287 in 1988 to .257 in 1989. Meanwhile, Fred McGriff had just hit .300 with 35 home runs. A season earlier, he had led the American League in home runs with 36. The Jays had stolen McGriff in a trade with the Yankees in 1982—one of the most lopsided in history—in which they also picked up Dave Collins, who was a terrific hitter and baserunner. The Yankees got basically nothing. McGriff appeared to be a franchise player, but at the same time, his laid-back demeanor didn't emulate the intensity that the Blue Jays front office wanted the team to have. They felt they could use a little more passion in the clubhouse.

Meanwhile, Joe Carter was in the middle of a great career but had just come off a down season when he hit .232 with a terrible .290 on-base percentage (his worst since his rookie year). He was, however, an experienced leader. He was vocal and intense—exactly what the Jays needed. Alomar was only 22 years old, with two seasons behind him as the Padres' second baseman. The Jays needed an upgrade in that position, but Alomar was inexperienced. The Padres were in the National League (before there was interleague play), so he was essentially unknown in Toronto.

"We had gotten close and not gotten over the hump in '89 and '90, and there was some desire to change the makeup of the club," says Gord Ash, likening the Jays to the Buffalo Bills teams that made it to four straight Super Bowls but never won a championship. The Jays decided they needed to fine-tune something, even if that meant tweaking the core of the team. "We needed to change the dynamic of the club. Adding Joe Carter was easy. Everybody knew who he was. He was a run producer. He was a power guy; a good defender. The Alomar part of it is a tribute to Pat Gillick's scouting background."

Though the deal seemed like a huge gamble at the time, Gillick and his team of scouts knew what they were doing. In fact, in their minds, the most important piece in the trade was the guy that nobody seemed to know.

The Jays had been scouting Roberto Alomar since he had been a kid in high school. Gillick had known the Alomar family since 1974, when Sandy Alomar was playing for the Yankees. Sandy would bring his two kids out and have batting practice with them before games. When Roberto got older and started playing high school baseball in Puerto Rico, Bobby Mattick flew out to watch him play. He told Gillick that Alomar was the best high school infielder he had ever seen. When he was 17, in 1985, the Blue Jays tried to sign him. But the San Diego Padres had signed his older brother, Sandy Alomar Jr., and given his father a coaching job with the team. The Jays offered Roberto more money, but he signed with the Padres.

The Jays' scouts continued to watch Alomar in the minor leagues, monitoring his progress. They watched his situation in San Diego closely. When there appeared to be a falling-out between Sandy Alomar Sr. and manager Greg Riddoch, who replaced Jack McKeon as the Padres' manager partway through the 1990 season, Gillick made his move at the winter meetings in Chicago.

"He really was the heart of the deal," Ash says about Alomar. "Not that I could say that we knew he was going to be a Hall of Famer, but we knew he was a pretty good player."

As soon as Alomar took the infield in the 1991 season, it was clear why the Blue Jays were so bullish on him. Despite his lack of big-league experience, there was no question he was a big-league player. He could see things that nobody else saw. This was a player who had been immersed in baseball his entire life. As a five-year-old he was asking his father what was happening on the field—why players did certain things, why they hit to certain parts of the field. In the majors you could see how Alomar anticipated things. You could see that he was always watching the flight of the ball. When it was outside, he was leaning to his left. When it was inside, he leaned to his right. He got a jump on everything.

You'll tell a player to watch the plane of the bat, and most don't get it. They will look at you like you have three eyes. And Robbie goes, "Yeah, I got it—watch the bat and see where the ball is coming off the bat." He would get an extra step that way. There might have been guys who were quicker than Robbie, but there wasn't anybody who anticipated as well as he did.

That's how special he was. You can't teach that kind of thing. You just have to identify it—and the Blue Jays did.

WHILE THE BLUE JAYS were bolstered by the addition of Carter and Alomar, as well as the arrival of John Olerud in the early 1990s, they enjoyed the benefit of a homegrown pitching staff, upon which they were similarly able to improve with a few additions. As I mentioned earlier, in 1990 the entire starting rotation for the Jays was homegrown: Dave Stieb, Todd Stottlemyre, David Wells, Jimmy Key and John Cerutti.

But they had even more internal talent on the way.

Juan Guzmán was signed by the Dodgers in 1985, when he was 18 years old. But once again Pat Gillick and his scouting team had their eye on an emerging talent. In this case it was Epy Guerrero who noticed Guzman as a teenager in Santo Domingo. Even after Guzmán signed with the Dodgers, the Jays never lost sight of him. The Dominican ace played a couple seasons of A-ball in the Dodgers system before Gillick spun a trade that brought him to the Jays in exchange for utilityman Mike Sharperson partway through the 1987 season. The deal worked out for Sharperson, whom the Jays had drafted in 1981. He was a consistent fielder and batter who went on to win the World Series with the Dodgers in 1988. (Sadly, Sharperson was killed in a car accident in 1996, at the age of 34.)

Guzmán was called up to the Jays in 1991, when the rotation suffered a rash of injuries. He finished the season with a 2.99 ERA in 23 starts and came second in the voting for the American League Rookie of the Year Award. Toronto again made it to the ALCS in '91, losing to the Minnesota Twins in five games. Guzmán was on the mound in game two, for the Jays' only win. The Twins went on to win the World Series.

Guzmán wasn't technically a homegrown player, but he was someone the Jays had their eye on and managed to bring in while he was very young, just as they had with Roberto Alomar. These were savvy trades, the result of a remarkable scouting network that had been in place since day one.

Meanwhile, the Jays continued to develop the players they drafted. The Blue Jays drafted Pat Hentgen in the fifth round of the 1986 free-agent draft, when he was 17. He developed in the Jays' minor-league system for five seasons before joining the big-league bullpen in 1992. It was the same year that the Jays went a different route—tapping the free-agent market—to pick up a veteran presence with proven big-game experience. Jack Morris spent 13 seasons with the Detroit Tigers, becoming one of the most dominant pitchers in the game and winning the World Series in 1984. He signed a one-year deal with the Minnesota Twins in 1991, helping them to a World Series title. He threw a ten-inning shutout against the Braves in the deciding game and was named World Series MVP.

With a roster primed for the World Series, Gillick made an essential move after the 1991 season by signing the veteran pitcher from the team that had taken down the Jays in the ALCS that fall. But the signing was important for much more than what Morris could provide from the mound. When Toronto added a guy like Morris to its lineup, it made the rest of the pitchers swell with pride, knowing that a guy who had just pitched, arguably, the best game in postseason history was now on their side. He was one of them—and that meant a lot.

In his first season with Toronto, the 36-year-old Morris won 21 games. With an ERA above 4.00, he was helped in that category by the team's remarkable offense. In three playoff starts, he didn't pick up a win, losing two games in the World Series. The following season, in 1993, was the worst in Morris's career. He picked up 7 wins in 27 starts with a 6.19 ERA. He didn't make an appearance in the postseason after suffering a season-ending injury.

Despite that, Morris was a huge factor in both World Series titles. Gillick absolutely made the right move in signing him, and Morris earned his rings. This is a part of baseball that so many numbers-driven people get wrong today. What Morris contributed to the Jays could not be evaluated by an elaborate equation. It cannot be tabulated by a computer. Obviously, the Jays would have liked to see Morris post another spectacular season in 1993. But it didn't matter—they won the two World Series championships regardless of what Morris did on the mound. What he provided was leadership, guidance and confidence to a young, talented team. Gillick didn't just sign Morris hoping he would be able to force another stellar season out of his aging body. That would have been incredible. But Morris had the incalculable benefit of experience.

Pat Hentgen was only 23 years old when he joined the Jays' bullpen in 1992, after five years developing through the team's minor-league system. He gives credit for his growth during that time to Bobby Mattick and to Mel Queen, who became the Jays' farm director in 1990 and would later become the team's pitching coach. Like Mattick, Queen had an enormous impact on many of the Jays' homegrown prospects who went on to have success in the majors, including position players Shawn Green, Shannon Stewart, Jeff Kent and Alex Gonzalez and pitchers David Wells, Todd Stottlemyre and Chris Carpenter.

When Hentgen arrived with the Jays, he was surrounded by experience. He had access to two of the best veteran pitchers in the game in Dave Stieb and Jack Morris. Hentgen studied them. He watched what they did in between starts, learned their routines and how they went about their business. Most important, he saw how they competed. Hentgen was following his father's instruction: "Whatever Jack does and whatever Dave does, you do. When they throw, you throw. When they run, you run." That's what Hentgen's dad told him. And he added, "Morris started 15 Opening Days in a row. There's a reason."

Hentgen always thought of himself as a competitive guy, but watching Stieb and Morris redefined his understanding of what competitiveness is. Hentgen says their example made him take things to another level. Even at their age, near the end of their careers, Stieb and Morris were both incredibly athletic. And they both worked incredibly hard. Despite their status on the team, they worked their asses off in infield drills. Neither slacked or came off as lazy. Neither complained about having to practice covering first base. "It was always at game speed," says Hentgen. "I think that was one of the things that really stuck with me."

Stieb was the best pitcher I ever caught. His movement was ridiculous. He could have pitched with one pitch, his fastball, but his slider was so good, he wanted to throw that all the time. But what stood out to me, too, was his competitive side. He didn't just want to win every battle on the mound. He wanted to *embarrass* people.

Neither Morris nor Stieb were overly verbal leaders on the team. But they led by example. They knew how to keep it simple. Stieb told Hentgen that, as an outfielder in college, he could throw the ball accurately to any bag. Then, when they moved him from the outfield to the mound, he just couldn't believe how close the target looked. Throwing it to the catcher's mitt was easy because he'd been doing it from center field all the way to third base all the time. With that in mind, when he moved to the mound, Stieb just kept things simple. Hitting that target is pretty easy, he thought. So he didn't rush himself. Didn't overthink. He just threw the ball right to that glove and let his movement take care of the rest.

Likewise, Stieb taught Hentgen to relax on the mound and to keep the game simple. He taught him how to rebound after a bad game— how to get out of a funk and get back into a groove. Even though he came off as emotional, or testy, in the press, Stieb really kept the game to the basics. He remained calm.

"He didn't overanalyze," says Hentgen. "It was always 'Keep the ball down, be aggressive, throw strikes, throw the ball up and in, trust your stuff'—all the same clichés that you hear pitching coaches talk about. But when you see a guy go out and execute it every fifth day, it just rings home."

Growing up in Detroit, Hentgen was a huge fan of Morris long before they were teammates. So when he was suddenly on the same roster, it was a big moment for him.

The first thing he noticed about Morris was his swagger.

"It was just a confidence," says Hentgen. "He basically just took over and said, 'I'm the man, and I'm going to show you the way'—and I think guys were better around him because of it. I mean, it was a confidence, it was a swagger, it was a competitiveness."

Hentgen basically followed Morris around, taking in any information he could glean. "He could have said, 'Hey, kid, quit bugging me.' But he never did that," Hentgen says. "He always took me under his wing."

After batting practice one day, Hentgen and Morris sat in the sauna together.

"You know what, kid?" Morris said. "You know how you win games in this league?"

"How?" Hentgen asked, all ears.

"You pitch longer than the other guy," Morris said. "They'll bring in a reliever, and the reliever will start to give up runs—and you'll be in there to win the game. You put your balls in your cup and compete as hard as you can until the manager comes and gets you."

"It's a story that stuck with me my whole career," says Hentgen, who won a Cy Young Award in 1996 and became a mentor to some of the game's future pitching icons. "I tried to pass it on to [Chris] Carpenter. I told that story to Rick Ankiel in St. Louis. I told that story to Doc [Roy] Halladay. I told all those guys that same story because it just resonated in my head over and over."

Injuries kept Stieb from returning to the dominant form he had shown in the 1980s. His biggest moment remains the no-hitter he pitched on September 2, 1990, after three previous attempts that took him into the bottom of the ninth with two outs, only to see him give up a hit. (He had back-to-back attempts in 1988 and a near perfect game in 1989.) But as Hentgen says, Stieb remained an enormous part of the pitching staff in 1992 as the Jays tracked down the team's first World Series. He made only 14 starts, and seven appearances in relief, going 4–6 with a 5.04 ERA. But like the addition of Morris, Stieb's veteran presence was essential to the pitching staff.

The Jays didn't have to lean on one or two guys to carry the whole load. Having the ability to send out Juan Guzmán, Pat Hentgen and Todd Stottlemyre was pretty impressive. That bullpen had confidence. And at the back end of that bullpen, Duane Ward had 45 saves and only gave up 49 hits—that's a pretty dramatic way to close out ballgames.

"It was just an incredible pitching staff," says Hentgen. "And it was led by Jack. It was led by Dave. It was led by Tom Henke. There's a reason why we were good. It's because they made other people around them better. I think that's the sign of a real leader—and I think that those guys did that."

In many ways the mentorship that occurred on the Jays' pitching staff in those World Series seasons was a lot like what has occurred with the Blue Jays today. The Jays have a great bunch of young arms, led by emerging ace Marcus Stroman. A key part of Stroman's jump to being one of the most feared pitchers in baseball came under the mentorship of Mark Buehrle, a guy who had seen it all and knew what it takes to win. Buehrle and Stroman developed a close bond, even though their personalities seem like polar opposites. During the 2015 season, the always-subdued Buehrle promised Stroman that he would react with emotion during a game if the ever-enthusiastic Stroman promised to pitch a game without getting excited. Buehrle held up his end of the bargain with an in-game fist pump.

Now it was over to Stroman in his next start. The requirements: no emotions after a strikeout or any good defensive play while he was on the mound. But Stroman struck out the very first batter of the game and marched off the mound with a huge fist pump and a big "YEAH!" He didn't last a single batter. Oh well, he had good intentions—and promised to try again next year!

Buehrle provided Stroman with the kind of mentorship a young, talented pitcher in the major leagues needs. Even though the aging Buehrle was left off the Jays' 2015 postseason roster, he played an enormous role on the team, supporting and guiding young pitchers like Stroman. When you look at the Jays' current batch of young, home-grown pitchers—guys like Stroman, Aaron Sanchez, Roberto Osuna and Drew Hutchison—you can see reminders of what the Jays had back in the early 1990s. And with veterans in the bullpen like Mark Lowe and LaTroy Hawkins, it was clear that Alex Anthopoulos had learned the lesson the Jays of that era taught: If you want your young players to develop, you need to surround them with teammates who have been there before.

Back in the early '90s, the Jays had developed enough quality pitchers to carry the load, with Jimmy Key, Juan Guzmán and Todd Stottlemyre in the rotation, and weapons like Tom Henke, David Wells, Duane Ward and Hentgen in the bullpen. And on top of Jack Morris, they added another veteran presence in late August of 1992, when they traded for David Cone.

Stieb left the Jays after the 1992 World Series, but Toronto signed Dave Stewart through free agency. Stewart had been dominant against the Jays in the ALCS in 1989 and 1992 while playing with the Oakland A's. The Jays added Hentgen to the starting rotation in 1993, and he won 19 games with a 3.87 ERA.

As a broadcaster I experienced a unique side of Jack Morris's influence over Hentgen that season. The Jays clinched the division title in Milwaukee, with Hentgen on the mound. He went six innings but didn't have his best stuff that day. Still, he kept battling in typical Hentgen fashion. During the broadcast, I said something to the effect of "Isn't that typical Pat Hentgen? He didn't have great stuff today, but he's leaving having given his team a chance to win in this clinching game."

Well, Morris had been listening, and he took exception to my observation that Hentgen didn't have his best pitches working for him that day. During the team's postgame celebration, I waded into the elated mob to a podium in the middle of the room, where I was to interview the Jays on live television. Morris jumped up on the platform, grabbed the mic, looked into the camera and said, "Is this live? Don't listen to this guy [meaning me!]. He doesn't know what he's talking about." That seemed a bit much in the middle of a celebration, but I thanked Jack and moved on. It was an awkward moment. But Morris was trying to defend his young teammate from a perceived slight. We didn't talk for a while after that, but during the World Series celebration, Morris bought me a bottle of champagne and apologized.

He and I still laugh about it today, as we've become good friends and were partners on television for a season with Sportsnet. Jack is a good broadcaster because he speaks his mind.

NINETEEN NINETY-THREE WAS the year of WAMCO. But while the Jays' hitting was tops in the American League, the foundation of that team was really the pitching we just discussed—and the defense lined up around those arms.

Consider what Gillick had put together with that 1993 roster. There was Pat Borders, who was athletic as hell, behind the plate. Olerud was terrific at first base. Alomar was *Alomar*. Then they brought back the great Tony Fernandez at shortstop. Meanwhile, 25-year-old Ed Sprague was an exceptional athlete at third base. And on top of that, they signed my old teammate Paul Molitor, who was destined for the Hall of Fame. Behind all of those guys the Jays had athletic veterans in Darnell Coles, Darren Jackson, Turner Ward and Alfredo Griffin on the bench.

"We had three shortstops all the time," says Hentgen. "They weren't playing short, but we had Gruber at third [and then Sprague], we had Tony at short, we had Robbie at second. We just had tremendous defense on that fast [artificial-turf] surface. And I think you forget one word, one key word is youth. There weren't a lot of old guys." The average age of the 1993 team was 29.3.

There was leadership on the field too.

Consider the presence of Molitor. He had such a dramatic impact on the whole team. He was just always a very intense, very focused, hard-driving player. When he came to Toronto, there was such a high regard for him because of all the success he'd had. The addition of an impact player coming from a team that had just won the World Series stoked the competitive fire. He was 36 years old, but he still played every single game. That was one thing that really turned things around. He came over and led the league in hits. Had it not been for John Olerud's phenomenal season, Molitor would have won the batting title. He had a remarkable presence that just kind of calmed everything down for the Blue Jays and validated again that they were doing whatever they could to win a World Series. He was just such a great addition. He was the designated hitter for most of the year, but knowing that he would always come up with a clutch hit was pretty special.

Another leader on that team—quietly and more intensely—was Pat Borders. He doesn't get the credit he deserves for the impact he had on

Sal Bando takes a swing with the Milwaukee Brewers. He was one of our leaders on and off the field. Of the teams I played on, that one was the best in the clubhouse, and Bando was a huge reason why. —MILWAUKEE BREWERS

Buck Rodgers (left) was one of the best coaches I ever had. We called him "Hollywood" because he was so handsome. He had a knack for teaching and a clear passion for the team. Any major-league coaching staff should have a guy like Buck on it. —MILWAUKEE BREWERS

Harry Dalton (right) was one of the best general managers in the game, developing the Orioles Way that led to the powerhouse teams of the late '60s and early '70s. George Bamberger (left) was the manager who helped create the chemistry that marked a team that would become known as Bambi's Bombers. —Milwaukee Brewers

Bobby Mattick, one of the finest judges of talent the Jays ever had. He and scouts such as Al LaMacchia and Bob Engle helped build the foundation of the Blue Jays' early success.

—Toronto Blue Jays

Two of the game's great managers, Sparky Anderson (left) of the Detroit Tigers and Bobby Cox of the Blue Jays, shake hands as their respective teams push for the pennant. Bobby was one of the most hands-on managers I ever played for, involved in every aspect of the team. —Toronto Blue Jays

Paul Beeston (right) and Bobby Cox share a laugh at Exhibition Stadium. Before retiring in 2015, Beeston was one of the most influential people in Blue Jays history. He was famously the team's first employee and helped Pat Gillick build the team that made the city's first run at the pennant. —Toronto Blue Jays

Few people may recall that Cecil Fielder was a Blue Jay. But Pat Gillick made a great trade with the Kansas City Royals for the young slugger in 1983. Fielder first appeared with the Jays in 1985, and he hit 31 home runs over parts of four seasons (and just 506 at-bats) with the team.

—TORONTO BLUE JAYS

Manny Lee was a product of Pat Gillick's savvy use of the Rule 5 draft. The Jays picked him up from Houston in 1984, and Lee remained an important piece of the Jays' lineup until Toronto won the World Series in 1992.

—TORONTO BLUE JAYS

Pat Gillick and Dave Stieb at the press conference announcing the signing of Stieb to a long-term contract. Gillick was the architect of the franchise; Stieb was the best starter the Jays have ever had. —Toronto Blue Jays

George Bell and Tony Fernandez high-five in this iconic shot taken after Bell caught the last out to clinch the American League East, their first-ever division win. —Toronto Blue Jays

I became an announcer after my playing days were through, and it gave me the chance to see the game from a whole new perspective. Here I am chatting with Joe Torre while working for TSN in 1999. —COURTESY BUCK MARTINEZ

During my days managing the Toronto Blue Jays. I'm front and center, Number 13. This was my dream job, but in retrospect it was one I just wasn't quite prepared for. I'm glad to be back up in the broadcasting booth! —TORONTO BLUE JAYS

It was such an honor to manage Team USA at the World Baseball Classic in 2006. I got to manage guys such as Álex Rodríguez, Chipper Jones, Vernon Wells, Roger Clemens, Chase Utley, Ken Griffey Jr. and the inimitable Derek Jeter.

—COURTESY BUCK MARTINEZ

With some of the "Drive of '85" Jays. From the left: Dave Stieb, Rance Mulliniks, Garth Iorg, Tom Henke (back), me, Jesse Barfield, Lloyd Moseby, George Bell, Willie Upshaw, Cito Gaston and Tony Fernandez. They brought the same kind of excitement to the city that Josh Donaldson, Troy Tulowitzki, Russell Martin, José Bautista and company delivered when the Jays almost went all the way in 2015. —TORONTO BLUE JAYS

Dayton Moore, GM of the world-champion Kansas City Royals. Born in Wichita, Kansas, Moore learned his trade in Atlanta under John Schuerholz, the former Royals and Braves general manager. It may have taken Moore longer than he had hoped to turn the organization around, but he has them in position to be a consistent contender with homegrown, two-way, athletic players—the same formula the Royals used in the 1970s and '80s.

—Kansas City Royals

I've been a player, coach, manager and broadcaster in baseball for nearly six decades, and the beautiful game teaches me something new every year. I'm so lucky to have spent a lifetime in baseball.

—Michelle Prata/Sportsnet

that team. A neat story about Borders: He was in his fifth year in the minors when a coach came up to him and said, "I don't think you are going to make it as a first baseman or a third baseman."

"What about catcher?" Borders asked.

He made the transition, putting his whole soul into the position, and in two years he was catching in the big leagues. It was another example of Gillick loading the Jays organization up with athletes and allowing them to find their place on the team. If players are athletic enough, their skill will get them to the major leagues. Borders became a tremendous catcher, and he had a staff of very difficult guys to catch. He played in 138 games—he was back there just about every single day. He was truly that guy you looked to. That's exactly what earned him the World Series MVP Award in 1992, when he went 9-for-20 with three doubles, a home run and three RBIs.

Even the young guys, like Ed Sprague, and the extra guys, like Turner Ward, had an impact on that team, even though they weren't really star players. Stottlemyre's intensity had a big impact on the team too. And he could cut your legs off at the knees anytime your head got a little bit too big. Dave Stewart had that death stare that was his trademark for years. And Danny Cox was a fantastic leader.

There were just a bunch of character guys on that team who always made sure that nobody took success for granted and that nobody felt they were too important for the team.

Character guys. Leaders. Homegrown youth, guided by veterans. The intelligent addition of key free agents. Athleticism. Pitching. Defense— and yes, hitting. That was the blueprint behind the Blue Jays' success in 1992 and 1993. It built on our success in the 1985 season, which was in the works from the very beginning of the franchise. I don't think Gillick and his team were surprised by anything. They had been building this team for years. Once they got to that point, they anticipated that they'd be a championship team, year in and year out.

The city felt it too. Toronto was elated. From the moment SkyDome opened in 1989 until 1994, when the baseball season was stopped because of the strike, it was packed every night. It's just what everybody expected. Toronto was a winner. Fifty thousand people every single night for an entire five-year span. It was remarkable.

For years, everyone had talked about Toronto not being a baseball destination. Now it was the center of the baseball world with back-to-back World Series championships.

It was hard to fathom for a long, long time. For 22 years, to be exact. That drought of postseason appearances would end in 2015, when the Jays won the AL East. In the American League Division Series, they stormed back after losing the first two games at home to the Texas Rangers, and they won game five in dramatic fashion. Despite losing to the Kansas City Royals in the AL Championship Series, a statement had been made, and the team is once again set up for several years of success.

16

WHAT I LEARNED AS A MAJOR-LEAGUE MANAGER

My time as manager of the Toronto Blue Jays started out as a dream job. By the end, it was a nightmare. But over the course of a season and a third, I learned some valuable lessons about the leadership it takes to turn a group of individuals into a winning team.

Through the late 1980s and 1990s, I was a baseball commentator on Blue Jays broadcasts on TSN with my good friend Dan Shulman. I also did work as an analyst on ESPN. My broadcasting career was going very well—14 years and counting. I loved traveling around, getting to chat with some of the smartest people in the game. And I loved to share their insights with the fans.

But a large part of me missed wearing the uniform. I missed being down in the dugout with a team. I missed being part of the action.

There is no substitute for that. I think any retired player knows what I'm talking about. The game always calls you back. Of course, I got to be part of the action in the broadcast booth, but not in the same way I had known it all those years on the field.

Gord Ash and I first discussed the possibility of my becoming the Blue Jays' manager in 1997, when Toronto was looking for someone to follow Cito Gaston. Gord and I were good friends. He had taken over as the Jays' general manager in 1995, in a move that was the culmination of his lengthy career with the organization. He started out in the box office back in 1978, well before I arrived as a player. He then served as the Jays' administrator of player personnel in the mid-1980s and became assistant general manager under Pat Gillick in 1989. He was a key part of the franchise's glory days in the early '90s.

I was excited by the idea when Gord first discussed it with me, but the timing just wasn't right. Along with my broadcasting duties I had agreed to help coach my son's baseball team at California State University at Sacramento. It was a great opportunity to spend more time with Casey. It was a volunteer position with the team and it was a lot of fun. The season ran from February through the end of May.

"I can't manage right now," I told Gord. "I promised my son I would travel to California."

The Jays hired Tim Johnson instead.

Coaching with the college team was a different experience for me. With my years as a player and broadcaster, I took on the role hoping that I'd be able to impart some of the wisdom I had gleaned through the decades. I had learned how to catch in the big leagues under such great coaches as Charley Lau, John Sullivan and Buck Rodgers. They taught me so much. But as a coach, I quickly learned that there was much more to imparting wisdom than simply understanding the game. You have to be able to figure out how to motivate people. You need to know how to get a team to work together. And you have to know how to teach them to get better. That's not an automatic skill. It takes time and practical experience.

I was coaching alongside my childhood friend John Smith, who had a long career as a college coach. It was fun to spend time with my son and be part of his playing days through college. But in the few years that I worked with the team, I can't say I really had much of a lasting effect. As a volunteer, it was difficult to have much of an impact. I tried to stay as neutral as possible and to help out everybody as well as I could, without overstepping my bounds.

In hindsight, I could have been more vocal. I could have been tougher. These were lessons that I was about to learn under a much brighter spotlight.

I did learn a lot about coaching, though. I had learned a lot about the difference between baseball knowledge and running a team. And more than ever, I knew I wanted to be a manager. So when Gord Ash approached me again about the Blue Jays' managerial position in the fall of 2000, there was no doubt that I would be interested. At the time, I was working as a postseason analyst with ESPN. Johnson had been fired after one season and had been replaced by Jim Fregosi, who lasted two seasons before being fired after the 2000 season, in which the Jays contended for the American League wild-card playoff berth before tailing off down the stretch, finishing third in the AL East with an 83–79 record.

Toronto was a solid-hitting club with some serious talent led by Carlos Delgado, who had just signed a four-year contract extension worth $68 million. The Jays also had Homer Bush, Alex Gonzalez, Tony Batista and Shannon Stewart. The lineup suggested they could be contenders, though the rotation and bullpen needed work. David Wells had won 20 games, but he would demand a trade in the off-season. Chris Carpenter's best years were ahead of him (mainly with the St. Louis Cardinals) and Roy Halladay was just developing. The Jays were playing in the American League East, when the New York Yankees had won three World Series titles in four years and were about to win another—anyone taking on the managing vacancy faced a significant challenge. Still, I knew I wanted the job.

When it was reported that I was in the running, many in the press wondered why I'd want to take on such a high-profile gamble. As I said, everything was going very well with my broadcasting career, which is something I had worked very hard at.

"It's because I'm a ballplayer," I said, when asked about my interest in the Jays job. "The attraction of competing again is there. It's always there."

I was 51 years old and eager to get back in the game.

When I spoke with Gord Ash about the position, I told him I believed that with some improvement on the mound, the team would have more success if they worked within a system that required a lot of communication, a lot of preparation and a lot of encouragement. I also told Gord that I believed that we needed to develop a team-first mentality again—a sense of pride in the uniform you wore and the city you played for—just like it was when I arrived in Toronto for the first time. We had that back when I played for Kansas City, and again when I played for Milwaukee. Through the mid-'80s in Toronto . . . boy, did we *ever* have it. Anyone who was watching in 1985 knows that.

But baseball had become an individualistic game. Players were more worried about their own stats than about wins. They were concerned more with what their agents thought than what their managers said. It was all about the bottom line—the game had become so money-conscious.

As a result, image was the most important thing. I understood that. I spoke with players regularly about the anxiety of always having to be concerned with image. I had hosted the Major League Baseball Rookie Career Development Program for several winters, trying to correct preconceived notions players might have before they made it to big leagues. "Players perceive that the media's against them," I told them. "They say, 'He's trying to make me look like a jerk.' I tell them, 'We make ourselves look like what we are. They're just reporting it.'"

That anxiety doesn't exist if players are playing the game because they love it. If you play with genuine enthusiasm for winning, every-thing else follows. I wanted to reintroduce that aspect of the game. Fun—what a concept! You look at guys like Robin Yount with the Brewers and George Brett with the Royals. They were competitors, but they had fun. Al Leiter was full of energy, always pounding his fist into his glove after a big pitch or a good play in the field. If only everybody interacted with teammates the way he did when he was on the mound. That's the way the game is meant to be played.

That's what I told Gord Ash. We needed to create an environment where winning would flourish! Gord believed I could provide that, because I possessed the most important "three Ps" in baseball: posi-tivity, perseverance and patience. I still believe that those are three key characteristics of leaders—and three key traits that a quality manager should possess.

I had several chats with Gord about my approach to specific situations—how I would handle them. And one of my last interviews was with a whole bunch of great baseball minds within the Jays organization—including legendary scouts Bobby Mattick, Al LaMacchia and Bob Engle—on the same subject. They'd ask questions like "What would you do if you had a guy who didn't run hard to first base?"

I thought of all the great managers I had played for and against, and tried to answer the way they would have.

"Well, I'd like to think that he would," I said. "But if he didn't, I'd like to think I could take him out of a game."

Of course, it's always easier said than done.

While I was in Seattle covering the ALCS between the Mariners and the Yankees, rumors swirled that I was in the running for the manager's job, along with Ernie Whitt, my old catching partner with the Jays, and Paul Molitor, the 1993 World Series MVP. I was talking to Gord throughout it all, and it looked like I had a very good chance of being given the job. With my years of experience in the game, I was confident that I had something valuable to bring to the job. But I didn't have experience as a manager, and of course, that made me nervous. I'd be up against established managers like Lou Piniella and Joe Torre, two of the best the game has ever seen.

During the series, I was walking near the visiting dugout at Safeco Field before one of the games. Someone gripped my neck from behind. It was Joe Torre. He asked if I was serious about this quest to lead the Blue Jays. I told him I was.

"I think you'd be great at it," Joe told me.

It gave me chills when he said that to me. I told him later that it meant more to me than anything anyone else had said leading up to my taking the position. I admired Torre so much. He was about to win his third straight World Series championship. I studied his management style, along with others, like Piniella. I wanted to keep learning from the best, just as I had throughout my careers as a player and broadcaster.

My commitments with ESPN at the time were set to take me right up to the end of the World Series. After that, I'd decided, I was ready to put down the microphone and put a jersey back on. I told Gord that I was all in.

In early November I officially accepted the job and became the eighth manager in the history of the Toronto Blue Jays. But as I mentioned, I was also the team's third manager in four seasons. At the time, I had a four-year contract with ESPN, so I insisted that any contract I sign with the Blue Jays be for the same term. I may be the only manager to ever get a four-year contract, first time out with no managerial experience whatsoever. Thankfully, it offered me some security from the revolving door that the position had become.

I could barely sleep for two days leading up to my first press conference. When I got to the podium, I couldn't help but get emotional. This was a dream job. As I faced the bright camera lights, my 23-year-old son, Casey, stood off to the side. He had been selected by the Jays in the 47th round of the amateur draft that year.

I teared up and had to compose myself.

"This," I said, when I finally found the words, "is a very happy day."

WE HAD A HELL of a team, I felt. We were on the verge of being a championship club. We just had to find a way to make 25 guys treat each and every game like it was the most important of the season. It was going to take a team effort, and I was surrounded by experienced hands that could make it happen. Our coaching staff was battle-tested. It included three former major-league managers. Cookie Rojas was our bench coach. He was a five-time All-Star who had managed the California Angels in 1988. Terry Bevington was our third-base coach. He had managed the White Sox from 1995 to 1997. We also brought back Cito

Gaston to work with our hitters. Mark Connor was our pitching coach and Garth Iorg was our first-base coach. It was a very experienced group, and I intended to utilize the collective wisdom. I wanted our team to be fun and emotional. I wanted to build trust with our players, to build a relationship that fostered a winning environment.

"Players are smart," I said during that first press conference. "You aren't going to fool them about stuff. I figure the best way to approach a player is to be honest with them, work with them and let them see where you're coming from. If I see something that I think is going to make a player better, then of course I'm going to let them know. But I'm going to tell him why I think that's the case and I'll listen to what they have to say about it. And at the end of the day, I might not agree with them. At the end you have to do what you think is right as the manager. But I will listen."

At first, my philosophy worked.

We opened the regular season in San Juan, at Hiram Bithorn Stadium, where I had played winter ball in the early 1970s. It was the first-ever major-league Opening Day to be held in Puerto Rico. The atmosphere at the game, played in front of more than 20,000 fans, was incredible, and it took me right back to those days. We cruised to an 8–1 win over the Texas Rangers and their star shortstop, Álex Rodríguez, who had just signed a record-breaking ten-year, $252 million contract in the off-season.

The momentum of the Puerto Rico trip carried through the first month of the season. We went 16–9. But the wheels fell off in May, when we went 10–18. By the trade deadline, we were ten games under .500 and had just been outscored, 30–5, in a three-game series with the New York Yankees.

The season had quickly become a write-off. While we managed a resurgence in the second half, it wasn't enough to make up for the ground we lost earlier. We finished 80–82 and third in the AL East.

When the season was over, Gord Ash was fired as the Jays' general manager. I knew my days were numbered. After Gord was released, team president Paul Godfrey and I met to have a private discussion.

At a press conference announcing that Gord had been fired, Godfrey said he wanted to set a new tone for the franchise. I knew this wasn't good for me. But I had been released three times as a player; I knew that the game could be harsh. Columnists and radio pundits were going to look at me and say, well, "He didn't improve on what we had. . . . He didn't make any dramatic differences in this team." I had thick skin. I had no problem handling that.

"It's important to understand that until and unless the entire organization is united in one goal, you're not going to have chemistry and enthusiasm," I told reporters after Godfrey's press conference. "You need one agenda set by the GM and the president. . . . Everybody has to be on the same page. You can't have divisions in the front office, on the field, or in the clubhouse. You have to abide by what the people in charge do. Paul Godfrey is in charge. And his challenge is to turn the organization around."

That November, J.P. Ricciardi was hired as the Jays' new general manager. He had been director of player personnel with the Oakland A's, where general manager Billy Beane was in the midst of his Moneyball movement.

I knew I was fired the first time I met him. It was just a matter of time.

THE 2002 SEASON STARTED rough. We went 8–18 through April. Our pitching staff was beat up. Chris Carpenter was the Opening Day starter in Boston, but he was hurt and went on the disabled list right after that start. Roy Halladay, Brandon Lyon, Scott Eyre, Brian Cooper and Luke Prokopec were the other starters to begin the season.

The press was all over us, suggesting that players had quit on the team. I defended them; I didn't think it was true. But we weren't playing together. We weren't on the same page. It didn't help that Ricciardi had made it clear that this wasn't really my team to begin with. In the middle of our difficult start, he announced publicly that my status with the team was "series to series."

The regime was much different under Ricciardi. Gord and I used to talk every night. We were on the same page. "What do you think about this, and how about that? Can that guy pitch?" That kind of communication is essential. But when J.P. came over to Toronto, there was no communication. Two or three times, he left me short a player by making transactions. In May we designated Homer Bush for assignment, and Darrin Fletcher sprained his ankle getting out of a cab at the ballpark. We called pitcher Scott Cassidy up from Syracuse, just a few days after we'd sent him down. I asked Ricciardi, "Do you realize we don't have enough players now?"

Ricciardi pulled the trigger in early June, after a three-game sweep of the Detroit Tigers that ended with my 100th win as the Blue Jays' manager. I was called up to the front office before the opening game of a three-game series against the Tampa Bay Devil Rays. Ricciardi told me, "We are going in another direction." And that was it!

I was replaced by third-base coach Carlos Tosca, whom J.P. had brought in along with John Gibbons, who was the new first-base coach. (Gibbons would become the manager in 2004, and would be fired in 2008 and rehired in 2013. In 2015 he led the Jays to the AL East title.)

It was a tough pill to swallow because we were in the middle of a winning streak, and I felt we were getting close to putting things together. But it just showed that my fate had already been sealed. It was his right to fire me and I understand—he was the new general manager and he was going to be judged on his record. He felt like he had a better solution to the situation. It didn't exactly turn out that way, but that's what he thought.

I didn't do any exit interviews. It wasn't an amicable split. I was so distraught at the way it ended that I didn't want anything to do with any of the platitudes that often follow the firing of a manager. There was nothing positive to say, so I didn't say anything at all. Being fired didn't catch me off guard, but it did hurt.

Looking back many years later, I realized I was poorly prepared and didn't come close to managing the way I had anticipated I would. It is the toughest time in professional sports to lead teams, unless you have a roster loaded with homegrown talent that plays hard day in and day out for each other. Managers like Bruce Bochy, Ned Yost, Mike Matheny and Joe Girardi have long-term relationships with their GMs, and that is vital to their success.

It took me a long time to get over the firing. I was deeply embarrassed by what had happened. I also felt that the relationships I had built with the organization and the community had been taken away from me. I felt like I didn't complete the job, that I didn't do what I had wanted to do and was capable of doing. In the end, though, it was nobody else's fault but my own.

I don't think I stepped on the field at SkyDome (later the Rogers Centre) for three years after that.

In the years that followed my tenure as manager, I spent a lot of time reflecting on what I could have done better.

In retrospect I was ill prepared for the job. At the time, I thought it was something I could do. It was something I *wanted* to do. I knew the Blue Jays better than anyone—I had been doing the broadcasts since 1987. Managing was an opportunity to get back down on the field and prove that I still had something to offer. There was no question about wanting to do it. But it had been 15 years since I was on the field. The culture of the game had changed. And to adapt, I lowered my standards.

I didn't have the experience to manage the way I wanted to. I let things go rather than standing up for my beliefs—for the way I knew the team should be run. Too many people on the outside influenced me. "You can't do that. . . . Players won't accept that." I allowed those voices to take me away from my philosophy of the game.

When I first agreed to sign, Gord Ash was as good a GM as anyone could have had in that situation. He brought me up to speed on the whole organization. I remember he gave me a binder with everybody's contract, the number of options they had, what their arbitration status was, how long they had been signed for. So I knew the organization from the non-baseball side of things and who was involved. He introduced me to all the people who made things happen on that side of the franchise. Even though I'd been around, I didn't know them on that level.

But you know, there were so many scouts and managers and coaches in the minors that I had known forever.

In my second year as manager, I should have insisted on having more input on the roster, on the players we picked up. Under Ricciardi, we added players to the team that I knew weren't a good fit. But I didn't want to speak up under a new general manager. Instead, I decided to go with the flow. And in the end, I lost control.

I thought back to my interview for the Jays position, when I sat across from guys like Mattick, LaMacchia and Bob Engle and told them that I would be an assertive manager who would demand that our players live up to the standard of effort the Blue Jays demanded. That's what Whitey Herzog had done with Garry Templeton, and what Billy Martin had done with Reggie Jackson. It's what Bobby Cox was doing with Andruw Jones. Those managers had an impact, not only on those particular players but on the mindset of the entire team. And you know what? I never got to that point.

We had Kevin Cash in camp as a young catcher. I thought he could be a good, everyday player. He had a good spring with the bat and was growing at the position, but Ricciardi didn't want his arbitration clock to start ticking. We had Ken Huckaby in camp as well. He could really catch, but he was sent to the minors out of spring training. We called him up for a short time on May 8 but designated him for assignment two weeks later. He cleared waivers, went to the minors and came back to the Jays the day after I was fired. Another pitcher I wanted out of spring training was Chris Baker, who reminded me of Pat Hentgen— but again we ran into the ticking clock for arbitration.

There were times when I wanted to take players out of the lineup, and I knew it was the right thing to do, but I just didn't do it, and I knew it was wrong not to. I didn't have the experience or the backing to make the call. My inaction jeopardized my authority over the team. That's something any manager has to worry about these days, with players making the money they do. But the best managers still find a way to lead—to be in complete control, with everyone on the roster buying into the team's system. That's where I failed.

There were a lot of veteran players on the Jays' roster while I was manager. We had Raúl Mondesí and Carlos Delgado. These guys were stars. Alex Gonzalez, Tony Batista, Brad Fullmer, José Cruz Jr., Shannon

Stewart—this was an established lineup, one with potential. I came in just hoping to bring it all together. I tried to find ways to get the best out of them. What I needed to do was to set the standard: *This* is the way the Blue Jays are going to play the game. We were going to play sound fundamentals. We were going to execute.

And we started out on that path, but then I got so much resistance. I never managed to do exactly what needed to be done. I tried to run drills in the infield—basic but important stuff. We worked on utilizing the cutoff man and a system for backing each other up on defense. The players hated it, and some of them complained.

During a round of infield drills one day, one of the players asked me why they were being punished.

"How are we punishing you?" I asked him.

"Well, we had to do cutoffs and relays today," he said.

"That's not punishing," I said. "We're not very good at it!"

But that was the mindset they had. It was like: "Well, the Yankees don't do that . . ." Yeah, well, the Yankees were winning championships. We weren't.

This was the sort of stuff we had to deal with all the time. And I kept thinking, "Really? *That's* what you're worried about?" They felt they had attained a status where they didn't have to cover the basics. That has become standard—nobody takes infield now. It's gone. And the game has suffered because of it.

It's remarkable how we've allowed players to dictate what we do with teams.

It has been a progression. I did it when I was managing, and I know it's an industry-wide issue today. Teams listen to the players *too* much, instead of management saying, "This is what we're going to do." I've discussed this many times with some of the game's great minds. Pat

Gillick, the architect of the Jays' glory days, shares my feelings. "We are not as demanding of the players as we should be and we used to be," he says.

I remember Danny Murtaugh, the great Pittsburgh Pirates second baseman who went on to become their manager, sitting on the cage during batting practice, watching his team hit. When Roberto Clemente, Manny Sanguillén and others weren't hitting the ball well, he'd kick them out of the cage. These were Hall of Famers! But today we don't want to hurt anyone's feelings.

It happened to me.

We had Mondesí, Delgado and Stewart in the lineup. I wanted to have Stewart hit third, with Delgado batting cleanup and Mondesí fifth. Stewart was our best hitter and got on base all the time. But Delgado wasn't driving in runs very well, and neither was Mondesí. I sat in my office in the SkyDome, telling Mondesí what I was thinking of doing. He seemed receptive. Then we brought Stewart in, and they both agreed to do it. Everything seemed fine. They didn't raise any objections to the move. After they left my office, I took off my uniform and hopped in the shower. As I was drying off, I got a call from Gord Ash.

"Boy, you've pissed everybody off now," he said.

"What do you mean?" I asked.

Mondesí and Stewart had both called their agents after they left the office and complained about the moves I was making. They didn't tell me to my face. The agents called our general manager, who passed the concerns along to me.

I couldn't believe it.

I learned a lot about myself after my time managing the Blue Jays. I realized where my strengths and weaknesses are. I had thought that my patience, positivity and perseverance would give me an edge as a manager. But I didn't account for just how much the game had changed. There is a lot I would do differently if I could go back and do it all again. I'd have been tougher with the players. I'd have hammered home a stronger team philosophy—one that centered on the *team*. At least that's what I'd like to think I would do. But I also know that managers today face a whole new world of challenges. The job is tougher than it has ever been. It's not negative; it's just a different challenge.

That's why I have such respect for guys like the Cubs' Joe Maddon, the Orioles' Buck Showalter, the Giants' Bruce Bochy, the Cardinals' Mike Matheny and the Angels' Mike Scioscia. They are all old-school managers who understand the challenges faced in the modern era. They aren't afraid to bench a star. And their players respect them for it. That's a fine balance. They are also the face of the franchise in front of the media. They answer for their players—they take the heat. They know the Xs and Os of the game, but also the intangible elements that so many people seem to want to discount these days. Each is the kind of manager who is as valuable as any player on a team. They hold everything together.

During the 2014 season, young Blue Jays outfielder Kevin Pillar reacted with a bit of a tantrum when he was pulled from a game for a pinch-hitter. It was a big mistake. John Gibbons didn't take too kindly to his attitude. Kevin was demoted to Buffalo and drove with his father to Triple-A, on what he described as the worst drive of his life. He didn't know if he would ever be back. But he learned his lesson. Embarrassing as the demotion might have been, it was a critical moment for Pillar. He returned to the Jays in 2015 as the consummate team player. He earned his spot in center field by playing incredible defense. Having been a great hitter in the minors, Pillar had been frustrated by his lack of opportunities to prove himself at a major-league plate. But when he made himself indispensable in the field, he finally had regular opportunities to show how valuable he could be when it came to rounding out the Jays' batting order. He became one of the young leaders in the Jays' roster.

Pillar's great 2015 campaign can be traced back to his outburst and demotion in 2014. It takes leadership to make those calls, and that's exactly what John Gibbons showed. Gibbons was also a big influence in insisting that the makeup of the Jays' roster had to be changed. He told Alex Anthopoulos that the team needed a major face-lift. To his credit, Anthopoulos finally began to understand "what a winning player looked like," as Troy Tulowitzki later commented.

My time in the Jays dugout taught me to look at the game differently. It got me thinking about the bigger picture. Not just how the game is managed, but how a quality franchise is developed.

People often ask me if I would consider managing again. My answer is always no. I had my chance. It was an important part of my career. These days, I love sitting up in the booth, sharing the game with all of you.

17

WHAT WE CAN LEARN FROM
GEORGE STEINBRENNER'S YANKEES

Before George Steinbrenner bought a share of the Yankees in 1973, the organization had become an abysmal mess. They had lost everything that Casey Stengel had developed as manager through the 1950s.

As the Yankees' manager, Stengel won five consecutive World Series championships between 1949 and 1953, and then won again in '56 and '58. (He also won the 1923 World Series as an outfielder with the Dodgers.) He was nicknamed the Old Professor because of his wit and remarkable knowledge about the game. He was at the helm of one of the most famous dynasties in the game, when the Yankees boasted the likes of Joe DiMaggio, Phil Rizzuto, Yogi Berra, Whitey Ford and Mickey Mantle, to name a few.

As manager, Stengel developed a distinct identity for the Yankees. Tony Kubek, the great broadcaster—a mentor of mine—grew up in the Yankees system in the 1950s before emerging as the American League Rookie of the Year in 1957, when he helped the Yankees to the World Series, which they lost to the Brewers. (New York would get revenge over the Braves in the 1958 World Series, this time winning in seven. It was the Yankees' second championship in three years.)

Kubek clearly recalls how Stengel and the Yankees developed a distinct culture that reflected what it meant to be part of the organization, regardless of where you sat on the hierarchy of players and prospects.

Stengel held a camp in advance of spring training every year. He brought all the first- and second-year big-leaguers in the Yankees organization—every manager, every coach, every scout—down to St. Petersburg, Florida, for the first of February each year. He focused primarily on about 50 young players. If you had only been in the big leagues for a year or two, you'd likely be required to attend.

Stengel had an offensive routine and a defensive routine, each of which was applied throughout the organization by all the managers, coaches, training staff and players.

You wouldn't hit during his offensive routine. The Yankees had a hitting instructor for that. Instead, everyone sat in the clubhouse, and he went over what they should look for from their opponents, what their strengths and weaknesses were. Then he would take the players out to the dugout—one step closer to the field—where he went over the signs and explained what he wanted his players to be looking for in the other team, assessing their strengths and weaknesses while they played. Then they moved to the batter's box, into the perspective of being on deck. He'd tell his players that he wanted them to be watching what the outfielders were doing, where they were playing—getting a sense of their defensive coverage. Then he would put a runner on first, second and third base and show his players exactly how he wanted them to take the lead: how many steps to take, which foot to put first, what angle to take toward the next base—all of the details that could give the baserunner an edge.

After taking his team through every aspect of his offensive plan, Stengel showed them how he wanted them to play defense. Not just playing the hitter according to what the pitcher might throw and how the batter has hit before, but playing him according to the situation in the count. Stengel always wanted his players to be thinking ahead. If they were playing first or second base or shortstop, he wanted them to be prepared for everything, so he ran through all the possible plays that could be made in any given scenario. Stengel wanted his guys to know where to play to be in the cutoff position every time. He wanted this knowledge to be ingrained in his players, whether they were in the minor leagues or the big leagues. He'd run through these drills with the players almost every day in the spring. Something that never happens today.

The Yankees lost the 1960 World Series to the Pittsburgh Pirates after Bill Mazeroski hit his famous home run over the left-field wall in the ninth inning of game seven. The Yankees lost the series, but they outscored the Pirates, 55–27; outhit them, .338 to .256; and outhomered them, 10–4. But still, Stengel was fired. He was forced out as the Yankees' manager after the loss because he was deemed too old for the position. He is reported to have said that he was fired for turning 70, and that he'd never make that mistake again.

The Yankees had success for a few years after Stengel left, including the historic campaign in 1961 when Roger Maris hit 61 home runs. They won the World Series that year. They repeated the following season, making it ten world championships in 16 years. The Yankees won the American League pennant again in 1963 and '64, making their fourth and fifth consecutive World Series appearances, but losing both times. After that the Yankees' success ran dry. CBS purchased the team in 1964, launching the franchise into nearly a decade of mediocrity.

The Yankees were affected by the advent of the amateur draft in 1965, which meant that they could no longer outbid teams for young talent as they had done for years. (The Yankees also often purchased young players from the Kansas City Athletics.) Instead, the Yankees would have to draft according to their standing in the league the previous season. And because they didn't have a top-notch farm system, and no longer had Stengel to dictate the real Yankees Way, the team's talent pool dried up. The players New York did draft weren't properly developed, so there was no one to replace the Yankees' aging stars.

New York had some awful years. I remember going to Yankee Stadium when there were just 8,500 people in the stands. The team was no good, so the fans wouldn't go.

Of course, Steinbrenner had his share of quirks, and he made his share of enemies, but he knew what he wanted his franchise to look like. When Charlie Finley owned the Oakland A's, he was a rogue, but what was he doing? Winning. Similarly, when Steinbrenner was a rogue and everybody hated him, what was he doing? Dominating the game. Everybody has always hated the Yankees. Why? Because they've wanted to stand out; they've wanted to be the best.

Steinbrenner came in and raised the standards. He made the Yankees better. There were things that seemed silly along the way, like making players shave their moustaches and cut their hair (over which he went to war with Don Mattingly). He also wanted the players to wear their pants a specific length, so their stirrups were visible. But it was part of a process. Steinbrenner wanted his players to look and act like a team. He didn't want individuals. He wanted a team, playing for the uniform.

Steinbrenner's background, after all, was in football. He was an assistant to Ohio State Buckeyes coach Woody Hayes in the early '50s, when that team was undefeated, won the Rose Bowl and was named the national champion by the Associated Press. Steinbrenner was later an assistant coach for the football teams at Northwestern University and Purdue University. Like Branch Rickey, Steinbrenner approached baseball with many of the principles found in football.

I remember interviewing Derek Jeter for *Baseball This Morning* on XM Satellite Radio after the Yankees had won their fourth championship in five years. Jeter and "The Boss" had developed a close relationship. Steinbrenner wanted to win more than anything; he and Jeter had that in common. Steinbrenner identified Jeter as the kind of player who had what it took to be a champion for a very long time. And Jeter quickly came to respect Steinbrenner's thirst for winning. "He's got the old football mentality where you have to win every single day," Jeter told me. "Sometimes, in 162 games, it's tough to do."

It *is* tough to do. But that mentality permeated the Yankees, especially in the late '90s, when they were led by Jeter and a homegrown core of stars like Andy Pettitte, Jorge Posada, Bernie Williams and Mariano Rivera. All of them were developed within a system that emphasized the way Steinbrenner wanted his team to play. Jeter, Posada, Rivera and Pettitte became known as the Core Four. These were homegrown players who learned under the Steinbrenner policy that winning the World Series was the only thing that mattered. Anything less than a World Series trophy was a failure in the Boss's eyes. That attitude disappeared with the passing of George Steinbrenner.

Sometimes, it seems that it takes a larger-than-life, eccentric personality like Steinbrenner to set the tone for how an organization will be run. But I don't necessarily think that has to be the case. For all of the Boss's quirks, he had a clear sense of how he wanted his Yankees to conduct themselves on and off the field. He wanted there to be pride in the pinstripe uniform. And he certainly achieved that.

I believe that any team that wants to win has to create a clear culture, a distinct way of doing things, that helps shape the team's identity. A team can't be made up of individuals with their own approach to the game. It has to be unified. It has to be cohesive. In his own way, George Steinbrenner helped create that environment with the Yankees. When you look back at the great teams in the game's history, most are rooted in some kind of identity. It may not require trimming a mullet or shaving off a moustache, but it does require a set of expectations for how your players approach the game, approach the team and, in many ways, approach life.

18

WHAT IS THE BRAVES' SECRET SAUCE MADE OF?

After building the Kansas City Royals team that won the world championship in 1985, John Schuerholz took a job as the general manager of the Atlanta Braves in 1990. Schuerholz, remember, learned the trade from Harry Dalton, Frank Cashen and Lou Gorman. He carried the same principles of building a franchise with him that he learned with the Orioles in the 1960s and the Royals in the 1970s.

Under Schuerholz's leadership, the Braves won the World Series in 1995 and won their division 14 times. A big part of the Braves' success was the leadership of Bobby Cox as manager. As I discussed earlier, I experienced Cox's incredible talent as a manager with the Blue Jays. He returned to Atlanta in 1986 in a general manager's role. Through those three years with Cox as GM, the Braves were abysmal. In 1988 they lost

106 games! But the system was changing from within. In the late '80s the Braves picked up young stars like Tom Glavine, Steve Avery, Pete Smith, David Justice and Chipper Jones (who was drafted in 1990). They were multitalented athletes who could play on both sides of the ball. Pitching and defense were always a major focus. The Braves were building a winner.

The Braves brought in Schuerholz to take over as GM after the 1990 season, giving Cox the ability to jump back into the manager's job, from which he could guide his team to success on the field. The pieces were in place. Schuerholz had done his due diligence before joining the Braves. He was watching what they were doing from afar, and he liked what he saw. The Braves had committed themselves to scouting and development, which was encouraging for a guy like Schuerholz, who believed that both were fundamental to building a great franchise. Schuerholz had seen this in Baltimore and Kansas City and now was implementing it in Atlanta.

"Homegrown players are the secret sauce," Schuerholz says. "Good players are necessary—you can be a good team [and be] a championship team—but homegrown players are really the secret sauce, because you see them grow up, you see how they handle success and adversity, you see their character, you see their clarity of thought, you see their bounceback, you see their commitment, you see all of that."

With a homegrown core, Schuerholz used trades and free agency to pick up pieces that bolstered the Braves' defense. That was the philosophy—pitching and defense were the primary focus. He picked up Terry Pendleton, Rafael Belliard, Sid Bream and Otis Nixon. He wanted a quarterback at catcher, a veteran presence who could help his young, talented pitching staff. He signed veteran Mike Heath for the position, but he didn't work out. The catching job would belong to Greg Olson and then Damon Berryhill, before homegrown Javy López took over the job in time for the Braves' 1995 championship.

Schuerholz focused on building a strong defense behind his pitching staff because he knew that they would be more confident if they were convinced that the team on the field would be able to back them up. The Braves' pitchers could rely on the fact that if the ball was hit, a play was going to be made. It was a lot like the Earl Weaver Orioles and the Whitey Herzog Kansas City Royals.

LEO MAZZONE WAS ONE of the most renowned pitching coaches in the game, having worked in the Atlanta Braves organization for more than two decades. He is credited for helping develop one of the most dangerous trios of pitchers in the game: Tom Glavine, John Smoltz and Greg Maddux. Mazzone was a student of Johnny Sain, who was a pitcher with the Milwaukee Braves along with Warren Spahn, and who later won three world championships with the Yankees. As a coach he worked with the Yankees as they won three straight pennants from 1961 to 1963, and he helped Whitey Ford retool his pitching motion. Ford had career seasons with Sain's help. Sain also coached with the Minnesota Twins, where he worked with a starting staff that included Mudcat Grant, Jim Kaat and Jim Perry. In his first year, the Twins won their first American League pennant. Then he moved on to the Detroit Tigers, helping them win a World Series.

Mazzone taught with a philosophy based on what he had learned from Sain. It was a very simple theory, one that makes all the sense in the world: On his first pitch, Sain advised, a pitcher should throw at 80 percent effort, aiming for the middle of the plate. Strike one. On the second pitch he should choose one half of the plate and throw at 90 percent effort. Strike two. On the third pitch he should throw at 100 percent effort, biting a corner. Strike three.

What many of our pitchers do in this generation is throw at 100 percent effort on the first pitch, trying to make it perfect. Ball one. Then they'll go at 90 percent effort, aiming for half the plate. Ball two. Then they have to throw a strike, so they're throwing for the whole plate at 85 percent effort. Instead of working from the inside out, they work from the outside in. They are pitching backwards.

For pitchers to have success, they need to get ahead in the count. When you look at the pitchers who throw first-pitch strikes, they're always among the best in baseball. First-pitch fastball, with a little movement. Or a first-pitch breaking ball. But *always* a strike. It's a simple philosophy.

But the formula has changed so much because of the information that is available. Everyone is overthinking. Hitters stand up and they know everything about the guy they are facing. They know what he throws, how he throws it, how fast it is and how often he throws it. Well, sometimes while you're calculating all that in your head, it's strike one. Then if he throws you something that he doesn't throw often, you get messed up completely. "He never does that. How come he did that?" Oops, strike two.

Hitters have so much information that they get overwhelmed instead of just seeing the ball and reacting to it. But instead of taking advantage of that, pitchers are often just as guilty of overcalculating and thinking too much. Yogi Berra always said, "You can't think and hit!"

Look at what Mark Buehrle always did on the mound. He worked incredibly fast, so hitters never had time to think at all. It was effective. Buehrle would pitch and pitch and pitch, and the hitter never had time to think about what he had seen on the video of Buehrle that he had watched the night before. Buehrle just didn't give him the chance. He'd give up a lot of hits because of this approach, but he also went deep into games. Before 2015 he had pitched at least 200 innings in 14 straight seasons; he missed doing it a 15th time by only an inning and a third.

This was how Mazzone and Sain taught pitching. Maddux pitched like Buehrle. Glavine pitched like Buehrle. They worked fast and they were efficient. They threw a lot of strikes. When you look at the major-league leaders in fewest pitches per inning pitched, they're among the best pitchers in baseball. The best pitchers don't waste a lot of pitches. In 2015 the most efficient pitchers were Bartolo Colón (13.9 pitches per inning), Mark Buehrle (14.2), Mike Leake (14.3), John Lackey (14.3), Zack Greinke (14.5), Clayton Kershaw (14.6), Max Scherzer (14.7), Corey Kluber (14.7), Erasmo Ramírez (14.7), Matt Harvey (14.8) and Sonny Gray (14.8). Jake Arrieta and Dallas Keuchel, the Cy Young Award winners, were next, at 15.0 and 15.1. There were lots of wins in that list! At the other end of the spectrum, there were five pitchers who averaged more than 17 pitches per inning: Hector Santiago, Yovani Gallardo, Lance Lynn, Ian Kennedy and Chris Tillman.

The best pitchers keep it simple. They throw strikes. They get hit sometimes, but they trust the team behind them. They don't worry about groundballs or fly balls. They know that their team has the defense to make the play. You can't overstate how important that is. When a team is built on a strong defense—the backbone of any successful club—a pitcher can keep it simple because he knows that, no matter what, he can trust the support behind him. What does that do to a pitcher's mindset? He actually *wants* the batter to hit the ball. And if batters are making contact more often, the pitcher is throwing less—and he's pitching later into the game, giving his team a better chance of winning. What a concept! If I stay out on the field longer, my team's going to have more opportunities to score runs for me. So as a pitcher, that's what I want to do. Look at how the Blue Jays' pitchers improved in 2015 with Donaldson at third, Pillar in center field, Martin and Navarro behind the plate, and eventually Goins at second, Tulowitzki at shortstop and Ben Revere in left. The pitchers had total confidence in the defense and weren't afraid to throw strikes.

And you know, there are a couple of things that have corrupted the game almost beyond repair: the radar gun and a statistic called the quality start. They have ruined how we evaluate pitchers. Tommy John once described the radar gun as a tool to give the uninformed another way to evaluate. We get very excited when a pitcher throws 98 miles per hour. But is it a quality pitch? Is Brandon Morrow's 98 the same as Aaron Sanchez's 98? Not even close. Sanchez has tremendous movement on his fastball, while Morrow's might be hard but is relatively straight. The movement on Edinson Volquez's fastball during the postseason in 2015 was the root of his success. Hall of Famer Tom Seaver identifies the three components of pitching: movement, velocity and location—with velocity being the least important. Marco Estrada and Mark Buehrle both know a little something about that.

PITCHING AND DEFENSE FORM the backbone of any good organization. Schuerholz has never forgotten that, though in the last decade he admits that the Braves lost sight of what made them great, and the consequences have been a few rough years in a row.

As president of the Braves today, Schuerholz has steered the organization back towards its roots, focusing on scouting and development. In September 2014 he reconfigured his front office. He fired general manager Frank Wren and brought in his longtime friend, veteran baseball man John Hart. "We really reconstituted our amateur scouting program," says Schuerholz. "We reconstituted our Latin American program, our international scouting programs—we have refocused on how major-league teams have to be built. . . . Everybody's enthused and energized and going in the same direction and getting back to being the old Braves again. That's our goal."

Don't bet against him. Despite a dismal year in 2015, it won't be long before the Braves are back on top with a team built on the tried-and-true principles that Schuerholz grew up with.

19

HOW THE ROYALS ARE CARRYING
ON AN OLD BUT EFFECTIVE PHILOSOPHY

The Kansas City Royals were a surprise contender in 2014. They earned a wild-card playoff spot and made it all the way to the World Series, where they lost to the San Francisco Giants (the NL wild-card team) in seven games. The success of the Royals that season followed nearly a decade of terrible results, in which they posted nine straight losing seasons—including three consecutive 100-loss seasons. The turnaround began when Dayton Moore was hired as general manager in 2006. Building the Royals into a winning organization took a lot of time and patience. And, yes, a lot of losing.

Moore developed as a baseball executive under John Schuerholz with the Atlanta Braves, whom he joined as a scout in 1994. He went on to become the Braves' assistant director of scouting, assistant director of player development and director of international scouting. Later, Moore became the Braves' director of player personnel before he was named the team's assistant general manager in 2005.

Asked to name the traits that made the Braves franchise successful, Moore says several stand out in his mind. The first is that the people in the organization, from top to bottom, were selfless.

"It was truly about what's best for the Atlanta Braves," says Moore. "No minor-league manager or hitting coach or pitching coach was overly concerned [about] whether they were in Double A, Triple A or Short Season A." (Short Season is made up of summer Rookie-league teams. The schedule starts after the June draft and generally consists of 60 games.)

Under the direction of Paul Snyder, who was in charge of the Braves' farm and scouting systems for years, Atlanta put coaches where he felt they best suited the players coming up through the organization. He would sometimes move them from level to level, along with the players they had been working with, to make sure there was some consistency in the players' development. At the top of it all, the team's executives had complete trust in the way Bobby Cox operated as manager. The Braves created a consistent atmosphere that way.

It wasn't just the coaches throughout the organization who were expected to be selfless. It was the players too. If a player didn't fit into the system, the Braves had no qualms about getting rid of him. If a player had a hard time adjusting his approach to the game so that it was in line with what Cox wanted—which meant giving 100 percent all the time, whether in the middle of a game or in fielding practice— there was no question that he'd be gone. If you were part of the Braves organization, you did what was best for the organization—otherwise, you'd play elsewhere. It created a very strong, distinct culture throughout the organization.

During his time with the Braves, Moore soaked in the wisdom of the great baseball minds around him. Among them he credits scouts Donnie Williams and Bill Lajoie with teaching him so much about the game when he first joined the organization. Every morning, Moore would try to get to the office before Paul Snyder, but he never could. He'd sit in Snyder's office as the boss chewed cigars and drank Diet Coke, and they'd evaluate and break down all the players in the Braves organization. In spring training Moore would sit with José Martínez, who was with the Royals through the '80s and worked in the Braves front office with Schuerholz. They'd talk about baseball every night, with Moore specifically taking in Martinez's insights on Latin players. (Player development doesn't just happen.) Their conversations always seemed to come back to the same idea: You wanted guys who loved to play the game, had the tools to play it and understood the rhythm of it.

It was a lesson that Bobby Cox himself stressed with the Braves' scouts. During one of his first meetings with the organization, Moore remembers Cox telling them to make sure, when assessing talent, that they also considered a player's ability to understand what it takes to win. That's an intangible quality that doesn't show up in a score sheet, but it's equally important. Cox said a world championship team needs role players like Jeff Blauser and Mark Lemke, who understand the rhythm of a major-league baseball season and understand how to win. Players who may not be superstars, but who, in the eighth inning with a one-run lead, will turn the tough double play to get out of a jam. The kinds of players who always advance the runner with a good at-bat. Players who never make mental mistakes. They are like gold; you can always count on them. On the current Jays roster you can see those kinds of traits developing in young infielders like Ryan Goins and Devon Travis.

When Moore left the Braves to take on the job of general manager of the Royals, he brought the same culture and mentality with him to Kansas City. He set out to build a winning franchise that was founded on homegrown players and focused on pitching and defense. He wanted to develop the prospects that were already in the Royals system, and he wanted to discover more talent. He wanted to reintroduce a Royals Way of playing the game.

By the time the Royals started winning again, the team's core was mostly homegrown. Billy Butler, Alex Gordon, Salvador Pérez, Mike Moustakas and Jarrod Dyson were all homegrown players. On the mound the Royals had developed Yordano Ventura, Danny Duffy, Greg Holland and Kelvin Herrera. The Royals also had success making use of their homegrown ace, Zack Greinke, whom they traded to the Milwaukee Brewers in 2010 for key pieces in shortstop Alcides Escobar and center fielder Lorenzo Cain, along with pitchers Jeremy Jeffress and Jake Odorizzi, who was spun to the Rays for James Shields and the monster closer Wade Davis.

The basis of Moore's approach was to develop a team that could win. He wanted to build a sense of pride and unity within the organization. He wanted to develop an identity. "I think the way you do that is you get a group of players and you raise them your way," says Moore. Paul Snyder would always say that the Braves wanted to raise their own, Moore says. They didn't mind inexperienced high school players, because they planned to develop them their way. The Braves would still look to get a talented college player, but if they could get a prospect while he was young, they knew they could mold him in the Braves Way.

"I think that's what you saw with our group," Moore says. "We tried to get a group of players from day one, teach them to respect the game, respect their teammates, respect the umpires, respect the community, and we started from day one, when they would get in the minor leagues, get involved with the community service. It's about the fans." The Royals acknowledge that so many of the team's comebacks, especially at home in Kauffman Stadium, were fueled by the support of their great fan base.

That's an important point, because one of the frustrating things that Moore realized when he first arrived in Kansas City was that the organization had lost a generation of fans. When he saw grandparents arrive at the ballpark in his first few years with the Royals, he'd see them wearing Amos Otis, Willie Wilson or Frank White jerseys. But their grandkids all wore hats for teams like the Yankees or the Boston Red Sox. "We knew for us to get that [generation of fans] back, we had to start winning games. Kids want to be associated with winners."

Moore had learned that lesson in Atlanta, where through the '90s it seemed that every boy wanted to be Chipper Jones when he grew up. It was a sense of community connection that stretched back to Ewing Kauffman's goal when he founded the Kansas City Royals.

After the Royals' World Series run in 2014, and after finishing first in the American League and winning the World Series in 2015, it's safe to say that the Royals have won back their fan base. If you go to a game in Kansas City today, you'll see kids in Salvador Pérez jerseys and wearing Royals caps. And Moore is looking at the long-term connection to the city. He took local prospect Bubba Starling with the fifth-overall pick, straight out of high school, in the 2011 draft.

"If a guy like Bubba Starling makes it, every kid in Kansas City is going to look at it and say, 'You know, what, I want to be like Bubba, I want to play,'" says Moore.

ONE OF THE REASONS that Moore has had success with the Royals lately is because he had the sense to stand back and let his prospects mature and develop. When he was with the Braves, he was taught to not even look at a player's stats for the first two years of his minor-league career. It sounds crazy today, when statistical analysis measures every angle of a player's development. But the philosophy was to not worry about what a prospect does during his first stint in Short Season A, or what he does during his first run in A-ball.

Statistical analysis has always been part of the game. It's true that baseball has always been a game of numbers. The numbers are more accessible now, and in some cases they measure the game in new and interesting ways. In other cases they represent pure nonsense. Stats may help validate a scout's perspective on a player, or perhaps identify a talent that everyone has overlooked. But too often, teams are making snap judgments on players based solely on the numbers.

"We really don't know, when a player goes from A-Ball to Double A to Triple A and certainly the major leagues, how they're going to adjust as a hitter," says Moore. "Because they've never faced that level of competition and they only know what they know."

Baseball has to be careful as an industry, says Moore, that it doesn't give up on players who are top-notch athletes just because their numbers don't work out right away. Players need time to develop.

Because the culture of how we view players these days has changed, it's a challenge for scouts to have the freedom to discover unpolished talent the way they used to. When we evaluate for showcase skills, we don't see the whole picture. It has become hard to spot the talents of— as Cox said—a Blauser or a Lemke, because players are being evaluated in a different, less complete way.

You have to give young players a chance to fail. A successful pro knows how to manage failure. But if we don't give prospects the opportunity to put up bad numbers and figure it out along the way, we actually skip an important step in their development as ballplayers. At the same time, the current system doesn't teach young players how to be part of a team. In the showcase-skill era we have players who learn to focus only on making their pitches, getting their hits, making their plays—but they don't have any idea of how to do that within a team context.

"I've learned that, until players can play fearless and just play for the team, they can't really reach their ceiling because they are just focused on themselves," says Moore. "That's what the showcase events are telling our kids . . . but until those players learn to just play for the team, do anything they can each and every night to help the team win, I think they're always going to be swimming upstream."

When he was rising through the Royals system as a highly touted prospect, Alex Gordon had to learn not to worry about what he was accomplishing as an individual. Royals fans wanted him to be the next George Brett. But he realized that all he needed to do was focus on what would help the team win. He needed to do whatever he could to be a great teammate, and not a great individual player. That realization took the pressure off of him, says Moore.

It also made him a better player.

In fact, one of the things that Moore regrets during his time as the Royals' general manager is that he didn't acquire enough veteran players who understand the importance of teamwork. "I could have done a much better job, probably, of trying to get the Raúl Ibañezes around this group of players, and the Josh Willinghams and the Jamey Carrolls a little sooner than I did," he says. "Looking back on it, I would have probably tried to add one or two of those guys a little sooner and maybe kept a young player in the minor leagues an extra six weeks." In 2015 Moore brought in Jonny Gomes to be that guy.

Reflecting on it now, Moore is reminded of what one of his scouting mentors, Bill Lajoie, once told him: "If you think a pitcher is ready for the major leagues, give it another month. If you think your hitter is ready for the major leagues, give him 50 to 75 more at-bats. You'd rather break him in a month too late than a month too early."

Still, Dayton Moore's philosophy in Kansas City has worked. He stuck with the approach, enduring several losing seasons and loads of criticism before the Royals emerged as World Series contenders. He built a team with a distinct identity, a tough and competitive personality, built on the backs of homegrown players and bolstered by intelligent signings. He came to the Royals Way, via the Braves Way, which descended from an earlier generation of the Royals Way, its roots all the way back in the Baltimore Orioles of the 1960s.

20

HOW ALEX ANTHOPOULOS
RETOOLED THE JAYS

Born and raised in Montreal, Alex Anthopoulos became the general manager of the Blue Jays when he was just 33 years old. He was learning then, and he hasn't stopped learning since.

Alex was a Montreal boy who didn't care much for baseball at an early age. He had taken over his father's air conditioning company when a friend insisted he join him for an Expos game. Alex was intrigued by the experience and wanted to find out more about the game. He didn't mess around. He called the Expos' GM, Jim Beattie, to inquire about working for the team. When Beattie actually answered, Alex was so surprised that he hung up. Eventually, he would begin working as an intern with the team, and over time he worked his way into scouting. The rest is history.

I sat down with him to chat about his philosophy on the game during spring training in 2015, just as he was in the midst of orchestrating one of the most remarkable series of moves that baseball has seen in quite some time.

In 2014, despite leading the American League East as late as July 3, the Blue Jays had finished third in the division with a record of 83–79. It was 21 years since the team had last reached the postseason—and when Kansas City nabbed a wild-card berth, it meant Toronto owned the longest postseason drought in the majors.

On paper the Jays looked like a team that should have been a playoff contender. But they just didn't seem to have all the right pieces. Manager John Gibbons said that the roster needed revamping with more athletic, energetic players—and Anthopoulos finally saw the light. So, in the dreary month of November, he made two bold moves that changed the course of a franchise that seemed to have reached the ceiling of its once-promising potential.

Conventional wisdom suggested that Anthopoulos would want to shop around for an ace on the mound and add a replacement in left field for Melky Cabrera, who was clearly on his way out as a free agent. Instead, he initiated two transactions that, on the surface, didn't seem to directly address the immediate needs of the franchise.

First, he signed veteran catcher Russell Martin to a five-year, $82 million deal. Martin was born in Toronto and grew up in Montreal, so he certainly had some Canadian appeal for Jays fans. He was also one of the best catchers in the game, both offensively and defensively. Martin was also incredibly experienced, having played for the Los Angeles Dodgers, New York Yankees and Pittsburgh Pirates—and made it to the playoffs in seven of his nine big-league seasons, each time in his first year with the respective teams.

Even though the incumbent catcher, Dioner Navarro, was coming off a decent season, Martin was unquestionably an improvement. (Both men had actually broken into the league with the Dodgers, with Navarro initially winning the starting job out of spring training back in 2006. But Navarro suffered a wrist injury about a month into the season, and Martin took his position and never looked back.) But still, to some, investing in an All-Star catcher like Martin seemed like a misplacement of funds, given the Jays' other needs.

A few days later, Anthopoulos sent shockwaves through the baseball world by trading high-octane third baseman Brett Lawrie, pitching prospects Kendall Graveman and Sean Nolin and infield prospect Franklin Barreto to the Oakland Athletics for Josh Donaldson, arguably the best third baseman in the game. Donaldson was under club control for four years when the Jays made the trade, so he could be a long-term fix. It was clear he was about to become a cornerstone of the franchise. The Yankees' Brian Cashman had checked in with Billy Beane on Donaldson's availability and was told, "He's not available." But Anthopoulos persisted and finally put together an offer that Beane accepted. The price was steep. Defensively, Lawrie was a promising infielder who played third base as well as second and had plenty of room to develop. And the surrendering of three prospects left some concerned that the future had been mortgaged—a sensitive subject, given the prospects the Jays had given away before the 2013 season in big deals to acquire veterans Mark Buehrle, José Reyes, Josh Johnson and R.A. Dickey, among others, hoping an influx of talent would shake up the franchise and the fan base.

Both acquisitions helped alter the culture of the Toronto Blue Jays. Martin and Donaldson were winners.

When I sat down with Anthopoulos at spring training, he offered a rare look inside his thought process. He is a man who is always evolving, reconsidering his views and looking to past examples for guidance. A man who is willing to reconsider his perspective if a more compelling one is presented to him.

Anthopoulos studied general managers the way that most kids study their favorite pitcher or slugger. As an Expos fan in Montreal, he sought out Dave Dombrowski after he had left the Expos for the Florida Marlins. Dombrowski would always sit in the stands when he was on the road. When young Anthopoulos spotted him, he nervously went over to make small talk. He asked Dombrowski the first question that entered his baseball-obsessed head: When was Quilvio Veras expected to come off the disabled list? (He wanted to show Dombrowski that he had done his homework!) It was a moment Dombrowski probably didn't think twice about, but one that Anthopoulos will always remember.

When you ask him about his influences, Anthopoulos excitedly dives into the conversation. Pat Gillick, he notes, is the only general manager in the Hall of Fame. And he read every page of John Schuerholz's book. Those are just the first two on a long list. "Guys that have had success in baseball, I'm very curious to pick their brains," he says. "I'm a big believer that you can't fast-forward experience. Scouting is all about recall, about comparisons, going back and talking about players. Guys that have been around a long time, guys that have done certain things—no disrespect to the young guys in the game today— I'm probably a little more interested to talk to them and spend time with them."

If there is a biography or memoir out there about or by a successful baseball executive, scout or coach, chances are Anthopoulos has read it. He can remember the lessons he's taken from every conversation he's had with a baseball executive that he admires. Because of his commitment to continually learning about the game, his perspective is constantly changing. Fresh from his trades for Martin and Donaldson, without yet knowing just how well their addition to the team would pay off, Anthopoulos explained how he had learned to better appreciate and understand character and experience in recent years. It was a lesson he was taught by Pat Gillick, he said, but one that he was slow to grasp. One of the concepts he struggled with at first was Gillick's advice that if he could get a player who makes another player better, he should pay a little extra for that guy.

"How do you quantify that? There's no analytical tool," says Anthopoulos. "But there's value in that, and there's plenty of examples of players that have gotten better."

Likewise, building on the principles of his favorite general managers, such as Gillick, Schuerholz, Dombrowski and Dan Duquette, he tried to build a roster that was stocked with athleticism. And not necessarily traditional athleticism, he says. He was looking for athleticism in regards to the action of a baseball game. He wanted to build a roster of young two-way players, with great defense, a deep bullpen and a strong rotation. From Marcus Stroman and Aaron Sanchez to R.A. Dickey and Mark Buehrle, he points out how athletic the Jays' pitchers are. A few years ago, the team actually added a new "athleticism" category to the evaluation form their scouts use when reporting on talent. Mel Didier, a man who has seen as much baseball as any person alive, put the athleticism category into words, and the team added it to their scouting priorities.

Character became another key point of assessment for the Jays under Anthopoulos. Attending the general managers' meetings for the first time, Anthopoulos introduced himself to Tony La Russa and said he'd read his book. They chatted for a long time. The Jays' general manager walked away contemplating La Russa's advice that if a player doesn't seem to be able to buy into the team's system within three years, it's best to cut your losses because the kid is never going to learn. If you can't get them turned around by that point, they're probably not going to change. Anthopoulos filed away that nugget of wisdom.

While talent still is the most important area to evaluate, Anthopoulos says he's learned to consider how much he *trusts* a player. He tries to get a sense of background and character before he can assess whether or not the player would be a good fit for his roster, regardless of what the numbers say.

The numbers, after all, don't see or explain everything.

"I think you need both. I love to cross-check one with the other," says Anthopoulos about the convergence of sabermetrics and traditional scouting. "Anyone can look at numbers and statistics and analyze them and break them down. I think the instinctive side, the feel, it's a separate thing."

The numbers, he says, can't account for adjustments in a player's game. Aaron Sanchez had better numbers in Triple A than he had in Double A, because he made a simple adjustment. While someone might look at his numbers and see a red flag because his walk rate was too high, a seasoned scout might see that his motion is just a few small adjustments away from being flawless.

"With Aaron Sanchez, when we talked about calling him up, I went and saw three of his last four outings. I know the walk rate was high in New Hampshire and so on. He made that adjustment; he was on top of the ball. He became a strike machine, and I could care less what he was doing before," says Anthopoulos. "I'm not a subscriber to the theory of 'Oh, it happens.' There has to be a reason. If the numbers are telling me one thing, let's cross-check that with deliveries, mechanics, swings, makeup, character. Let's have a reason. [And if] there's something we're seeing from a scouting standpoint, is there anything we can do from an analytical standpoint to merge those things?"

So many factors go into a player's development: his aptitude, his coachability, his athleticism, his ability to adapt. Some catch on quickly; some take a little while longer to pull it all together. José Bautista was a relatively late bloomer. Analytics couldn't have shown us what he would become. That took coaching and adjustments, and a willingness to adapt.

Bill Bavasi—brother of former Jays GM Peter—was farm director and director of player development for the California Angels before becoming their GM between 1994 and 1999. He later worked as the Dodgers' player development chief and as GM of the Seattle Mariners. Anthopoulos points out that he would always be aggressive about moving guys in the minor leagues because he thought failure was such an important part of the game. The idea was that they'd better learn to fail now. Failing was part of their player-development plan. Other players need to be fast-tracked through the minors to get to the pros. Each is different.

Looking at the moves Anthopoulos made in 2015, it's clear that he has a strong understanding of how to build a franchise that takes the best of past and current approaches to the game. He knows how important talent is, but he also knows how important character is. He knows that a team needs to have a culture, and that it takes the right pieces to establish that culture. Early in his career as a general manager, Anthopoulos had focused primarily on acquiring talent, but he has come to understand that it is not talent alone that matters. A case in point: Infielder Yunel Escobar, acquired in a trade with Atlanta in 2010, was highly talented, but he had a questionable reputation. The knock on him was he lacked maturity. Those issues resurfaced toward the end of the 2012 season, and Escobar was sent to Miami as part of the 12-player trade that brought Mark Buehrle and José Reyes to Toronto. Anthopoulos recognized that, in addition to skill, a player also needs character and the ability to contribute to the chemistry of a clubhouse.

The Jays' emphasis on scouting led to the emergence of home-grown position players like Kevin Pillar and Ryan Goins, who broke out during the 2015 season. A desire for experienced, talented guys with character paved the way for the heroics of American League MVP Josh Donaldson. It also led to the steady, consistent presence of Russell Martin behind the plate, anchoring the team's defense. The Jays' exhaustive scouting and development system was also responsible for the stack of pitching prospects they shipped out of the system in order to bring in such All-Stars as shortstop Troy Tulowitzki and ace pitcher David Price at the trade deadline, along with key pieces such as outfielder Ben Revere, utility infielder Cliff Pennington and experienced relievers LaTroy Hawkins and Mark Lowe.

After the trade deadline the Jays went on a remarkable 43–18 run and surged toward the team's first division title—and trip to the American League Championship Series—since the glory days of 1993.

It suddenly felt like 1985 again. Thirty years later, a young GM who grew up watching Pat Gillick in action was using the same timeless principles to bring baseball back to life in Toronto again.

21

HOW TO CHANGE IT UP

I was given a tour of the Louis Vuitton store in Toronto last year. My wife had been in there shopping and met the regional director, and it turned out he was a big baseball fan. He invited me to go behind the scenes. He showed me the customization room, where you can pick out the material, the hardware, even the color of the high-end bags they make. He showed me a whole wall of leather in all of the different colors.

"We do everything," he told me. "We raise our cows. We tan our hides. We make our shoes. We make our clothes."

Everything they sell, they make. They make glasses in Switzerland. They make sunglasses. They make their watches in Switzerland. They don't sell anybody else's stuff. Because of that, Louis Vuitton is associated with rare quality. From start to finish, only the finest materials are used, and products are manufactured to meticulous standards.

During the tour, I realized that there isn't much difference between what they do at Louis Vuitton and what a winning baseball organization seeks to do. It's the whole point of what I'm talking about.

So far, we've seen a lot of examples of how great teams were developed in the past. My argument is that the best teams still use those philosophies today. And above all, they set the standard for pride and excellence. Every aspect of their team is built and developed with care. To meticulous standards. Building a winner is about paying attention to the details.

That's what I experienced when I broke into the league as a pro with Ewing Kauffman's Kansas City Royals. The Royals Way became the standard by which everybody else played. We had the best coaches. We had the best players. And we had the homegrown talent. But it's interesting how similar principles are at work in a business context. Louis Vuitton is regarded as a premier fashion house, and they've been doing it since the 1850s.

It hit home to me that *that's* how you build a baseball team.

IF YOU COULD BUILD a baseball organization from the ground up, what would you do? It's a fun question to consider, and it's something I've thought about a lot over the years. When I look back on all the experiences I had in the game as a fan, player, manager and broadcaster, there are so many examples of how to build a winner. And not just a team that wins for a season—a team that knows how to win *consistently*.

Look at the teams that had the most success over the past two decades. You have the Yankees' dynasty of the late '90s. You have the Atlanta Braves, who made the playoffs for 14 straight seasons. You have the San

Francisco Giants, who won three world championships between 2010 and 2014. And of course, the St. Louis Cardinals, who have made the playoffs in 12 of the last 16 years and have won four National League pennants and two World Series championships since 2004.

What does it take to be a winner like that?

There is no exact science. But if you were to borrow from the game plans of the game's great innovators, you'd have the foundation to build an organization from the ground up. You'd start right from the moment prospects enter the organization as rookies, with a manager who teaches them 40 percent baseball and 60 percent life and tells them how to be a pro. You would have a system in place to show the players how to come to work every day, how to be ready to play. To respect the uniform. To respect the game. To play hard and know that if they don't, you'll get somebody else who will.

Accountability, reliability and consistency will win over talent every day of the year. It's not an accident that team players, grinders like David Eckstein and Pat Borders, end up in the World Series. That's a product of consistency and everyday effort. Yes, you need to have stars. But more important, you need a team built on these attributes.

If I had the opportunity to build an organization today, I would modernize the approach that Ewing Kauffman and the Kansas City Royals took. I just don't think that, as an industry, baseball is doing enough to develop players. And I believe that's where the foundation of any franchise should begin. You have to create an identity and then find a way to implement your philosophy across the board.

Before you do anything, you have to decide what you want. What kind of players do you want? I want an all-around player who plays defense, runs the bases well, hits home runs, hits for high average and doesn't strike out. I want a pitcher who throws strikes, can change speeds, can pitch a long time, is durable and never misses a start. I want a Mark Buehrle level of durability. How do you do that?

The atmosphere of the Kansas City Royals Academy was the perfect mold for creating the kind of players and culture that led to a winning franchise. The focus should be on coaching. It has to be. Prospects aren't complete ballplayers. You hope they will turn into polished professionals. But for some reason we don't put the emphasis on actually giving them the necessary instruction to get where they need to be. Minor-league coaches are paid a pittance compared to their major-league counterparts. Money goes into so many other areas of a franchise, but for some reason it's never used to pay top coaches to instruct at the levels of the game where they are needed the most. As I've discussed, if you look at successful organizations, they all invested heavily in coaching and player development.

So this is the first thing I would do if I had my own organization: I would recruit three quality coaches at every level in my farm system, and I would pay them the highest salaries of any group of minor-league coaches in baseball. I would sign them each to five-year contracts for $200,000 a year. I'd tell them, "You're going to be here for the next five years. You'll move your family here, your kids—and you'll live on a comfortable salary." The catch is that they would know that they would remain at the same level for the duration of their contract. If they are A-ball coaches, that's what they would remain. If they are Double-A coaches, that's what they would be for the duration of their contract. And each coach would take a different approach to the development of the players he got, according to their age and experience level.

In total, I would invest about $4 million in coaching across my farm system. It's such a small investment compared to the money spent on the game today. These days, we are paying some minor-league managers around $40,000 a year, which is much less than their major-league counterparts—let alone the players they coach. (When the 30 MLB teams are spending $3.7 billion on 897 major-league players, as they did in 2015, then $200,000 should be rather easy to find. It really isn't much when you consider the minimum salary for major-league players in 2016 will be $507,500.)

How do we expect quality coaches to stay with an organization when the franchise isn't willing to spend the money to keep them there? It's crazy how little some of these guys get paid. You have to pay for quality instruction. But it will be difficult to change things. Beeston told me that franchises will always hesitate to spend on the minor leagues, because it is seen as taking money away from the big-league club. The problem today is that teams, despite the enormous sums they fork out for players, try to cheap out in an area that matters so much to the players they are investing in. It's backward. Where do successful corporations put their money? Research and *development.*

Think about it. If you sent your entire draft class to your own version of the Royals Academy, you would have complete control over the development of your prospects. I believe if you took your draft class in July and put them into the Academy atmosphere until the next spring, you'd be head and shoulders above the game.

Prospects would play in the Gulf Coast League in Florida, and that's where they'd be all year long. But this isn't just about the instruction on the field—which would be key, of course. This would be about teaching aspiring players how to be professionals. How to put on their jerseys and act like professionals. I would bring back the concept of baseball immersion.

It would be a page right out of the Royals Academy. Players would be taught about public speaking. Taking care of finances. Nutrition. They would be taught things that will make an impact on their lives as baseball players. On top of that, they'd be taught how to play baseball.

Practice would be just as important as games. Every aspect of the players' lives would be focused entirely on the game. And it would be the same throughout the organization. Players would know exactly how to approach their at-bats and their positioning on the field. When a prospect closed his eyes, he'd know exactly what the third-base coach's signs are. With one strike, you hit it this way. With two strikes, you do this thing. You bunt this way. You steal bases this way.

There's no way a computer can spit out something that's going to make a ballplayer better than pure immersion in a team's system. He has to play the game.

After all, you're trying to create a long-lasting situation, right?

Well, instead of rebuilding your team through free agency, spending millions of dollars on players who are more than likely past their prime, why not produce a steady stream of young, homegrown talent that you have nurtured, developed and taught to play the game the way you want?

Why not sign a guy who seems less talented up front, but give him the training to become a ballplayer? You can say, "Here's how *we* play the game." You can develop his skill in the mold of the kind of ballplayer you want in your organization.

You may end up with less-talented players, but they'll be more reliable players, more consistent players. Players you can count on. Players you can trust!

It's a simple concept. You have to groom your own players. You have to build your own organization. They have to be homegrown. And the organization that does that first will dominate the game.

22

THE VIEW FORWARD

B y the end of the 2015 postseason, the Kansas City Royals had completed a circle that brought the team back to the heights it reached with its first world championship in 1985. As I discussed earlier, general manager Dayton Moore set out to build a championship team on a foundation of pitching, defense, speed and athleticism. That vision was fully realized when the Royals walked over the New York Mets to win the World Series in five games.

The Royals were a thrilling team to watch. Even fans of the defeated Blue Jays have to acknowledge that much, as frustrated as they might have been to watch the best team Toronto had fielded in more than two decades fall in the AL Championship Series. The Royals simply refused to quit. They refused to believe a game was over until the final out, and every single player on the roster was focused on one thing: winning.

And boy, was it thrilling to watch them get there.

The Royals' 2015 title was no fluke. The club's rise really started two years before. Since 2013, Kansas City has posted the fourth-most wins in baseball with 270, behind only the St. Louis Cardinals (287), Pittsburgh Pirates (280) and Los Angeles Dodgers (278). Kansas City made the playoffs—for the first time in 29 years—in 2014. Now *that's* a playoff drought that Blue Jays fans can truly appreciate. It should also be a positive reminder that, with the right approach, years of apparent misfortune can turn around very quickly.

Since his arrival in 2006, Moore had worked to revamp the team's farm system and to use the draft to assemble what would become the core of a franchise built on homegrown talent. The season before Moore arrived, the Royals picked Alex Gordon second overall. Then, in 2006, they signed catcher Salvador Pérez as a 17-year-old amateur free agent out of Venezuela. The same year, they drafted pitcher Luke Hochevar, who had played at the University of Tennessee. In 2007 the Royals drafted third baseman Mike Moustakas second overall, and in 2008 they took first baseman Eric Hosmer third overall.

To summarize, the Royals didn't miss on their first-round draft picks. And then they developed a core that grew up together, learned to play for the Royals together, and ultimately learned how win together.

Consider this: On July 23, 2014, the Royals were 50–50. The next day, they beat the Cleveland Indians with a walk-off single in the bottom of the 14th inning—a win that, today, looks like a trademark victory for the World Series champions. Lorenzo Cain hit a single to lead off the inning, and then stole second during the next at-bat. Nori Aoki then singled to left field and Cain ripped around from second to home, winning the game.

At the time, the Royals were in the midst of a retooling process that would bring them the final pieces that Moore knew they needed to become a contender. He had signed veteran Raúl Ibañez as a free agent at the end of June. Then, in July, he traded for pitcher Jason Frasor. The experience the two veterans offered would play a key part in bringing the Royals together. In August the Royals traded for Josh Willingham and claimed Jayson Nix off waivers. Again, both were veterans who brought leadership to the clubhouse. The Royals' homegrown core was bolstered by character guys picked up through free agency, waivers and trades.

That walk-off win on July 24 signaled the start of a 39–23 run to finish the season. After a few weeks atop the AL Central in August and early September, the Royals ended up a game behind the Detroit Tigers, but their record earned them a spot in the wild-card game against the Oakland A's. That was all they needed.

In a do-or-die battle, Kansas City trailed Oakland, 7–3, going into the bottom of the eighth, with ace Jon Lester still on the mound for the A's. That's when the Royals truly showed what they were made of. Alcides Escobar led off the inning with a single to center field and then stole second. Aoki grounded out, moving Escobar to third. Cain singled to center, scoring Escobar. With Eric Hosmer at the plate, Cain stole second. Hosmer walked, and Lester was pulled for Luke Gregerson. It didn't help. Billy Butler hit a line-drive single to right field, scoring Cain and sending Hosmer all the way to third. Terrance Gore came in to pinch-run for Butler and promptly stole second. At this point the Royals were a freight train barreling down on the hapless A's. (Looking back, it doesn't even seem all that shocking, considering the setbacks the Royals have overcome since.) Gregerson threw a wild pitch, allowing Hosmer to score and putting Gore on third. Two strikeouts in a row, and Gregerson was mercifully out of the seventh inning.

But the damage was done. Kansas City had stormed back to make it a 7–6 game, playing the kind of baseball that everyone would soon recognize as the Royals Way.

In the bottom of the ninth, still trailing, 7–6, the Royals didn't flinch. Willingham led off the inning with a fly-ball single to right field. Manager Ned Yost took him out in favor of speedy pinch-runner Jarrod Dyson, with Escobar back at the plate. What came next was textbook baseball. Escobar laid down a sacrifice bunt, moving Dyson to second. Then, with Aoki at the plate, Dyson stole third. Aoki hit a sacrifice fly to right and Dyson motored home to tie the game and complete the remarkable comeback.

It wasn't the last hole the Royals would pull themselves out of. In fact, it was the first of several they would face on their way to becoming the best team in the game. The next test came in the bottom of the 12th, after Oakland had pulled ahead, 8–7. Once again, the Royals responded. After Cain grounded out to lead off the inning, Hosmer hit a triple. Up came Christian Colón, who had come into the game as a pinch-hitter for Terrance Gore in the tenth. Colón was another first-round pick by the Royals, taken fourth overall in 2010 out of Cal State Fullerton.

Despite having spent most of the game on the bench, Colón came through with a season-saving single. After Alex Gordon popped out in foul territory, Colón stole second base with two out. All he had to do was get into scoring position. All the Royals seem to *ever* have to do is get into scoring position. On the next at-bat Pérez hit a single to left field and Colón sprinted home from second. Game over. The Royals won, 9–8, in 12 innings, in one of the most remarkable comebacks in the history of the game.

And they didn't look back. Yes, the Royals went on to lose the seventh game of the World Series to the Giants, but they had taken that first step. As Hal McRae would say, "You have to knock on the door before you can kick it in."

And if the Royals knocked on the door in 2014, they certainly kicked it down the following season.

In 2015 the Royals got off to a 7–0 start. They were in first place for 164 days of the regular season. They were never under .500. The longest winning streak they had was seven games. The longest losing streak was four.

They were the definition of consistency. The Royals were never too high and never too low.

And once again, they took advantage of every possible opportunity and buried opponents with speed and effective hitting. The Royals had a .278 batting average with two out and runners in scoring position. That was 33 points higher than the league average. They scored 301 runs with two outs, which was third most in the majors.

They were also stellar on defense. Under Moore's tenure in Kansas City, the Royals have won 12 Gold Glove Awards and 20 All-Star selections. Once again, Moore brought in the necessary pieces to improve the roster. At the interleague trading deadline, he brought in veteran Ben Zobrist and pitcher Johnny Cueto. He signed pitcher Ryan Madson— who, while recovering from Tommy John surgery, had pitched only one minor-league inning since 2011—to replace Jason Frasor. Madson was one of the reasons the team's bullpen ERA improved by half a run in 2015. The Royals had the third-most saves in the major leagues with 56, behind St. Louis with 62 and Tampa Bay with 60. Even when the Royals lost closer Greg Holland to injury in September, Wade Davis was ready to step into the job. They didn't miss a beat.

When Kansas City faced the powerhouse Blue Jays in the ALCS, the Royals beat them down with singles. They took advantage of openings and mistakes. They made the Jays pay for every lapse.

It happened in the seventh inning of game two, with the Jays leading, 3–0, and David Price on the mound, having retired 18 consecutive batters. Ryan Goins misplayed a pop-up to shallow right off the bat of Ben Zobrist, and an easy out turned into an opportunity. It was like a broken record. Cain singled, Hosmer singled and Zobrist scored. Kendrys Morales grounded out, scoring Cain, while Hosmer managed to get to second base and avoid the double play. Next up, Moustakas, who hit another single, sending Hosmer in from second to tie the game. After Price appeared to recover from the onslaught by striking out Pérez, Alex Gordon beat him back down with a double to center field. Moustakas scored on the play, giving the Royals the lead. After Price was finally chased from the game and replaced by Aaron Sanchez, the Royals managed to pick up one more run off a single from Álex Ríos—and the death by a thousand singles (or rather five singles and a double) was complete. Kansas City added another run in the eighth (the product of two walks and a single) to win, 6–3.

In game four we once again saw the Royals' ability to cause serious damage with efficient hitting and speed. It was a nightmare for Toronto. Before the Jays even had a chance to get up to the plate at the Rogers Centre, the Royals had managed to take a four-run lead. Escobar led the game off with a single. Zobrist hammered a two-run homer. Cain walked and stole second. Hosmer singled and Cain went to third. Russell Martin missed a pitch from R.A. Dickey, and Cain scored on the passed ball. Hosmer, who had advanced to second on the passed ball, moved to third on a groundout by Morales—and then scored on a sacrifice fly by Moustakas.

The hole was too big to crawl out of. The Royals knew that if they could get the first run, their defense would have the advantage, even against an offensive juggernaut like the Jays. *If we get one, they have to get two.* They were right.

The Royals finished off the Jays. But Toronto was knocking on the door. Something special had happened that should leave Jays fans with a lot of hope for the season. If the Jays can gain anything from losing the ALCS in 2015, it's what they can learn from how the Royals played the game.

Kansas City went on to kick the door in and become World Series champions by playing against the New York Mets exactly as they always played. Once again, their pitching and defense took over. Despite trailing, 4–3, in game one, the Royals still wouldn't go down. In front of a wild crowd at Kauffman Stadium, Alex Gordon hit a solo home run to center field off of Jeurys Familia. They went on to win it in the 14th inning by loading the bases and scoring on a sacrifice fly by Hosmer, who dutifully flipped his bat in celebration. Singles, stolen bases and sacrifice hits are all key aspects to the Royals Way. In game four the Royals did it again. Trailing, 3–2, in the eighth, they scored three runs on a series of walks, a Mets error and singles—and went on to win, 5–3.

With a chance to win the World Series in game five, the Royals were dominated by Mets ace Matt Harvey all game. It was no contest. Kansas City trailed, 2–0, heading into the top of the ninth. Mets manager Terry Collins sent his star pitcher back out to finish off the job (after some serious lobbying by Harvey himself). It was a bad idea, especially given the Royals' history of refusing to die. Cain walked, stole second and was driven in on a double by Hosmer. We'd seen this movie before. The Royals never tried to do anything dramatic. They rarely swung for the fences. They just wanted to get on base. Up next, Moustakas grounded out, advancing Hosmer to third. Then we saw just how gutsy the Royals really were. With everything on the line, they relied on their scouting reports and sent Hosmer home on a routine groundout by Pérez. The Royals had done their homework. Mets first baseman Lucas Duda had trouble throwing the ball to home plate under pressure. His panicked throw was way beyond the reach of catcher Travis d'Arnaud, and Hosmer slid safely across the plate, tying the game.

The Mets were wounded, and the Royals smelled blood in the water. Pérez led off the 12th inning with a single and Dyson came in to pinch-run. He stole second. Gordon grounded out and moved Dyson to third. Up came Christian Colón, the hero from the wild-card game in 2014 who had sat on the bench all through the 2015 postseason. He was pinch-hitting for pitcher Luke Hochevar. Colón hit a single to left field, Dyson scored and the Royals had the lead. They didn't let up. When all was said and done, the Royals had scored five runs on four hits and taken a 7–2 lead. Wade Davis took care of the rest by striking out three of the deflated Mets in the bottom of the inning.

And the Royals were kings, once more.

What a remarkable run it was. What an example they set. We watched a team play as one unit, each man doing his part to help out. No one was concerned with individual statistics. No one cared about hitting home runs. They cared about winning and did whatever it took to get there.

Watching the Royals' run to the championship in 2015 reminded me of so many of the great teams I have watched through the decades. They played the game the way it was meant to be played. They changed things up. The Kansas City Royals started as a great, inventive organization with an approach to winning that ultimately led to a World Series championship in 1985. Then the organization lost sight of what it once was. To regain that sense of purpose took 30 years. And it took a Dayton Moore—who, remember, developed his philosophy of how to build a franchise while working for the Atlanta Braves, under John Schuerholz. And in turn, Schuerholz had developed his philosophy with the Royals all those years ago.

From my seat in the broadcast booth, I smile at that thought. We have learned so much about this game. We have found so many new ways to analyze it. So many new ways to evaluate and judge talent. We have, in many ways, come a long way. But if you really think about it, for all this talk about how the game has changed, the formula for winning has stayed the same: homegrown talent, pitching, defense and a team that knows how to play together.

Sometimes a clear view forward requires a good, long look back. And that's how you change it up.

ACKNOWLEDGMENTS

I WOULD NEVER HAVE BEEN ABLE to enjoy all of my experiences in baseball without my life's partner by my side. My wife, Arlene, didn't know much about baseball when we met in 1971 in Puerto Rico. But over the years she has become as knowledgeable and wise about the game as anybody who has touched my life. Arlene has more passion and fire than anyone I know. Thank you for joining me on this long, wonderful journey.

I'd like to thank Dan Robson for all our conversations over the course of writing this book, and for helping me put my thoughts into words. Thanks to the whole team at HarperCollins Canada—especially Jim Gifford for his baseball passion and his editorial direction. Also, thanks to Lloyd Davis for his careful copyediting and meticulous attention to detail through this process.

I'm very fortunate to work with a great group at Sportsnet. One of the many excellent people I work with is Scott Carson, who is a wizard with historical facts and stats. He was a big help in putting this book together. Thanks, Scott.

While broadcasting, we never have as much time to tell the stories as we do in a book. Through this process, while talking to many of the good friends who grew up in the game with me, I was reminded of the many stories the game has blessed me with over the years. I also want to thank all the players, teammates, coaches, managers, general managers, scouts and broadcasters who helped me recall the many wonderful memories that helped inform this book.

In particular, I'd like to thank Alex Anthopoulos, Gord Ash, Sal Bando, Don Baylor, Paul Beeston, Larry Bowa, Chris Buckley, Mark Buehrle, Steve Busby, Chris Colabello, Jon Daniels, Mel Didier, Josh Donaldson, Pat Gillick, Dr. Bill Harrison, LaTroy Hawkins, Richie Hebner, Liam Hendriks, Pat Hentgen, Torii Hunter, Clint Hurdle, Reggie Jackson, Buzzy Keller, Tony Kubek, Al Leiter, Russell Martin, Bob McClure, John McLaren, Hal McRae, Dayton Moore, Jim Palmer, Kevin Pillar, Tim Raines, Aaron Sanchez, John Schuerholz, Buck Showalter, Art Stewart, Marcus Stroman, Gorman Thomas, Ron Washington and Tim Wilken.

—*Buck Martinez*

I'D LIKE TO THANK the wonderful Buck Martinez for the opportunity to work with him on this book. It was an education from start to finish: a journey through the game with one of the people who know it best. Buck, thank you for your patience and understanding throughout the process. And thank you for trusting me with your words.

ACKNOWLEDGMENTS

A huge thanks to Jim Gifford and HarperCollins Canada for their support through this process. It was an honor to work on another project with you. Another huge thanks to Lloyd Davis for his thorough copyediting and help fact checking.

Several books proved key in researching *Change Up*. We owe a debt to the authors whose work helped inform the arguments laid out in this book. In particular, I'd like to thank John Helyar for *The Lords of the Realm*, Lee Lowenfish for *Branch Rickey: Baseball's Ferocious Gentleman*, Stephen Brunt for *Diamond Dreams: 20 Years of Blue Jays Baseball*, and Jeff Blair for *Full Count: Four Decades of Blue Jays Baseball*.

As always, thank you to my tireless agent and friend Rick Broadhead.

Thanks also to:

John Intini and *Sportsnet Magazine*, for giving me the chance to live out my writing dreams and always supporting my endeavors.

My family and friends who supported me through the process of working on this book, among so much else this past year.

Jayme Poisson, who holds my world together.

And my father, Rick Robson—a builder and fixer—who was so proud when this project started but didn't live to see it end. Every word I've written, and every word I'll write, belongs to you, Dad. Miss you always. Love you forever.

—*Dan Robson*

APPENDIX
My All-Time Team

PART OF THE FUN of thinking about how to build a perfect franchise is to dream about what you would do if you had the chance to actually create one yourself. I've been fortunate to be able to spend my entire life in this beautiful game. There are so many people who have influenced my understanding of baseball. I've often wondered, if I could go back and build my own dream team—a team that would best embody how I believe the game should be played—what exactly would that roster look like? Using people that I either played with, or played for, what would the perfect team look like to me?

I gave those questions some serious thought, and the next few pages show what I came up with. These are the people I played with who have the characteristics I'm looking for as part of a perfect *Change Up* roster.

STARTING PITCHERS

DAVE STIEB

Dave was the best competitor I've ever been around. He just *loved* to compete. And he was a terrific all-around athlete. He had the best slider I've ever caught, with a tremendous knack for throwing a dead-fish changeup. He was a *fifth-round* draft pick by the Jays in 1978. He went on to be a five-time All-Star, starting back-to-back All-Star Games in 1983 and 1984. Dave threw 103 complete games and 30 shutouts. He pitched a no-hitter and knocked on the door of five more.

STEVE BUSBY

Steve was a second-round pick of the Kansas City Royals in June 1971. He was an excellent all-around athlete, starring in several sports when he was younger and before he committed fully to baseball. He was a ferocious competitor, and as dominant a pitcher as I caught in the major leagues. From 1973 to 1975, he went 56–41 for the Royals, with 45 complete games—and two no-hitters!—in three seasons. In 1974 alone, he went 22–14. The only blemish on his attempt for a perfect game on June 19, 1974, was a walk. Just one baserunner! But then he hurt his shoulder in 1976 and his career was cut short. It's too bad, because he was something special.

DENNIS LEONARD

Dennis was a tough competitor on the mound. He pitched a dozen seasons for the Royals after being a second-round pick in 1972. He won more than 20 games in a season three times, with 103 complete games and 23 shutouts. Dennis had a heavy fastball and a great curveball. And he just ate up innings! He threw 292⅔ innings in 1977 and

294⅔ in 1978. Dennis was a perfect example of a homegrown player, drafted in the second round from Iona College in New York in June 1974. He played his entire career with the Royals and moved to the city full time, just as Ewing Kauffman had envisioned his players would do when he started the franchise. Leonard still lives in the area.

JIMMY KEY

Jimmy finished in the top four of Cy Young Award voting in three different seasons and was a four-time All-Star. Not bad for a third-round pick in 1982. Jimmy threw more than 200 innings eight different times in his career. He also had 37 career pickoffs. He was 116–81 in nine seasons with the Blue Jays. On top of that, he was 3–1 in two World Series. I will never forget game four of the 1992 Series against the Braves at the SkyDome, which featured two of the best lefties in the game: Tom Glavine of the Braves and Jimmy. Key went 7⅔ and left the game with a 2–1 lead. As he crossed the foul line, he had tears in his eyes when he tipped his cap to acknowledge the crowd, realizing he had pitched his last game for the Jays at home, ending a nine-year run with the team.

PAUL SPLITTORFF

Also a lefty, Paul was a 25th-round pick of the Kansas City Royals in 1968, coming out of Morningside College in Sioux City, Iowa. He spent 15 years with the Royals—his entire career. He never made an All-Star team, but he had one of the best curveballs I have caught. Paul won the first game of our 1977 battle in the American League Championship Series against the Yankees. And he went 166–143 in his career. He'd be an important part of any rotation. Split, like Leonard, George Brett, Freddie Patek and many other Royals, made his home in Kansas

City, and he became a terrific announcer for the Royals and on college basketball games. Sadly, we lost Paul in May 2011.

BULLPEN

ROLLIE FINGERS

Rollie is a Hall of Famer who won the Cy Young Award and was the American League MVP in 1981 with Milwaukee. So he's an obvious choice. He spent 17 years in the major leagues, posting 341 saves. He was a seven-time All-Star. Rollie was also part of one of my favorite moments in World Series history. In game three of the 1972 Series between the Oakland Athletics and Cincinnati Reds, Rollie was on the mound with his A's trailing 1–0. The Reds had runners on second and third, and Johnny Bench was at the plate with a full count. Oakland's manager, Dick Williams, went to the mound and had a long chat with his pitcher. Then he signaled for an intentional walk to Bench. Catcher Gene Tenace stood up, ready to catch the fourth ball. But at the last second, he crouched back down as Rollie rifled a slider over the outside corner of the plate, striking Bench out. Bench was caught completely off guard. It still makes me laugh. What a moment!

TOM HENKE

Tom spent eight years with the Toronto Blue Jays and was a complete warrior for the team. He saved 217 games for Toronto—including 34 in 1992, en route to the World Series. Tom was a Missouri boy who grew up in a small town outside of Jefferson City. He was drafted three times before signing with the Texas Rangers in 1980. Tom is a perfect example of Pat Gillick's scouting system. Henke pitched a total of 60 innings for the Rangers over three years, and they didn't recognize what they had. (Remember Branch Rickey's grandfather, the horse trader: "You'd better know your horses better than the other guy.") Gillick saw Henke's potential as a closer. Henke was selected by the Jays as a free-agent compensation pick when the Rangers signed Cliff Johnson in the winter of 1984. Henke never forgot that Toronto had given him that opportunity.

TOM BURGMEIER

Tom had a 17-year major-league career. He was an all-purpose lefty who pitched a lot in the middle innings. Tom was athletic as hell. The Royals even tinkered with the idea of putting him in center field after the 1969 season. Joe Gordon, the team's first manager, watched Burgie all season long, shagging fly balls during batting practice. He was clearly the fastest, most athletic player on the field. Gordon, a former Yankee, thought Tom would make a great leadoff man and center fielder.

Tom and I were roommates in KC. After that first season, the Royals sent both of us to the instructional league in Sarasota, Florida, me to catch and Tom to play center. He played well and got a few hits, but that was the last of that experiment as Tom's true value was on the mound. Burgmeier played three games in the outfield, for a total of two and a third innings, but always kept himself in great shape. He pitched until he was 41, finishing with the A's in 1984.

DUANE WARD

Duane was a first-round pick by the Atlanta Braves in 1982. He had a terrific breaking ball and was a tremendous competitor. He pitched 100-plus innings five times in his career. He was an All-Star with the Blue Jays in 1993, posting 45 saves. Ward and Henke were the best one-two punch in the AL for a while. Teams knew that if you didn't get to the Jays before the sixth inning, you weren't going to beat them. Sound like the 2015 Royals?

BOB McCLURE

The final guy in my bullpen is Bob McClure. Another lefty! He was a terrific relief pitcher for 19 seasons. He also had 73 starts in his career and had 21 career pickoffs. Bob also once threw a complete-game shutout—I was behind the plate for it. It was September 19, 1980. Our manager, George Bamberger, told Bob that he could only start if he promised not to shake off the catcher. Bob reluctantly agreed and pitched a five-hit, complete-game shutout!

FIELDERS

CATCHER: TED SIMMONS

Ted Simmons would be my man behind the plate. He was a first-round pick of the St. Louis Cardinals in 1967, and he went on to be an eight-time All-Star and win a Silver Slugger Award in 1980. A switch-hitter, he batted .285 over his career. Ted was clutch at the plate. And he started 120 or more games behind the plate eight times in his career. Ted was a terrific leader, and having come up in the Cardinals system, he learned how to play from some of the greats. Remember, the Cardinals have been doing it right for a long time. Simmons had an immediate impact on the Milwaukee Brewers in 1982, in much the same way that Russell Martin impacted the Blue Jays in 2015.

FIRST BASE: CECIL COOPER

Cecil was drafted in the sixth round of the 1968 amateur draft by the Boston Red Sox. He turned into a terrific first baseman with a magic wand for a bat. Cecil was a two-time Gold Glove winner and a three-time Silver Slugger winner, and he finished in the top five of MVP voting three times. In 1980, Cecil hit .352, but no one noticed because George Brett hit .390! He drove in 100 runs four different times and was a career .298 hitter. He too became a big part of the turnaround of the Brewers, which led them to a World Series appearance in 1982.

SECOND BASE: PAUL MOLITOR

How could it be anyone else? Paul was a career .306 hitter who scored more than 100 runs five times. He won the Silver Slugger four times, and he racked up 200 or more hits four times in his career. As Toronto fans know, Paul was also clutch in the playoffs. He hit .368 in 29 post-season games and hit .418 in two World Series appearances! On top of all that, Paul stole 504 bases in his career. And he actually started at every position at least once in his Hall of Fame career, except pitcher and catcher.

SHORTSTOP: ROBIN YOUNT

Yount was an everyday player. An *exceptional* everyday player. He was the third-overall pick in the 1973 draft. He made the big leagues at the age of 18; we called him "The Kid." He just loved to play the game. And boy, could he play. He was named the American League MVP twice, at two different positions: in 1982, as a Gold Glove–winning shortstop, and in 1989, as a center fielder. He batted in more than 100 runs three times and finished his career with 3,142 hits. If there is anyone you knew you could trust at short, it was Robin Yount.

THIRD BASE: GEORGE BRETT

George Brett was great friends with Robin Yount. In fact, he named his son after him. So you can imagine what they would be like side by side in my infield. Brett was a second-round pick of the Royals in 1971. He went on to become one of the most prolific hitters the game has known. He had 3,154 hits in his career (good for 16th all time, two spots ahead of Yount). George won the Gold Glove in 1985 and was a three-time Silver Slugger winner and 13-time All-Star. He actually led the league in hitting three different times in three different decades: in 1976, 1980 and 1990.

But it wasn't just his skill that set him apart. Like Yount, there was a special joy to the way Brett played the game. He never gave an out away. He never believed that he couldn't get a double on a base hit. George's intensity was unmatched by any of my teammates.

LEFT FIELD: GEORGE BELL

George Bell was as reliable a clutch hitter as I have ever seen. He was one of Epy Guerrero's best discoveries in the Dominican Republic. In a dozen years in the majors, he was a .278 hitter and a three time Silver Slugger. He won the American League MVP Award in 1987 and remained the only Blue Jay to have earned that honor until Josh Donaldson, after his remarkable season in 2015. One of Bell's most famous moments came on Opening Day of 1988, when he hit three home runs off of Bret Saberhagen. The outfield trio of Bell, Lloyd Moseby and Jesse Barfield remains the best I have ever seen.

CENTER FIELD: GORMAN THOMAS

Gorman took a great deal of pride in his defensive abilities, and he loved hitting home runs. He was selected 21st overall in the 1969 draft by the

Seattle Pilots. He'd go on to hit 268 home runs in his career, leading the American League in homers in 1979 and 1982. But he's probably best known to Jays fans as the guy who didn't run me over when I broke my leg! Gorman was one of Frank Howard's favorites while we were in Milwaukee. Hondo loved Gorman's passion and drive.

RIGHT FIELD: JESSE BARFIELD

Jesse Barfield was a ninth-round pick for the Blue Jays in the 1977 amateur draft. By far, he had the best arm of anybody I ever played with. He had 162 outfield assists in his career, including 20 or more in three different seasons. He took a lot of pride in his defense. But Jesse could also hammer the ball. He led the American League with 40 home runs in 1986. So Jesse is an easy pick for a right fielder. No one made stronger, more accurate throws from the outfield than Jesse.

THE BENCH

BACKUP CATCHER: BUCK MARTINEZ

I am the backup catcher, because for 17 years I was the only backup catcher on my team! My job was not to lose any games. I didn't win many, but rarely lost any.

UTILITYMAN: JIM GANTNER

Gantner was a 12th-round pick of the Brewers, and he played 17 seasons with them.

He never made an All-Star team, didn't win any Gold Gloves, but Gantner would beat you every day of the week. He loved to win, he loved to compete and he believed he was the best player on the field all the time.

SWITCH-HITTING INFIELDER: TONY FERNANDEZ

Tony was a four-time Gold Glover and a four-time All-Star. He was incredible, especially in the postseason, where he hit .327 in 43 games. His ability as a switch-hitter and his speed were incredibly valuable weapons on offense.

OUTFIELDER WITH SPEED: LLOYD MOSEBY

Lloyd was a remarkable defender. He could play all three outfield positions, which makes him ideal as a guy who can step in wherever needed. Lloyd also had 30 or more stolen bases five times in his career.

LEFT-HANDED BAT/FIRST BASEMAN: JOHN MAYBERRY

Mayberry was a first-round pick of the Houston Astros in 1967. He was a great-fielding first baseman, but he also launched 255 career home runs. He'd be the perfect left-handed bat coming off the bench.

EXTRA OUTFIELDER: LOU PINIELLA

I had such respect for the way Lou Piniella played the game, ever since he won Rookie of the Year honors in 1969. Lou was a clutch hitter who batted .291 over the course of his career. Lou was a very smart baseball man. Remember, he was with the Royals early on and was traded to the Yankees with Ken Wright for Lindy McDaniel (that's how Lindy and I were reunited). Piniella did about all you can do in baseball. He was a hitting coach, an announcer, GM of the Yankees (Steinbrenner loved his passion) and one of the best managers of his generation, managing 23 years for five different clubs. Lou won the World Series with the Reds in 1990 and managed the Mariners for ten seasons, leading them to an incredible 116 wins in 2001. Lou is one of the best I ever played with.

DESIGNATED HITTER: HAL McRAE

Hal focused more on winning than any player I ever had the chance to play with. His intensity was unmatchable. He was a career .290 hitter who never hit a groundball that he didn't think was a double. It paid off. He led the league in doubles twice. Hal was a middle infielder's nightmare on double plays. He did everything to beat an opponent (especially if it meant sliding hard into second base). Whether it was in batting practice, infield practice or the ninth inning of a game, Hal was entirely focused on beating the opposition.

MANAGEMENT

MANAGER: BOBBY COX

Bobby was an incredible communicator. He could be tense, but he was fair and he had a very short memory. That's an important characteristic for a manager to have. Bobby never let one game bleed into the next.

BENCH COACH: BUCK RODGERS

Buck was a terrific baseball mind. He was thinking two innings ahead, all the time. Buck was a great asset for a catcher, because he had such a great read on opponents.

FIRST-BASE COACH: FRANK HOWARD

Hondo was every ballplayer's favorite coach. He never let you get a big head, but he also never let you get too down. He loved the game and wanted everyone to love and enjoy it as much as he did. I wish everyone had Hondo's love of the game.

THIRD-BASE COACH: JIMY WILLIAMS

Jimy was the finest instructor I ever worked with. He was terrific on the fundamentals of baseball. He was the architect of the Bell–Barfield–Moseby outfield. Jimmy was also the master of split decisions.

PITCHING COACH: GALEN CISCO

Galen understood a pitcher's mindset as well as anyone. He lived his life as a pitcher—so he knew exactly what anyone on the mound was going through. He was a calming presence. Galen also played football for the Buckeyes at Ohio State. He had a tough football background. Another football link: Woody Hayes was Galen's coach, and Steinbrenner was a student assistant at OSU under Hayes.

HITTING COACH: CHARLEY LAU

Lau had the ability to break down an opposing pitcher for his hitters better than anyone in the game. He also helped me develop as a major-league catcher. He was big on improving a catcher's game calling and mechanics. He was great for me! Charley was a mentor to many of the game's great hitters: guys like Joe Rudi, Hal McRae, Lou Piniella and George Brett. Unfortunately, he couldn't do a thing for *my* batting average!

GENERAL MANAGER: PAT GILLICK

Pat has as complete a baseball mind as you'll find. It has to do with his scouting background. Ask him about anything in the game today—he remembers. Pat also loved his players, sometimes to a fault. But his record stands for itself. He was a fantastic GM. Gillick is the only GM in the Baseball Hall of Fame who is solely there for his role as a general manager.

TRAINER: BILLY JONES

Billy was my favorite all-time trainer. He was with the Royals for years. He was such a sharp personality. He was as good a character influence as a young player could ever have. He also had a long career in the NBA, with the Kansas City and Sacramento Kings.

EQUIPMENT MANAGER: AL ZYCH

Al never let a ballplayer get too full of himself. It didn't matter who you were. He would always tell me, "I'm not ordering you any bats. You don't play!" Al was also the master of the "gong show," in which he managed to get his hands on a gong and would go around after a game and gong a player who had been key. *The Gong Show* was a very popular TV program in the 1970s, and Royals players were actually guests of the show after they learned about the Zych tradition.

WHAT A TEAM THIS WOULD BE! I was so fortunate to play with or for all of these guys. I was so fortunate to have learned from each of them. If I had the chance to build my own team today, I would be looking for players with the kind of character and athletic ability that all of these guys had.

When I think about it now, I realize how lucky I was to play the game when I did. I wouldn't change that for anything.